PRESTON ST(on)OUR

A Two Thousand Year History

PRESTON on STOUR

A Two Thousand Year History

HANNAH SPENCER

Matador
9 Priory Business Park,
Wistow Road, Kibworth Beauchamp,
Leicestershire. LE8 0RX
Tel: 0116 279 2299
Email: books@troubador.co.uk
Web: www.troubador.co.uk/matador
Twitter: @matadorbooks

ISBN 978 1785893 407

British Library Cataloguing in Publication Data.
A catalogue record for this book is available from the British Library.

Printed and bound by CPI Group (UK) Ltd, Croydon, CR0 4YY
Typeset in 11pt Adobe Garamond Pro by Troubador Publishing Ltd, Leicester, UK

Matador is an imprint of Troubador Publishing Ltd

Acknowledgements

Firstly I owe sincere thanks to everybody who has shared their memories, photographs and family stories of the 'good old days' and brought this book to life.

Also thanks to Robert Howe, Will Spencer, Richard Parnham and the late Peter Foster for sharing research; Professor Ian Green, Professor Judith Green and Mick Jennings for advice on the manuscript; Sally Jennings for providing the cover photograph.

Acknowledgement must also go to Preston's early historians, schoolteacher Dorothy Unett and Revd J. Harvey Bloom, and also to the Preston Women's Institute, who did so much to keep the lanterns of memory alight.

Extracts from Preston enclosure records, estimates for rebuilding Preston church and settlement certificates are used by permission of Shakespeare Birthplace Trust.

Extracts from wills and inventories are used by permission of Gloucester Archives.

Photographs by Frank Packer are used by permission of Oxfordshire County Council – Oxfordshire History Centre

Contents

Introduction

They fashioned more than they could ever know,
These men who built our village, long ago.
Ruth Irons; from a poem in WI archives.

The village of Preston on Stour lies in a remote part of the Warwickshire countryside near Stratford upon Avon. Unusually untainted by the modern world, its character and structure can be considered unique. There is something haunting about this village. Something that remains in people's hearts and draws them back, time and again.

Preston's story began two thousand years ago when a Romano-British settlement was formed on its hillside. A few centuries later the land was granted to the Anglo-Saxon priory of Deerhurst, and its history began in earnest.
By the 13th century it comprised two separate settlements, Preston and Alscot, divided by the River Stour. Alscot has long disappeared, with the exception of its name. Preston's lords of the manor named their mansion Alscot Park.

Many stately homes are now tourist attractions or conference centres with their estates fragmented, but Alscot Park remains the home of the family who purchased Preston over 250 years ago. For this reason the village retains its character, its beauty and its history.

Preston has played host to countless lives, and has made brief forays into national history. Generation after generation have been nurtured within its bounds. They worked and wed and bore their children. They grew old and died and were laid to rest within its churchyard walls.

Time passes, but the land still holds high the lantern of memory. Their names are inscribed in church records, letters, wills and leases. Their stories are whispered by the walls of the houses they built, the farms and forges they worked, the fields they tended, the gravestones they raised for their loved ones. The village tells the story of the past to those who listen. A thousand lives and deaths, loves and losses, joys and tragedies have played out in Preston's bounds.

This is the story it has to tell.

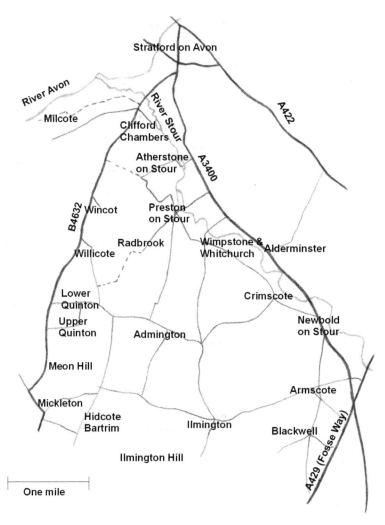

Preston on Stour and the surrounding area. Dashed lines indicate non-vehicular rights of way.

One: A Tour Around the Village

The Village Today

Preston would be unusually recognisable to a former resident of the 18th century. The main village street was rebuilt in the 19th century; farmsteads stood in what is now the Lower Park; and the road called Shakersway is now a footpath. These are the only substantial changes to the village size and structure.

Many farmhouses were divided into two or three dwellings in the 19th century and their outbuildings were demolished. Some are now single residences again. Only six new dwellings were created in the 20th century, and over thirty buildings have been listed as of special historical interest.

Before the 19th century, dwellings were identified by their occupants' names. Whitehill Farm was called Widow Phipps' House in 1723 and Thomas Heydon's House in 1740. The practice of giving each dwelling a name or number followed the advent of the Penny Post in 1840. People could now send letters and postcards just as we send a text or email today, and each dwelling now needed an individual address.

Most of Preston's houses were numbered by 1861, the sequence beginning with the houses built between 1852-56. The farms were known by name; the Beer House and others were known by trade. Others left unnumbered were probably marked for demolition.

All houses are referred to here by their current names or numbers, even though these may not have been used at the times in question.

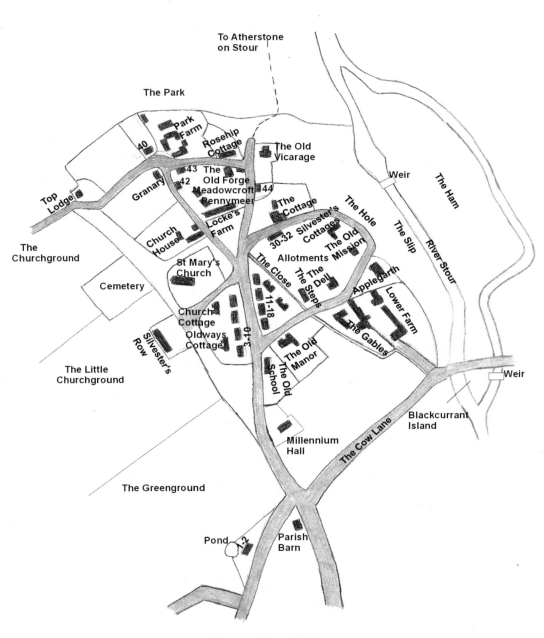

Preston on Stour, 2015.

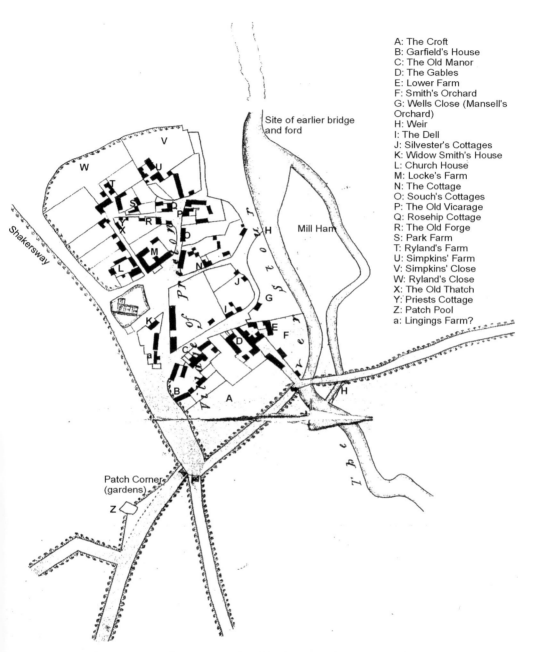

A: The Croft
B: Garfield's House
C: The Old Manor
D: The Gables
E: Lower Farm
F: Smith's Orchard
G: Wells Close (Mansell's Orchard)
H: Weir
I: The Dell
J: Silvester's Cottages
K: Widow Smith's House
L: Church House
M: Locke's Farm
N: The Cottage
O: Souch's Cottages
P: The Old Vicarage
Q: Rosehip Cottage
R: The Old Forge
S: Park Farm
T: Ryland's Farm
U: Simpkins' Farm
V: Simpkins' Close
W: Ryland's Close
X: The Old Thatch
Y: Priests Cottage
Z: Patch Pool
a: Lingings Farm?

Site of earlier bridge and ford

Mill Ham

Shakersway

Patch Corner (gardens)

Map drawn c.1760 after a new road and bridge across the Stour were built. Many former farmhouses have outbuildings, now demolished. Note the church is depicted from a sideways perspective: only God was fit to look down upon a church. Roads were gated to prevent livestock straying.

3

Numbers 1-18

These model semi-detached houses were built in nine pairs in the 1850s by James Roberts-West. They are still owned by Alscot Estate. One pair was built on the Admington Road, and eight pairs stand along the village street. They were numbered consecutively rather than the more usual odds and evens. Number 10 was the village Post Office for over fifty years.

Many were homes to the same families for several decades. Giles Horseman lived at No.1 for over forty years. Giles Samman lived at No.3 for a similar time, as did William Paxton at No.18. Village residents between 1861 and 1957 are given in the appendix.

The village street c.1926. Frank Packer collection.

Numbers 19 & 20: The School Houses

These flank the school built in 1848 by James Roberts-West. They were intended for the schoolmasters and mistresses, although it seems only No.19 was used for this purpose.

The Old Manor House (Numbers 21-23)

The earliest section of this black-and-white, timber-framed house was built in the early 17th century. A later section is inscribed with the date 1659. It was once the village manor house – the capital messuage of the lords of the manor – and is likely a rebuild of an earlier manor house, although it wasn't used for this purpose in its later history. In 1618, during Sir Richard Brawne's lordship, it was leased to John Jackson, who seems to have been the steward or bailiff. It was then the second largest house in the village, even before the 1659 extension.

It was purchased by wealthy farmer Thomas Smith from Thomas Marriett in the 1660s. It passed to Thomas Smith's son Thomas, then to Thomas junior's son-in-law William Salmon. William's grandson sold it to James Roberts-West in 1840. By this point it was divided into three four-roomed dwellings.

The house was sold into private hands in 1978 and converted back into a single dwelling.

The Gables

This black-and-white timber-framed farmhouse was built in the late 16th century. It is believed to have been owned by the Mansell family, an ancient line of yeoman farmers, from this point. Its timber-framed barn dates to the 17th century.

It was a working farm until the early 1900s. Robert Mansell, the last of the family, died in 1905 and the farm passed to his sister Ann Smith's children. It was sold out of the family in 1945.

The Gables and thatched barn, early 20th century. Frank Packer collection.

The Dell

The earliest part of this black-and-white, timber-framed house dates to the late 16th century. The remainder is early 17th century. It was the home of a wealthy man, as indicated by the quality of the structure, but wasn't a farmhouse, at least by the 1720s.

In 1793 it was owned by blacksmith John Elvins. It was now divided into two. It became the property of the Mansell family in the mid 19th century. One half was occupied by carpenter William Dodd for over thirty years. The other was occupied by various tradesmen including cordwainer John Hone, tailor John Gardiner and wheelwright Frederick George.

It was converted into a single dwelling after Frederick's death in the 1920s and became the home of Kate Smith, a descendant of the Mansell family. It remained in the family until the 1970s.

The Dell, early 20th century. Frank Packer collection.

Lower Farm

This is an early 19th century rebuild of a much earlier farmhouse. It was owned by the Smith family from the 1650s until sold to the Alscot Estate in 1875.

In 1922 it was taken by Harvey Smith of The Old Vicarage, of no known connection to the earlier family, who swapped houses with farmer Harry Gould. Harvey's son Harry took over in the 1950s and remained until his death in 2003. It is no longer a working farm.

The Steps: Numbers 28 & 29

This pair of late 18th century cottages are Preston's only cob cottages: layered mud and straw with an outer layer of brickwork. They are adjacent to the steps taking the footpath onto the road.

The Cottage

Despite the quaint name, this is a 16th century farmhouse, largely rebuilt in the 19th century. Timber-framing at the rear betrays its antiquity.

The farm belonged to the Timbrell family by the late 17th century. It was sold to Richard Salmon *c.*1820, then inherited by his nephew Samuel Silvester. Samuel's son Frederick sold it to James Roberts-West in 1872. It ceased to be a working farm soon afterwards and became the land-agent's home until the 1920s. It was then occupied by Miss Mary Fortescue, a distant cousin of the West family. It is now in private hands.

Silvester's Cottages (Numbers 23-25)

The earliest part of this building – a timber-framed section with brick panels – dates to the late 16th century and formed part of a substantial building, possibly a farmhouse. By 1785 it was owned by William Timbrell of The Cottage and divided into two.

William died in 1790 and his niece Elizabeth Sheldon inherited the building. It was then rebuilt in brick as three dwellings. On Elizabeth's death the property passed to her son Thomas who sold it to Richard Salmon, the recent purchaser of the Timbrell farm. Richard added a fourth cottage.

The property passed to the Silvester family from whom it got its name, and was sold to James Roberts-West in 1872.

One dwelling was removed in the 1890s and the others were numbered 23-25. Confusingly, The Old Manor was already numbered 21-23. The dwellings were converted into a single residence in the 20th century.

1, 4, 7 & 8 Silvester's Cottages, Silvester's Row or Scrapers Row

This was originally a terrace of nine meagre cottages, built *c.*1840 by Samuel Silvester for his farm labourers. They were sold to James Roberts-West in 1872 and are still owned by Alscot Estate.

By 1881, perhaps badly neglected thanks to a decade of agricultural depression, they were the homes of the poorest families. Two were occupied by farm labourers. Martha Hancox and Elizabeth Gibbins, both elderly paupers, and John Parker, an 82-year-old disabled former labourer, lived in others. The rest were empty.

The 1891 census records only five dwellings, two empty. This may indicate rebuilding work. By 1901 there were eight thatched cottages with their own pigsties and a washhouse. They were combined throughout the 20th century; four dwellings now remain.

Numbers 30-32

This terrace of three labourer's cottages, comprising a single storey and a garret, was built in the late 18th century.

The Old Vicarage

This timber-framed and brick-paned farmhouse was built in two stages in the late 17th and early 18th centuries. It was owned by the Souch family by 1721, and remained so until sold to James Roberts-West in 1838. It ceased to be a working farm in the 1850s. It was briefly a vicarage when Charles Quesnel, vicar of Preston from 1876 to 1887, took up residence. It belonged to Alscot Estate until 1978.

No.44; formerly No.45A or The Beer House

This was one of three timber-framed cottages belonging to the Souch family. It was sold to James Roberts-West in 1838, and was owned by carpenter Robert Fletcher by the 1850s. He may have purchased it when the other cottages were demolished. It became a licensed Beer House where beer and cider could be bought but not consumed on the premises.

Robert remained until his death in 1889. The property, now old and dilapidated, was sold by his son William. The sale price was set at £60 (£3600 today). It was soon pulled down and the present brick cottage, owned by Alscot Estate, was built in its place.

The Beer House. Reproduced from an old photograph by Dorothy Unett, c.1950.

Numbers 36-38 (Rosehip Cottage)

This timber-framed house with brick panels was built in the 17th century in two stages, as betrayed by the change in roofline. It was almost certainly a farmhouse in 1721, but seems to have fallen into disuse soon afterwards. The house is L-shaped with another building to the rear on the 1760 map: these may be farm buildings.

It may have been the tenement divided into three, with a barn and yard to betray its former farmhouse status, owned by farmer William Salmon in the 1760s. It was certainly three residences by 1841 and remained so until the late 20th century. It was owned by Alscot Estate until 1978.

The Old Forge (No.45)

The earliest part of this timber-framed and brick-panelled house dates to the 17th century, with a later extension. A small timber-framed building, now joined to the main house, may have been an apprentice's cottage. Local historian Dorothy Unett recorded that wheelwright Frederick George (1877-1922) said as much, but this could have been a more recent use.

The timber-framed blacksmith's forge dates to the 17th century and was in use until 1948. The property is owned by Alscot Estate.

No.40 (The Sexton's Cottage)

This was built in the early 19th century. Farm labourer Thomas Walton, who moved to Preston in 1814, was living here by 1841. His son John, grandson Thomas and great-grandson John all continued the tenancy.

It was later taken by George Nason, who married his Preston sweetheart Molly Westbury when he returned from active service in 1945. The couple remained for their lives and celebrated their golden wedding anniversary in the cottage. Owned by Alscot Estate, it is now under reconstruction.

The Old Thatch (No.42)

This is the only thatched building now in Preston. It was built in the 18th century, during the decline of timber-framed buildings, as betrayed by the poor-quality timber work.

This, however, is not the whole story. The presence of a cruck frame inside – two curved timbers rising from floor to ridge which support the entire structure – indicates that the cottage is a rebuild of a much older building, probably 15th century. Smoke-blackened timbers in the roof indicate an central open hearth; an upper floor was added c.1580 when a chimney was presumably built. The building is much larger on the 1760 map.

It was owned by Alscot Estate until 1978.

Priest's Cottage (No.43)

This black-and-white, timber-framed cottage dates to the late 16th century. The origin of its name is a mystery, but has no connection with the monks of Deerhurst. It is famed for its pronounced lean. The stone plinth collapsed soon after construction: the 17th century brickwork was an attempt to stabilise it.

In the 1860s it was occupied by farm labourer Thomas Gibbins and and his wife Ann, who raised nine children in this three-roomed cottage. The couple lived here until their deaths and their son George remained until at least the 1930s. It was owned by Alscot Estate until 1978.

Top Lodge (No.41)

This single-storey, Gothic-style cottage was built in the late 18th century as a fitting entrance to James West's newly extended park. It was home of Alscot Estate's gamekeepers for around a century.

Priest's Cottage; Top Lodge.

Park Farm

This timber-framed farmhouse dates to the 17th century. It is the only working farm in Preston today. It was known as Church Farm in the 18th century, later renamed after the adjacent deer park. It has been owned by Alscot Estate for at least 200 years. The Spencer family who live here today are descendants of the Smith family who took the farm in 1860.

Locke's Farm (Numbers 46-49)

This late 16th century farmhouse crowning the village green was the home of the Locke family, yeoman farmers from the 15th century. Allen Locke purchased the farm, which his father had rented, in 1606. The house was either newly built or Allen demolished and rebuilt an older house.

The close panelling and decorative framework are hallmarks of wealth and quality. The house was once larger, evident on the 1760 map. A brick extension comprising a dairy and a stone-floored cheese room was added in the 18th century.

Thomas Locke, the last of his family, died a bachelor in 1781. The farm passed to his sister Elizabeth, wife of William Timbrell, and was sold. It was purchased by Alscot Estate in 1827 and ceased to be a working farm shortly afterwards. By the 1850s it was divided into four dwellings, two of which were combined in the 20th century.

Locke's Farm. The lime tree on the right is the Stocks Tree. From WI collection.

Church House (Numbers 50 & 51)

This farmhouse was built during the 17th century – timber-framing survives at the rear – and was largely rebuilt in brick in the 18th century. The large Georgian windows are typical of the period.

It was probably home of the Yeats family in the early 18th century. It was the property of Robert Burton of Radbrook by 1749 and was sold to Alscot Estate in 1842.

It was divided into two in the early 19th century. One half was the bakery until 1970. The 19th century bakehouse still stands behind. The house, now privately owned, is again a single dwelling.

Applegarth; Penny Meer; Meadowcroft

These dwellings all date from the late 20th century. Penny Meer and Meadowcroft were built in a paddock behind Locke's Farm. Applegarth was built in an orchard near Lower Farm, after which it was named.

Church Cottage; Oldways Cottage

These were converted from the disused outbuildings of the Victorian cottages in the late 20th century.

Buildings Outside the Village

Alscot Park

This Grade I listed mansion, beside the river Stour, was largely rebuilt in the mid 18th century from an earlier manor house. It has been the home of the lords of the manor since the early 17th century, and the home of the West family since 1747.

Alscot Park, early 20th century. The ferry transported the family across the river. This worked well providing the ferry was on the correct side. Frank Packer collection

The Lodge

This pair of gatehouses was built in 1840, flanking the entrance to Alscot Park on the turnpike road. One was a living area; the other a bedroom – the occupants had to cross the drive to go to bed.

In 1891 it was home of former gamekeeper Henry Whitrod, and following his death in 1894, former coachman Henry Kingston. Both were elderly men employed simply to open the gates if needed. It was a residence until the late 20th century.

The Lodge Gates, early 20th century. Frank Packer collection

The Gardener's Cottage

This was built in the 1840s. Head gardener James Knackston from Middlesex was the first resident, followed by a succession of gardeners into the 20th century.

The Stalls

A dwelling among some now-converted farm buildings beside Preston Lane in Alscot Park. It was the home of shepherds throughout the 19th century.

Other Dwellings in Alscot Park

Two cottages were built by the cricket pitch in the early 20th century. One was home to chauffeur William Jobe until the 1930s.

The Dairy Cottage was built amongst other ancillary buildings, and a hostel above the stables was used by stable lads until the late 20th century.

Preston Pastures Farm

This was built *c.*1760 by James West on his newly-enclosed allotment of land along the Admington Road. It was named after the pasture ground it incorporated. It was leased to a succession of tenant farmers. Robert Ashby from Tysoe took it in 1860, and the tenancy was continued by his son Henry and grandson Fred, who purchased the farm in the 1920s and sold it in 1936. Two farm cottages were built in the mid 20th century.

Sweet Knowle Farm

Built *c.*1760 by James West on his second allotment of land. 'Knowle' means land on a hillock: the farmland is on a slight rise. 'Sweet' may be a poetic description of fertile land.

It had a succession of tenant farmers, the longest-standing of which were the Jaques family. It was sold into private hands in the 1920s. Five farm cottages were built in the mid 20th century.

Whitehill Farm

This was built in Alscot Field *c.*1670 and largely rebuilt in the 19th century. The dairy, the oldest surviving part, bears a date-stone of 1797.

The first tenants were the Phipps family who remained until the 1720s. Thomas Heydon followed, succeeded by his son-in-law Thomas Smith and then Thomas' son Thomas, who remained until 1815. The Tipping family then took over, followed by Thomas James from Didbrook in 1868. Joseph Spencer from Park Farm took over in the 1950s, followed by his son Clive. It ceased to be a working farm in the 1990s.

Beecham (Beauchamp) Farm

Built in Alscot Field in the late 17th century and extended in 1736. It was leased by Nicholas Alcock from the 1690s until his death in 1714. In the 1740s it was taken by Thomas Townsend, followed by his son Edward. By the mid 19th century the farm was divided into two, then reunited in the 1900s. It was taken by Alfred Bishop in the 1910s, and his son Andrew remained until the late 20th century. It is no longer a working farm.

Rough Farm (Alscot Farm)

Built in Alscot Field, on ground known as The Rough, *c.*1730. It seems to have replaced an older farm, occupied by William Cotterell in the 1690s but gone by the 1720s.

The Greenway family were tenants from *c.*1735 until at least 1798. From the 1850s it was home of Alscot's farm bailiffs. It is no longer a working farm.

The Kennels

A gamekeeper's residence built in the early 19th century above the turnpike road. Alscot's hunting dogs were kennelled here.

Mansell Farm

Built in 1939 on the allotment of land belonging to the Mansell family along the Wimpstone Road. It is still owned by the family's descendants.

Radbrook Cottages

Farm workers' cottages built in the late 19th century on land formerly belonging to Robert Burton of Radbrook.

Field Barn Cottage

A three-roomed cottage built in the 1870s adjacent to Park Farm's buildings, a mile from the village. It was redundant by 1961 and demolished in 1972.

Non-Residential Buildings

The Parish Church of St Mary the Virgin

The oldest building now in Preston. Parts date to the 15th century although it was largely rebuilt in the 18th century.

The Mission Room

A Baptist chapel built in 1885 on land owned by the Mansell family. It was converted into a private residence in 1979.

The Village Hall

A wooden building named the Coronation Hall was built in the 1950s and opened during the coronation celebrations of 1953. It was replaced by a brick building named the Millennium Hall in 1999.

The Parish Barn

This Victorian brick barn at the crossroads was intended for the communal use of the villagers, particularly those who held allotments.

The Granary of Park Farm

This brick building opposite the farm was built in the 18th century. It probably had a set of steps leading to the upstairs door. The holes in the doors were to allow the cats in to catch the ubiquitous mice and rats.

Now-Demolished Buildings

Many dwellings were demolished in the 19ᵗʰ century. Most were impoverished dwellings whose existence is known purely from census data. They themselves replaced even older buildings, of which no record remains.

Souch's Cottages

Three timber-framed and thatched cottages near The Old Vicarage, property of the Souch family by 1721. They were sold to James Roberts-West in 1838. The largest became the Beer House in the 1850s. The other two, assigned numbers 34 and 35, were uninhabited by 1861 and demolished by 1871.

No.39

This four-roomed cottage stood somewhere near No.40. It was the home of painter George Wheeler and his family for over forty years. George died in 1899 and the house had no further recorded inhabitants. A village story tells that a falling tree destroyed this house and the upper part of No.40. The change in style of brickwork in No.40 supports this.

The Dame School

A thatched cottage near No.39. From the 1840s it was home of schoolmistress Elizabeth Salmon, who provided basic lessons for around a dozen children. She fell into poverty when the village school opened in 1848. The cottage was demolished after her death in 1864.

No.44

Possibly between No.43 and The Forge, where a building can be seen on the 1760 map. It was the home of 70-year-old labourer Richard Day in 1841, and his son George lived here until his own death in 1870. It was demolished soon afterwards.

A Dwelling near Lower Farm

This belonged to the farm and may have adjoined the farmhouse. In 1875 John Allin Smith, who had recently inherited Lower Farm, sold the farm and cottage to Alscot Estate. The cottage was demolished soon afterwards.

Numbers 24-27

These were probably near or opposite The Old Manor and were demolished in the 1870s. The numbers 24 and 25 were reassigned to two of Silvester's Cottages.

Houses belonging to William Salmon

William Salmon, whose grandfather had acquired The Old Manor in the 1750s, sold this house and three other properties to James Roberts-West in 1840. A cottage adjoining The Old Manor was occupied by labourer William Restall. Two cottages opposite, their exact locations unclear, were occupied by farm labourers Mary Emms and Richard Harris. All three were soon demolished.

Widow Smith's House

This timber-framed house was leased to Martha Smith, widow of wealthy farmer John Smith of Lower Farm, by 1721. It stood near the church, approximately where the garden of No.10 now is. It was present in 1760 but demolished soon afterwards.

Widow Smith's House. Drawn c.1750 by C.F. Prentice, possibly a Preston resident

Ryland's Farm and Simpkins' Farm

These were in the Lower Park. They were demolished in the 1760s to make way for James West's new parkland.

Lingings Farm

This was probably once the property of the Lingen family of Radbrook manor. By 1721 it was owned by Richard Marriett and occupied by farmer Giles Smith. It probably ceased working soon after this date. It may have been where Numbers 3 and 4 now stand.

The Green

Preston is a 'green' village: its houses are focussed around a village green. This hails to its earliest days, when a secure pasture for livestock, defensible against neighbouring settlements, Danish raiders and wolves was near essential. The green would have been surrounded by wooden palings, now long since gone.

As illustrated by the 1760 map, the green was the central point of the village, physically, religiously and socially. Roads radiated from it and homesteads faced it. The church was almost always on the green: in Preston it stands on the south side on a natural prominence.

The stocks were located on greens from Medieval times, as was the May Pole and a pound for straying cattle – this was against the church wall. No other building was permitted. This is why so many greens survive, long after the wolves and raiders were consigned to history books.

Gardens and Allotments

Many dwellings had gardens by the 18th century. It was considered a labourer's prerogative to have a patch of land for vegetables and soft fruit, and this gave the rural labourer a great advantage over his urban counterpart.

From the 19th century many people took allotments to boost their income. This was applauded as it gave labourers a means out of poverty. Allotment use was actively encouraged in many villages, but some commentators warned that labourers would be found on their allotments instead of at work – or, on Sundays, in church – so the times a labourer was allowed on his allotment were often restricted.

The allotments behind Numbers 11-18 probably date from the 1850s when the village was restructured. The Allotment Act of 1882 decreed that all landowners must designate an area for allotments and provide up to one acre of ground for anyone who wished, and part of the field now called the Allotment Field was turned into allotments. It was of little use for ploughing and in poor condition, probably filled with weeds, brambles and scrub. It was used as such until the mid 20th century.

Allotments and gardens became a hobby after the mid 20th century, but were still widely utilised. The annual Flower and Produce Show was packed with entries. Harry Westbury of Silvester's Row planted his entire allotment with strawberries, for which he was known as 'Strawberry Harry'.

A national challenge to grow the most potatoes from six seed potatoes was held in the 1960s. Farmworker and expert gardener Eric Dale managed an incredible 240lbs on his first attempt. But this was amateur when compared to the national record: 1548lbs. The trick was to cut up each seed potato, as each of its many shoots could form a separate plant, then feed them vast amounts of water, straw and manure.

Few people can match this now. It's cheaper and quicker to buy produce from the supermarkets. The vegetable plots are buried beneath patios and ornamental shrubs, and the allotments are now the haunt of brambles and nettles, no longer threatened by the gardener's hoe.

Orchards

Several houses, mainly the farmhouses, had orchards in the 18th century. The area of trees now called The Slip was orchards until the late 19th century, owned by the Smith and Mansell families. Another orchard beside the Cow Lane, called The Little Croft, was owned by Thomas Smith of The Old Manor in 1721. It is still planted with fruit trees today.

Beer and ale, made from fermented malt; cider from fermented apple juice and perry from fermented pear juice were staple drinks until the 20th century. Carrier Thomas Walton boasted he'd drunk nothing but home-brew and cider since aged ten. He was still championing their merits when he died in 1936, aged 84.

Water from wells and rivers was often contaminated with harmful bacteria, cholera a prime example. Centuries before the word 'sterilisation' became a household term, it was believed safer to drink cider or beer. The alcohol, as we know today, destroyed the bacteria.

Beer was easily made. Malt – sugar-rich grain allowed to germinate – was ground in a malt-mill, boiled and fermented with honey and hops. A dough kiver – a wooden trough for proving bread dough – was the traditional vessel for small-scale brewing. Farmer John Jones, who leased The Cottage in the 1730s, had a specialised brewhouse with five kivers. Robert Fletcher, the Beer House Keeper in the 19th century, used the same method.

Cider and perry were made in bigger houses and on farms. The fruit was crushed or 'scratted', then the juice was pressed out and fermented in barrels for several months. John Jones had seven barrels in his cellar. The fruit was originally scratted using stone wheels driven around a circular trough by a horse. A steam or petrol-driven scratter was later used. Mary Watts, nee Spencer (b.1923) from Park Farm remembers a portable cider mill touring the local farms. The cider was traditionally doled out to the farmworkers, who would all have a good drink when they finished work.

The Village Boundaries

Village boundaries were regularly and ceremonially walked by all members of the community, known as 'beating the bounds'. The custom originated in pagan times and survived into the 19th century, now involving Gospel readings and the symbolic driving out of the Devil – presumably into the neighbouring village's lands. The bounds of Preston and Alscot were recorded in 1740 as follows:

Preston: *Beginning at New Leasow stile leading from Preston to Atherstone; across the road* [Shakersway]*; along Shakersway Furlong, Short Six Acres, Crabtree Furlong, Upper Redlands, Lower Redlands, Clay Butts Furlong and Long Grinnel; into Horsegrass Meadow; to the brook* [Marchfont Brook] *next to March Meadow where there is an X; along the brook and into Preston Pasture; to Quinton Ditch which parts Admington and Preston manors; through Roundabout Close; across the Admington Lane at Admington Gate and into Furfield; along the Small Brook to the Humber Brook; to Broad Bridge and across the Wimpstone Road; along Humber Furlong to Dunsmore Ford where the brook discharges into the Stower; along the river into Moor Meadow; across the Stower into the Mill Orchard; along the back brook into the Mill Ham; across the back brook and over the stone bridge* [no longer present] *at Preston Mill; along the Stower to The Lenches; into Lake Meadow and along the Stower; then along the hedge of Lake Meadow to the stile aforesaid.*

Alscot: *Beginning at the capital house of Richard Marriett* [Alscot Park]*; along the River Stower through Little Meadow; across the lane from Stratford to Preston* [nearer to Alscot Park than today]*; along the Stower through Long Meadow, to an X where Gloucestershire and Worcestershire meet; through Lower, Middle and Upper Ram Closes, then along the Stratford-Shipston road to an X and into Pike Ground;*

along the hedge to the house of Thomas Heydon [Whitehill Farm] to an X on the fourth brick on the fifth row from the parlour door; to the brook and along to Bob Close; along the hedge to an ash tree in Little Rye Grass Close [the Three Shire Ash] where an X parts Warwickshire, Gloucestershire and Worcestershire; along the hedge next to Ailston Pasture and Ailston Field to the Stratford-Shipston Road; through the yard and gardens of the Park; along Ailston Lane to the Stower where there is a cross; into the Park and along the river to the capital messuage of Richard Marriett.

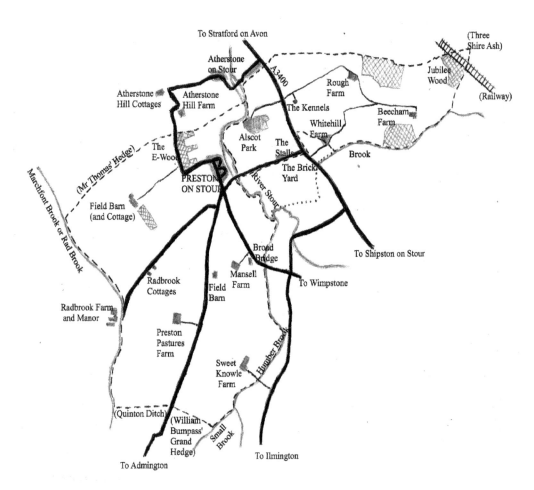

The boundaries of Preston and Alscot manors, denoted by dashed lines. The dotted line indicates land in Alderminster parish incorporated into Alscot Estate. Landmarks in brackets are no longer present or the names are obsolete.

These bounds still denote the parish boundaries, and may have considerable antiquity. Boundaries respected today were often in existence over a thousand years ago, as shown by Anglo-Saxon charters, and in some cases much earlier still.

There are no known Anglo-Saxon charters for Preston but some of the bounds follow county boundaries, often indicative of considerable antiquity. The Three Shire Ash, now long since gone, marked the joining of Warwickshire, Worcestershire and Gloucestershire. Mr Thomas' Hedge on the north-western bound once divided Gloucestershire and Warwickshire, as did the Humber and Marchfont Brooks.

Humber, a common river-name, may derive from the pre-Celtic word *humbr*, meaning 'river'.

Rad is generally interpreted as 'reeds'. March is a derivative of 'marsh'. Brook itself means 'muddy stream'. This suggests the area around the Marchfont was boggy and overgrown with reeds. The brook was meandering and poorly drained until straightened in the 1880s. Another plausible interpretation of March in this case may be *mearc*, an Old English word for 'boundary'.

There is a further element of interest in this name. The element *font* derives from the Old English *funta*, which in turn derives from the Latin *fontana*, meaning 'spring' or 'fountain'. Place-name historian Margaret Gelling states that settlements with this name element have a striking relationship to Roman remains. That Anglo-Saxon settlers adopted the Latin word, rather than their own *wella,* indicates a Roman association which the settlers respected, plausibly the mechanics to collect the water.

The source of the brook is near Larkstoke on Ilmington Hill, where many springs are found. One was known for its healing properties in the 17th century. A Roman road ran across the hill, and several Roman sites are known in the area. It is tempting to link these points, but this can only be speculation.

Building the Timber-Framed Houses

Preston's surviving timber-framed buildings mostly date from the 16th and 17th centuries. Earlier rural timber-framed houses typically lasted only a generation or two.

Enduring, quality buildings, surviving for over four centuries, began to appear during the Tudor period. Henry Tudor seized the crown in 1485 and proclaimed himself King Henry VII, ending a generation of war and uniting England under a strong and stable rule.

England began to flourish. People could divert time and money into architecture, aiming for grandeur and comfort rather than defence. The age of the castle was over. The country house was born. It is testament to this unprecedented quality that many of these buildings survive today.

They are often now called cottages, but were originally the homes of wealthy men, mostly yeoman farmers in Preston. Houses were built by their occupants according to their means, even if the site and therefore the dwelling belonged to the lord of the manor. A cottage – the home of a cottar or landless labourer – was often little more than a single-roomed hut which would scarcely last a generation.

The houses of wealthier men now followed a three-roomed structure – a central hall, a kitchen and a parlour – with an upper storey. The earliest substantial timber-framed houses were built using the cruck-truss method. The Old Thatch is the only surviving example of a cruck house in Preston, although it was largely rebuilt in the 18th century.

A cruck was a naturally curved timber, cleaved in two for a matching pair. They were joined at the top, giving a shape like an upturned boat. These supported the roof so the walls were less liable to collapse. The crucks were placed 16 feet (5m) apart. The method also applied to farm buildings, and this was the space needed to house two pairs of oxen.

Crucks were followed by the box-frame method. All intact timber-framed houses in Preston were built this way. Substantial straight timbers were used in the walls, which now carried the weight of the roof. A tie beam for each bay – still 16ft – linked the opposite walls and prevented them splaying outwards. Two or three full stories could now be built.

Large square panels were the cheapest method. Close studding – upright timbers placed close together – were favoured by wealthier builders. Close studding was often put at the front and square framing at the back, out of sight. Decorative framing was a mark of prestige reserved for the wealthiest builders. Locke's Farm and The Old Manor are the only surviving examples of this in Preston.

The Old Manor. Square framing, close studding and decorative work are all evident. Frank Packer collection.

The panels were filled with wattle and daub. Oak staves were woven with hazel wattles then coated with daub – a mixture of clay, straw and dung – and plaster. The dung may result from cattle being used to trample and mix large quantities of daub.

Priest's Cottage unusually has a jetty or projecting upper floor. Jetties have many benefits: they prevent the upper floor sagging; increase room size; protect the walls from rain water; and are often simpler to construct. They also add an element of status. Jetties were common in the 15th and 16th centuries but were rare in the countryside.

Timber-framing was used until the late 18th century. The heavily-wooded landscape had dwindled, and demand for timber for ships and industry left little for building. Softwoods were used instead of oak, thinly cut and providing little structural support. The Old Thatch, largely rebuilt in the 18th century, is an example. A new method of construction was now adopted.

Bricks and Mortar

Bricks were used by the Romans, but were then abandoned until Medieval times. Brick 'nogging' replaced wattles in timber-framed houses from the 17th century – Park Farm and The Old Vicarage are examples – but it wasn't ideal. The unaccustomed weight caused structural damage. By the 18th century, most dwellings were built entirely with brick. Older houses were restructured in the new fashion and the timbers stripped away or bricked over. Church House is an example.

The older bricks were less uniform in size and uneven firing caused dramatic variations in colouring, often used decoratively.

Clay pits are evident as hollowed-out areas in Park Farm's orchard and in the grass field called the Greenground. The field names of Old Brick Kiln Ground and New Brick Kiln Ground give clues to other kilns. A brickyard was built on the turnpike road near Preston Lane.

Concomitant with brick-making came tiled roofs. With the overwhelming advantage of being fire-proof, they quickly replaced thatch. Only one thatched building remains in Preston today.

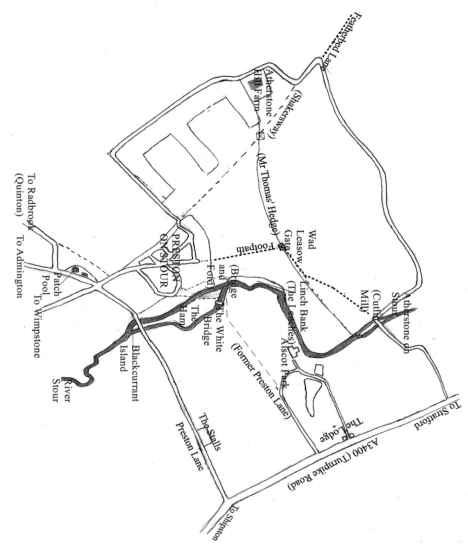

Roads around Preston. Former roads are shown as dashed lines. Dotted lines indicate footpaths

The Roads

The A3400

This is the nearest major road, and is of considerable antiquity. It is recorded as *'thaere ealdan straete'* on an Anglo-Saxon charter for Alderminster.

From the 16th century each parish was responsible for maintaining its own roads, but many hadn't the finances or inclination to do this, so turnpikes – roads on which a toll was demanded – were created from 1656. The tolls were used to finance repair work, resurfacing and drainage. The A3400 became a turnpike in 1730.

A coach and six horses was charged 1s; with four horses 6d. A wagon or cart with one horse or ox was charged 2d; 3d for two; 6d for four; 8d for five or more. A non-drawing horse or mule was charged 1d; cattle 10d per score; sheep 5d per score. No toll applied to pedestrians, vehicles travelling to church, harvest wagons, or cattle moving from farm to field.

David Hughes, a waggoner who worked for Preston farmer Richard Hughes, was adept at sneaking past the gates. Five times in autumn 1852, David left Stratford with a wagon and three horses. He drove over private land 'of which he wasn't the owner, occupier or the servant of the above' to avoid the toll gate. This could result in a £5 fine for each incident. William Masters, rector of the tolls of Stratford, took David to court, but David quickly paid the tolls and escaped the fines.

The tolls ceased in 1877.

Preston Lane

The original route from Preston to the A3400 crossed the Stour at a ford below the mill, at the bottom of The Ham, then continued past Alscot Park. It is marked as such on Henry Beighton's map of 1725. Prior to this it probably turned left to link to the Atherstone road. The ford, apparent as the wide area of the river on the 1760 map, was replaced by a bridge built by Sir Richard Brawne in the early 17th century.

After purchasing the estate in 1747, James West wanted to enclose the nearby meadows into parkland and remove traffic from near his house. He funded a new road and bridge in their current positions, the furthest point in his estate, so when his application to close the original road was investigated by the Chancery, the villagers would not object to his plans. The original road was used to access the ancillary buildings of Alscot Park.

The Cow Lane

The Cow Lane, running from the bridge to the crossroads, is contemporary to the new Preston Lane. It post-dates the field layout: it cuts across the ridge and furrow still visible in the adjacent field. Dairy cows from Lower Farm, walking from pasture to milking parlour for much of the 20th century, gave its name.

Shakersway

The primary road through Preston once ran up what is now the green; past the church; below Atherstone Hill Farm; down Featherbed Lane, now a farm track; and on to Binton Bridges ten miles away.

A dramatic change in elevation between the former road and the field called The Churchground betrays the antiquity of this road. The route is also evident in the topology of the Top Park. Countless feet, hooves and wheels eroded the ground away, and ploughed soil worked its way down to the boundary over many centuries.

Shakersway is of uncertain meaning, but may refer to Quakers, also known as Shakers. Wealthy Quaker William Barnes Esq owned Wincot and Talton manors in the 17th century; he may have regularly used this route between his properties and given rise to the name. Another possibility is that it derives from *Straker Way*, a road used to reach common grazing.

The road was diverted up the hill in the 1760s – although there is no indication this followed the correct legal process – when James West extended his park. Thanks to this, the back of Atherstone Hill Farm became the front. The section along the green may have fallen into disuse around the same time when the road was diverted past Park Farm.

Two short lanes either side of the church led from the central village green to Shakersway. They were probably used for droving livestock to the open fields. One is now tarmaced; the other a footpath.

The route of Shakersway, showing the drop from the adjacent field.

The Wimpstone Road

The road between Preston and Wimpstone was present by 1721, but post-dates the medieval field system: it cut Humber Furlong in two. It was known as the Greenway in 1721. It crosses the Humber Brook into Wimpstone parish at Broad Bridge, a name in use by 1721 but possibly a corruption of 'ford-bridge'.

The earlier road may have run nearer to the river, between Moor Meadow and the ploughed furlongs, where a footpath still exists, and crossed the Humber at the confluence with the Stour at Dunsmore Ford.

The Admington and Radbrook Roads

Both roads are contemporary to the field system: they mark the boundaries of the quarters of the ancient open field. The road between Preston and Radbrook once continued to Quinton. This latter section is now a footpath. It was known as Cotway in 1721, possibly a corruption of Quinton-way.

The road now turns to link to the Admington Road, but once ran directly across the grass field called the Greenground. This is now a footpath. There is evidence of a brick crossing point over the ditch where it reached Shakersway. This section was disused by 1721 but the route remains evident in the ridge and furrow pattern.

The Influence of the Enclosures Act

When the parliamentary commissioners rewrote the field boundaries in the 1750s, they also inspected the roads and footpaths. No new roads were ordered for Preston but the widths of the current ones were fixed, and they were also to be enclosed [hedged]. The roads to Admington and Radbrook were fixed at 60ft; Shakersway and Wimpstone 50ft; and the road from the New Bridge into the village [the Cow Lane] 40ft.

Without hard surfacing – stone was laid in the 19th century and tarmac later still – roads would soon become churned with mud and impassable if too narrow. The busier the road, the wider it had to be. When the roads were paved, only a single lane was now necessary for many rural thoroughfares, and the excess became the grass verges typical of country lanes today.

Farmers would sometimes move their hedges into the highway. The Wimpstone Road near Broad Bridge, where it passes through the Mansell family's land, is much narrower than the statutory 50ft. When the hedge was eventually planted, the unknown member of the Mansell family sneaked them out a bit!

Several footroads – most people had no choice but to travel on foot – were also laid out and fixed at 4ft wide. These led to Atherstone; Wincot; Admington; Wimpstone and the Radbrook road, and from Admington to Wimpstone. Most are still in use today.

The Tramway

The Stratford to Moreton-in-Marsh tramway opened in 1826 for commercial and then passenger transport. It followed the route of the turnpike road from Stratford to Newbold on Stour, then cut across to Ilmington and Moreton. The route can still be traced as the wide strip of land along with cuttings and embankments. The Stratford section of the route was closed in 1904.

Two: Land and Lordship

The Earliest Days

A settlement existed in the region of Preston before the Roman conquest. The Celtic culture, of which iron-working became a key part, dominated Britain. Shards of Iron Age pottery have been found in the field called the Churchground above the village.

Several hundred pieces of Roman pottery have also been found, mostly dating to the 2nd and 3rd centuries AD. The inhabitants were probably Romano-British by this point: Celts who had adopted the culture of their conquerors.

Most of the pottery is locally-produced 'coarse ware', but pieces of Samian ware, a fine pottery imported from Italy, and mortaria – pottery embedded with quartz or limestone for grinding foodstuffs – have been found, suggesting this was a farmstead of relative prosperity. Archaeological surveys have found evidence of a D-shaped enclosure, likely Iron Age, and other linear features, probably from the Roman period.

The site has a spectacular view of almost 360°; the adjacent field is still called Watching Hill. Meon Hill, the site of an important Iron Age hill fort, is three miles to the south-west, and a Roman fort stood two miles to the north-west. The Fosse Way, a major Roman road, is four miles to the east. These features may have influenced the location and longevity of the site.

Roman pottery shards found in the Churchground.

The Anglo-Saxon Period: The Birth of a Village

From the 6th century AD, the land around Preston was part of the Anglo-Saxon kingdom of Hwicce, which was absorbed by the neighbouring kingdom of Mercia in the 9th century.

In the year AD804, Ethelric, the last Ealdorman [a royal official or leader] of the Hwicce, granted some land at 'Sture' (the river Stour) to the Benedictine priory of Deerhurst, near Tewkesbury in Gloucestershire, 35 miles from Preston. Deerhurst was an important religious institution and Ethelric's father was buried there.

It is from this early settlement that the village derives its name: the priests' *ton* or farmstead. *Ton* is often erroneously translated as 'town' but Preston is not and has never been a town. Stour, also spelt Stower, is of uncertain definition but may mean a powerful or treacherous river. It was said in the 19th century that the river claimed a life every year. Records show this wasn't far off the mark.

The *ton* can't be linked to the older settlement. Its buildings had probably crumbled and its fields reverted to scrub, so there was likely no sign it was ever there. But that said, many Anglo-Saxon estates in the Stour Valley were already of some antiquity; Deerhurst may plausibly have accepted an existing estate.

There is no known documentary or archaeological evidence regarding the nature of the *ton* prior to the Norman Conquest. The Benedictines devoted their lives to prayer and study rather than manual labour, and Deerhurst probably installed a reeve or steward to manage the land on its behalf instead of sending monks to populate the site.

The *ton* probably comprised a farmhouse, outbuildings and a chapel. Tradition states that Alscot Park was built on the foundations of an ancient chapel. The Lion Ponds of Alscot Park – now overseen by lion statues – were described in a lease of 1496 as a fishery in water belonging of old to the Priory of Deerhurst. A plentiful supply of fish was needed for Fridays and Saint's Days when meat was forbidden.

The community was probably small and precarious – Mercia was repeatedly plundered by Danish raiders throughout the 9th century – but by the 11th century it seems to have comprised a substantial estate. Deerhurst also prospered, and consolidated its estates into a single *hundred,* an administrative subdivision of a county, and for this reason Preston remained a spur of Gloucestershire until 1931 when it was transferred to Warwickshire.

The Middle Ages

Deerhurst's prosperity didn't last. It was accused of greater interest in decadence than zeal and revolution, and in 1059 Edward the Confessor confiscated its lands and gave them to his physician Baldwin, a monk of the Abbey of St Denis near Paris. In the Domesday Book, compiled in 1086, Preston is recorded as the property of St Denis.

Preston now comprised ten hides of land. A hide was defined as the amount of ploughed land which would support one household. Each farmer typically managed a quarter of a hide, known as a virgate, yardland, ploughland or husbandland. This could be worked with one team of oxen. A hide varied from 60-180 acres according to the quality of land. In 1540, a yardland in Preston was 23 acres; a hide was therefore around 92 acres.

After the Norman Conquest there were increasing references to *manors*. A manor was an estate upon which dues were collected by its lord and services were rendered by its populace. Many manor boundaries had their origins in Anglo-Saxon times or earlier. They were often held on tenure of military service: the holder was bound to supply a certain number of armed men and horses for the king if required. This system was later replaced with monetary payments.

St Denis granted the freehold of Preston manor to a succession of wealthy men, although it remained nominally the property of the Abbey. Landowners often held several manors, so the owner of a manor may not live there or even visit it.

By the 13th century, Preston was divided into two manors, Preston and Alscot, divided by the Stour. They were separate administrative units although Alscot, also known as Alverscote or Allescote, was considered a secondary manor held by Preston. The first known record of Alscot as a separate manor is in 1238. It was eventually swallowed by history, with the exception of its name. The lords of Preston manor built their mansion, Alscot Park, on the site.

The etymology of Alscot is unclear. It may refer to a Saxon personal name; the nearby village of Alveston derives from *Alwih's ton*. The Saxon term *cote* means 'dwelling'.

In 1287, a number of peasants were living at Alscot, which had its own reeve or overseer. In 1327 six tax payers were recorded at Alscot, and nineteen at Preston.

In 1401, one William de Willicotes held land at Alscot and Quinton – probably the hamlet of Willicote from which he took his surname. When William died in 1411 he owned a house, two ploughlands and six acres of meadow at Alscot, all held of St Denis. A few years later his son John held freehold land in Preston and Alscot on tenure of military service.

Men began to use a surname as well as a given name during the 13th century, and their place of residence was a common choice: William of Willicote. Other surnames derived from an occupation – *Smith* – or family relationship – *Richard's son*. At some point this name was fossilised and bound to a man's descendants. An interesting example of this in progress comes from a record of Preston taxpayers in 1327. Godfrey Mercer was a *mercatore* or merchant; John Miller was a *molendinario* or miller.

Lords of the Manor of Preston and Alscot

Preston on Stour

Alscot

William de Willicotes	1401-1411
John Wylcotes (son)	1419
William Catesby	1485
George Catesby (son)	1485-1507
Richard Catesby (son)	1507-1553
William Catesby (heir)	1553-1562
John Hunckes (purchase)	1562-1571
Thomas Hunckes (son)	1571-1590
Henry Bartlett (purchase)	1590-1596
Thomas Bartlett son)	1596-1608
Sir Hugh Brawne (purchase)	1608-1617

Preston on Stour:

Roger Wakeman (grant)	1538-1545
John Dudley (purchase)	1545-1546
Thomas Hunckes (purchase)	1546-1558
John Hunckes (son)	1558-1571
Thomas Hunckes (son)	1571-1594
Edward Greville (purchase)	1594-1607
Sir Hugh Brawne (purchase)	1607-1617

Preston and Alscot combined

Sir Richard Brawne (son)	1617-1659
Thomas Marriett (son-in-law)	1659-1691
John Marriett (son)	1691-1709
Richard Marriett (son)	1709-1738
Richard Marriett (son)	1738-1743
Jane Marriett (sister)	1743-1745
Sidney Lowe (sister)	1745-1746
John Lowe (husband)	1746-1747
James West (purchase)	1747-1772
Sarah West (wife)	1772-1799
James Roberts-West (grandson)	1799-1838
James Roberts-West (son)	1838-1882
James Alston-Roberts-West (son)	1882-1918
Harry Charles John Alston-Roberts-West (son)	1918-1931
William Reginald James Alston-Roberts-West (son)	1931-1940
James William Alston-Roberts-West (son)	1940-1988
Emma Henrietta Holman-West (daughter)	1988-

In 1467, Edward IV gave St Denis' property to Tewkesbury Abbey. It's unclear who held Preston at this time, but Alscot eventually came into the possession of William Catesby. Catesby's maternal grandmother was one Phillippa Willicot, likely a descendant of William de Willicotes.

Catesby played an important role in English history. He was Chancellor of the Exchequer to Richard III, the much maligned king from 1483-85. Catesby was executed after the Battle of Bosworth in 1485, when Henry Tudor was pronounced King Henry VII, and Alscot manor passed to Catesby's son George, who held it until his death in 1507. It then passed to his son Richard, who was described as a free tenant of Preston manor.

In the late 1530s came dramatic upheaval. Henry VIII completed his systematic dissolution of the monasteries and Tewkesbury's lands were confiscated. Preston and Alscot passed into secular hands.

The Hunckes Family

The manors now were held directly of the Crown. Alscot remained in the hands of the Catesby family, and Preston manor was granted to Roger Wakeman, nephew of the Abbot of Tewkesbury, who sold it to John Dudley in 1545.

As Duke of Northumberland, Dudley served as Protector of Edward VI, the successor of Henry VIII, and after Edward's death in 1553 tried to install Lady Jane Grey, the nine-day queen, on the throne. Edward's sister Mary secured the throne and Dudley was executed.

Dudley had sold Preston manor in 1546 to Thomas Hunckes, High Sheriff of Worcestershire and lord of Atherstone on Stour and Radbrook manors. Thomas Hunckes obtained a decree that Alscot, now in the hands of Richard Catesby's heir William, was part of Preston manor. Only one house was now occupied at Alscot, leased to a farmer.

Thomas Hunckes died in 1558 and the manor of Preston, along with the advowson – the right to appoint a priest or curate – passed to his son John, who bought Alscot from William Catesby in 1562. The Catesbys disappeared from Preston, but not from history. William's son Robert was one of the Gunpowder Plot conspirators, fatally wounded after that fateful event in 1605.

John Hunckes' property now comprised diverse messuages, tenements and lands in Preston; the advowson of Preston church; the capital messuage of Alscot; and 560 acres of grassland, wood, furze and heath in Alscot manor. All this he held of Queen Elizabeth for £30/annum. Military tenure was now commuted to monetary payments.

John also owned Preston rectory estate, for which he paid £8/annum to the Dean and Chapter of Christ Church. When the manor was sold to his father, the rectory or parsonage estate – comprising two yardlands of farmland and the rectory – was granted to Christ Church, a newly-formed college of Oxford University. The Dean sold it to Thomas Hunckes, subject to a payment of £8 per year. This was still paid a century later.

John Hunckes died in 1571. The estates passed to his 19-year-old son Thomas, although John's widow Frances had a life interest in the estates. Thomas lived at Hidcote Bartrim while Frances lived at Preston. It seems Thomas had financial problems, presumably shared by his mother.

Preston's manor house, its farmland and the watermill were leased to gentleman Leonard Bennett of Ebley in Gloucestershire. Thomas then sold Alscot to Henry Bartlett Esq of Saintbury. It seems Thomas regretted this, and another indenture was signed two months later whereby Bartlett would sell the manor back to Thomas if he desired. This never happened.

Thomas next sold a sizeable messuage with some farmland to John Maunsell alias Alexander. Two years later the remainder of Preston manor, comprising fifteen messuages, the rectory and the advowson, was sold to Sir Edward Greville of Milcote manor.

Greville had financial problems of his own. He inherited large debts and lived an extravagant lifestyle. He mortgaged some of his Preston estates to Leonard Bennett then sold more to Rowland Berkley Esq of Worcester.

Henry Bartlett actually lived on his new estate at Alscot, as did his son Thomas. Thomas' daughter Elizabeth was baptised in Preston church in 1602.

The estates then caught the eye of Sir Hugh Brawne, a wealthy Surrey vintner who was buying up vast amounts of land in Warwickshire and Gloucestershire.

The Brawne Family

Sir Hugh Brawne purchased Preston Manor from Berkley and Greville in 1607. A year later he purchased Alscot from Thomas Bartlett. The two manors were united and have remained so ever since.

Sir Hugh didn't live on his newly-purchased estates. Preston manor house was leased out, and Alscot leased to yeoman farmer Richard Smith. Richard was bound to provide three days board for Hugh when he visited the estates, and Hugh could keep up to six horses there at Richard's expense.

Hugh died in 1617 and his son Richard inherited the estate. Richard lived in Westminster until Richard Smith's lease ended in 1626, then he took Alscot as his capital messuage or primary residence. He may have built the oldest surviving part of Alscot Park, which then comprised a hall, parlour, study, three bedrooms and a garret.

Richard divided his time between Alscot and Westminster. His ninth and last child, Richard, was born at Alscot in 1642 and baptised in Preston church.

During the Civil War (1642-1649) the Brawnes moved to Saintbury and Alscot was leased to the Milward family from Welford on Avon. Both families were supporters of Parliament. The district suffered regular incursions of both Royalist and Parliamentary forces, who exacted money, grain, livestock and anything else they wished from the unfortunate people. Radbrook Manor, now home of Royalist captain Roger Lingen, was garrisoned by the Parliamentarians. Forty foot soldiers and sixty horsed soldiers made liberal use of his resources. The lack of church registers in Preston from this period, a consequence of the upheaval, is now the only hint of the plight of the village during the Civil War.

Richard Brawne eventually returned to Alscot and died in 1659. His two sons, Richard and Hugh, had predeceased him, so his estates were divided between his three married daughters. His daughter Lucian was wife of Thomas Marriett Esq of neighbouring Whitchurch, and so the estates of Preston and Alscot estates were allotted to Thomas.

Portion of the Brawne estate granted to Thomas Marriett Esq of Whitchurch and Lucian his wife.

The manor, lordship or farm of Alscot alias Alliscot with all rights thereof.

All houses, messuages, buildings, barns, stables, outhouses, dovehouses, gardens, orchards, yards, hopyards, courts, waters, fishings, fish ponds, woods, underwoods, lands, tenements and common of pasture belonging to the said manor.

The meadows, leasows and pastures called Over and Nether Alvescott alias Alliscot, totalling 596 acres.

The manor or lordship of Preston upon Stower.

The capital messuage of Preston and 6½ yardlands.

A messuage and 1½ yardlands in the occupation of Thomas Jeffe.

A messuage and $1\,^1/_3$ yardlands in the occupation of Cuthbert Taylor.

A messuage and 1 yardland in the occupation of Humphrey Underhill.

A messuage, close and 1 yardland in the occupation of Roger Edwards.

Seven cottages in the occupation of Robert Mosse, Widow Bury, Roger Haddocks, William Moore, Henry Pear, Thomas Huntingdon and Thomas Brown.

The meadow ground called Moor Meadow.

Two water corn mills.

The rectory or parsonage of Preston with 2 yardlands glebe land and the tithes thereunto belonging.

The advowson and right of patronage of the vicarage of Preston.

All other messuages, cottages, meadows, waste grounds, furze, rivers, woods, underwoods, pastures, fishings and commons belonging to the said manor.

The Marriett Family

Thomas Marriett, an MP and also Sheriff of Warwickshire, was now the lord of Preston, Alscot and Whitchurch manors. As his mother-in-law, Dame Theodosia Brawne, was still living at Alscot, he had to settle her elsewhere at his own expense before he could move into the house. Aside from this, he had considerable financial problems.

During the 1670s, anti-Catholic hysteria grew, fuelled by a series of Papist plots to undermine the Church of England and the new constitution. Many men were arrested, imprisoned or fled the country. In November 1678, Thomas received a letter from H. Rugeley, the Under Sheriff.

> *To the Right Worshipful Thomas Marriett Esq, High Sheriff of War-wickshire, at Alscot.*
>
> *I have a warrant to apprehend Mr Ralph Sheldon of Weston and Mr Griffin his steward, accused of high treason to levy war against the king and subvert the government. Your personal attendance will be very requisite with half a dozen men well-armed, because in the same warrant diligent search is to be made for all arms and treasonable papers. It must be done tomorrow for I must give an account on Saturday night else you may be fined and I commit-ted, the parliament are so hot about this business.*

The men were able to conduct the search peaceably, with the full cooperation of Mr Sheldon, a Catholic antiquary, and no treasonable material was found.

More trouble followed. The childless King Charles II intended his brother James to succeed to the throne. But James was a Catholic. The Whigs, the opposition of the Tory government and enemies of Catholicism, proposed a Protestant successor. In June 1683, Whig leaders were accused of a plot to assassinate Charles and James. The Rye House Plot was followed by a major crackdown with state trials and widespread searches for arms.

Thomas Marriett had been in secret correspondence with Charles II before he regained his throne, but in 1679 had stood for parliament as a Whig. Doubts were now raised as to his loyalty. In July 1683, the Deputy Lieutenants of Gloucester ordered a search of the house at Alscot, occupied by Thomas' son John. Nothing untoward was found.

The men then received information that there was indeed a considerable number of arms in the house. Word was sent at once to Captain Theophilus Leigh, the Constable of Alscot, that he was to go immediately to Alscot and search the house and outbuildings. Any arms found were to be seized and details conveyed to the Lieutenants. If the party met with resistance, they were to enter by force.

'And you are not to fail at your peril,' the warrant ordered.

The search was successful. Captain Leigh seized six firelock muskets found between two floors in the house. They also took affidavits that many more arms had been conveyed away by night. Thomas was summoned before the Privy Council.

Both father and son, it was reported, were very disaffected men. Thomas was examined before the king for hiding the arms, but he managed to lay the blame on his son and was dismissed. John was then summoned.

It seems nothing more came of this. The small hoard could be innocently explained; Thomas was in the clear; John was perhaps considered insignificant through his lack of political influence. Both men kept their lives, lands and positions.

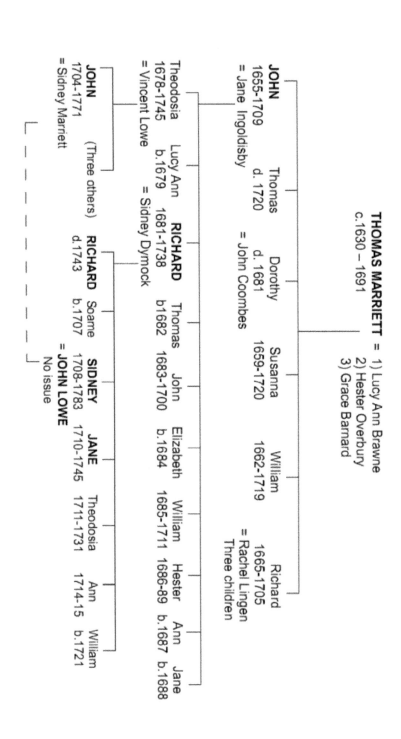

THOMAS MARRIETT = 1) Lucy Ann Brawne
c.1630 – 1691   2) Hester Overbury
                 3) Grace Barnard

JOHN
1655-1709
= Jane Ingoldisby

Thomas
d. 1720

Dorothy
d. 1681
= John Coombes

Susanna
1659-1720

William
1662-1719

Richard
1665-1705
= Rachel Lingen
Three children

Theodosia
1678-1745
= Vincent Lowe

Lucy Ann
b.1679

RICHARD
1681-1738
= Sidney Dymock

Thomas
b1682

John
1683-1700

Elizabeth
b.1684

William
1685-1711

Hester
1686-89

Ann
b.1687

Jane
b.1688

JOHN
1704-1771
= Sidney Marriett

(Three others)

RICHARD
d.1743

Soame
b.1707

RICHARD
1708-1783
= JOHN LOWE
No issue

SIDNEY
1710-1745

JANE
1711-1731

Theodosia

Ann
1714-15

William
b.1721

40

Thomas' wife Lucian died in 1681 and he soon remarried. His bride was the widow of his friend Sir Thomas Overbury of Admington – also embroiled in the Whig plots – and it was believed (correctly) that Thomas was marrying Hester purely for financial gain.

Hester died the following year and Thomas sought a third wife. Grace Barnard, a baronet's daughter from Huntingdonshire, accepted his offer. It seems the marriage wasn't happy, and when Thomas died in 1691 he left Grace just one shilling. His estates and debts were inherited by his son John.

John and his wife Jane lived at Alscot and had ten children. The church register records that their eldest daughter, Mrs Theodosia Marriett, married Mr Vincent Lowe of Denby in 1699, and the couple had several children baptised in Preston. Theodosia's marriage portion was a handsome £1000.

'Mrs', short for Mistress, denoted a woman with property or business assets. It didn't define a married woman until the late 19th century. Mr, meaning 'Master', had a similar meaning.

John Marriett died in 1709 and was buried in the family vault at Preston. His eldest son Richard then inherited the estate. Richard had seven children born at Alscot and became High Sheriff of Gloucestershire.

Thomas Marriett, painted by Cornelius De Neve (d.1678). Richard Marriett, painted by John Verelst (fl.1698-1734).

Richard died in 1738 and his son, also called Richard, inherited the estate. He died a bachelor in 1743 and the estate passed to his unmarried sister Jane. On her death in 1745, it passed to their sister Sidney, wife of their cousin John Lowe.

In 1746 Sidney signed the estates over to her husband. Perhaps she wasn't a businesswoman. Perhaps she was coerced by her husband who wanted control of her property, and more importantly, her money. A year later John purchased Locko Park in Derbyshire and sold her estates to antiquary James West of Lincoln's Inn.

The West Family

James West was born in 1703, the son of a London clothier who also owned estates in Prior's Marston in Warwickshire. He was educated at Eton and Balliol College Oxford, where his tutor wrote in 1723:

'He is a gentleman of exceedingly good understanding, of good nature and good manners, and will be a credit to his college and a comfort to his father and family. Most of his ready money has been laid out in books, in which he is very curious and takes abundance of delight.'

James married heiress Sarah Steavens in St Paul's Cathedral in 1738. A son and two daughters followed. It was in no small part due to this marriage that James was able to buy the estates from John Lowe in 1747. The sale price was £27,400; James contributed only £2700. The remaining £25,000 was money placed in trust for Sarah by her father.

The family moved to Alscot shortly after the purchase. The house had altered little since it was built by Sir Richard Brawne a century earlier, and Sarah wrote to her brother Thomas:

'It is the comicallest little old house I ever saw. The house itself is very bad and old but everything else is very delightful. The Park, though small, is finely planted and the river runs through it, and there is on the banks the most beautiful grove of full-grown firs that I ever saw. There is two fine pieces of water in the park stored with fish [the Lion Ponds]. The gardens consist of a bowling green, flower garden, wood walks and a very good kitchen garden.'

James West

James was MP for St Albans from 1741-1768, and then for Boroughbridge in Yorkshire. He was appointed secretary to the Chancellor of the Exchequer and secretary to the treasury. He became a Fellow of the Society of Antiquaries when in his twenties and president of the Royal Society in 1768. He collected books, coins, medals and curiosities. The library at Alscot, sold after his death, comprised over 1600 books, and his London library over 2200. Many of his manuscripts are now in the British Library.

James' only son James married Sarah Wren, a descendant of architect Christopher Wren. Harriet never married, and Sarah married Andrew, 2nd Baron Archer of Umberslade. She became a compulsive gambler and tyrannical mother, much satirised in the London publications.

The Preston church register records on the 4th September 1757 the baptism of:

George, a Negro youth of 13 or 14 years of age, a servant of James West of Alscot, whose sponsors were the aforesaid gent, Thomas Steavens [James' brother-in-law] *and Miss West.*

It became fashionable to own a Negro slave, generally as a domestic servant, in the 18th century. James came from London where slave traders would dock after returning from America, and where many slaves who served on board these ships were sold before the traders returned to Africa.

George's future is unfortunately lost to history.

Rebuilding Alscot Park

James had ambitious plans for the house and the park. He was advised to demolish the existing house and build a new one further from the river, but decided to develop the existing building.

He commissioned master mason Edward Woodward of Chipping Campden and the London surveyors and carpenters John Phillips and George Shakespear, whose portfolio included Hampton Court and St James' Palace, to turn the 'very bad and old' house into a modern stately home. The work began in 1751 and took nearly fifteen years.

At first, James remodelled the house into an early rococo Gothic style, with the distinctive ogee (curved) windows and battlements which characterise it today. Architects who favoured the Gothic revival adopted Medieval styles of architecture, abhorring the more popular Greek and Roman-styled buildings.

James later added a new three-storey block, followed by another new wing which doubled its size. It has been largely unaltered since and is now Grade I listed.

Three coach houses, a brewhouse, a wash house, a clock tower and stabling for thirty horses were added. Regency-style gardens were laid out and an orangery created. Wealthy landowners now strived for elaborate and beautiful landscaped gardens. At Alscot they extended for five acres, including flower beds, lawns, a walled kitchen garden and a lavender garden.

A large, landscaped park was a symbol of good taste and gentility. The park had been enlarged by Thomas Marriett in 1686 when he enclosed The Lenches, an area of common grazing by the river today overgrown with scrub, for which he gave the village one cow and six sheep per annum in recompense. By 1723 the park covered 58 acres.

James West decided to incorporate the meadows called Little Meadow, Long Meadow, and Hither, Middle and Further Ram Closes. But there was a problem with this. The public road from the turnpike to the village ran between these fields, close to the house. Too close, in his opinion. It would have to go.

James built a new road, the current Preston Lane, with a stone bridge over the river. The meadows were turned into a deer park, and remain so today. Deer parks were jealously protected. Anyone damaging the palings was fined £30 or received a year's imprisonment. James allowed the villagers to make hay in the former meadows with a stipulation that nobody was to disturb the deer.

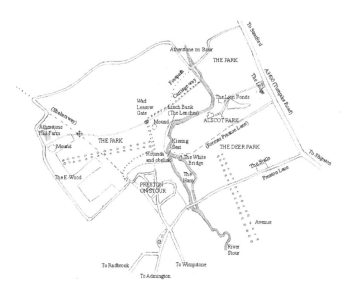

The extent of Alscot Park. Dashed lines: former roads. Dotted lines: footpaths.
Crossed lines: carriage ways.

The Parliamentary Enclosures of 1759 divided the common fields of Preston between individual farmers. James made sure he was allotted the land above the river, and fifty acres of this soon became parkland. He now had to divert another road, which today runs up the hill, skirting the former park.

James erected several buildings in the current fashion, including an obelisk; a Chinese-style building with steps leading from the river; and a 50-foot high rotunda with an octagonal tower and a domed roof. Edward Woodward was again commissioned. He gave quotes for the obelisk and the rotunda in 1757, two years before the enclosures were completed. James was obviously confident he'd be granted the land he desired!

A small building by the river, the only one still present and colloquially known as the 'kissing seat', was used for admiring the park and deer. The White Bridge stood until the mid 20th century. An earthen mound for the rutting deer to fight on is still a prominent landmark in the Lower Park, and gives the field's alternative name, The Mound. Another mound on the brow of the hill was intended as a viewpoint. Several avenues of trees were planted, and a carriageway was installed so the family and their guests could view the sights in comfort.

All these features inspired poet Richard Jago to write in 1767, when describing the river Stour:

Boasting as he flows of growing fame,
And wondrous beauties on his banks display'd-
Alscot's swelling lawns and fretted spires,
Of fairest model, Gothic or Chinese.

These features are now long gone. The avenues are felled, sheep graze over the ruins of the oriental buildings and corn grows over the carriageways. Only a few lone trees remain of the park's former glory.

Alscot Park with the deer and the White Bridge, c.1909.

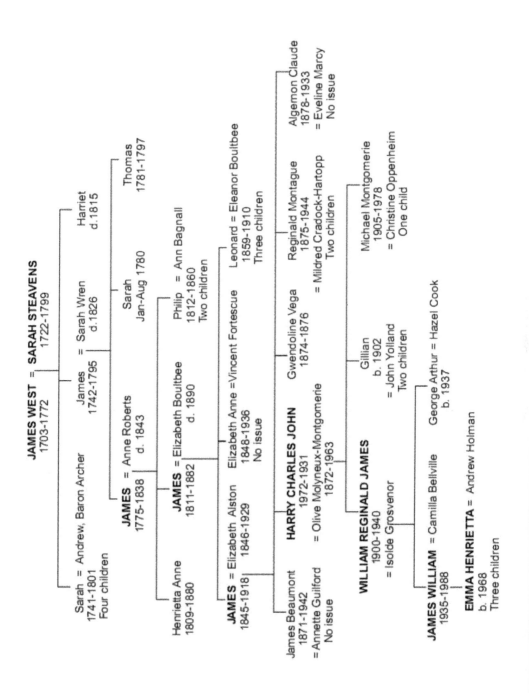

JAMES WEST = SARAH STEAVENS
1703-1772   1722-1799

Sarah = Andrew, Baron Archer
1741-1801
Four children

James = Sarah Wren
1742-1795   d.1826

Harriet
d.1815

Sarah
Jan-Aug 1780

Thomas
1781-1797

JAMES = Anne Roberts
1775-1838   d. 1843

Henrietta Anne
1809-1880

JAMES = Elizabeth Boultbee
1811-1882   d. 1890

Philip = Ann Bagnall
1812-1860
Two children

Leonard = Eleanor Boultbee
1859-1910
Three children

JAMES = Elizabeth Alston
1845-1918   1846-1929

Elizabeth Anne = Vincent Fortescue
1848-1936
No issue

Gwendoline Vega
1874-1876

Reginald Montague
1875-1944
= Mildred Cradock-Hartopp
Two children

Algemon Claude
1878-1933
= Eveline Marcy
No issue

James Beaumont
1871-1942
= Annette Guilford
No issue

HARRY CHARLES JOHN
1972-1931
= Olive Molyneux-Montgomerie
1872-1963

Gillian
b. 1902
= John Yolland
Two children

Michael Montgomerie
1905-1978
= Christine Oppenheim
One child

WILLIAM REGINALD JAMES
1900-1940
= Isolde Grosvenor

George Arthur = Hazel Cook
b. 1937

JAMES WILLIAM = Camilla Bellville
1935-1988

EMMA HENRIETTA = Andrew Holman
b. 1968
Three children

47

James Roberts-West (1775-1838)

James West died in 1772. The burial register records that:

The Honourable James West Esq of Alscot in the parish of Preston died in London on July 2nd and was buried in ye family vault in Preston church on July 11th 1772.

His widow Sarah, whose marriage portion had purchased the estate, remained at Alscot for her life. Her son James lived in the village of Snitterfield and had three children, two of whom died young. He died in 1795, and on his mother's death in 1799, the estate passed to his son James.

James married Anna Roberts, a wealthy heiress from Newcombe, and added her surname to his own. Two sons and a daughter followed. He lived at Alscot until his death in 1838 and his eldest son, another James, inherited the estate.

James Roberts-West (1811-1882)

James described himself in the 1851 census as a farmer of 1254 acres, employing 51 labourers. In 1861 he employed fourteen live-in servants in the house. He was a magistrate and also Deputy Lieutenant of Gloucestershire.

James bought five of the six remaining freehold farms in Preston, as well as Radbrook farm, Wincot farm, part of Alderminster and part of Clifford Chambers. He replaced several dilapidated buildings in Preston with new model cottages and founded a school, which received continual support from the family until its closure in 1974. He undertook similar work in Wimpstone and Alderminster.

James had three children. James, his elder son, would succeed him. Leonard became a JP and raised a family in Hampshire. Elizabeth was described on her marriage to Revd Vincent Fortescue of Alveston manor as an angel of charity and kindness amongst the poor.

'While her neighbours rejoiced at her wedding,' the *Worcestershire Journal* reported, 'they couldn't suppress a pang of regret that the fields of Preston and Atherstone would see her less often, and the pretty cottages would no longer so often be gladdened by her presence.'

Her wedding took place in August 1881. The arrangements were lavish. The two-mile route from Alscot Park to Preston church was lined with evergreen arches decorated with flags, wreaths and flowers. In the village the arches formed a continuous avenue, and every cottage gate was similarly decorated.

The schoolchildren were marshalled along each side of the road, those on one side wearing red hats; those on the other blue. More colour-coordinated children lined the avenue to the church to strew the path with flowers. A celebratory meal of roast beef and plum pudding was laid on for the village, followed by tea for the younger children including an immense iced cake.

The couple received many presents. The cottagers of Preston, Wimpstone and Atherstone gave a silver breakfast dish; the Preston schoolchildren a silver cruet stand; the tenants of Alscot Estate a silver centre piece.

Six months after Elizabeth's wedding, her father died. His funeral was held in a most simple manner, with all tenants and private servants invited, and he was buried in the family vault in Preston church. 'He was deeply lamented,' the *Stratford Herald* reported, 'and the moving signs exhibited at his funeral testified the respect in which he was held.' The estate then passed to his eldest son James.

Members of the West family, c.1880. It was considered immodest for a woman to look directly at a camera. From WI collection.

James Alston-Roberts-West (1845-1918)

James was a lieutenant in the Royal Navy Reserve and High Sheriff of Gloucestershire. He married heiress Elizabeth Louisa Alston and added her surname to his own. Five children followed. The family lived on the Isle of Wight before returning to Alscot in 1882.

James continued his father's altruism towards the working classes. The family provided soup for poor families in winter and distributed blankets, shawls and flannelling to the villagers on St Thomas' Day [21st December]. All tenants were provided with work – in 1921, thirteen employees had been at Alscot for over

21 years, including 81-year-old sawyer Giles Samman who had worked on the estate for 59 years.

Revd Beal of Whitchurch was passing through Preston in 1887 with a friend who commented on how well-clad the labourers' children were, and how well-housed they were, despite the low rents – 1s 2d/week – which in other villages would afford only the most meagre dwelling.

'That's due to having a good landlord,' Beal replied. 'Mr West always makes full efforts for anything affecting the happiness of individuals or the community at large.'

There seems to have been another side to James. In 1892, he evicted Preston labourer William Timms for his support of the Liberal party, whose policies of reform didn't please the landed elite. He also evicted Alderminster labourer Joseph Rouse for a similar reason. It seems he was a good squire, providing everyone remained in their rightful place.

It was tradition for the women to take tea at Alscot each year. In July 1912, the women were entertained by James' daughter-in-law, Olive West. Every year the women derived great pleasure from her singing, and this year was no exception. They were also entertained by her children, Master Michael, aged 7, and Miss Gillian, aged 10, who danced very prettily for the company.

The women then strolled about the grounds and looked over the house. The requisite National Anthem brought the evening to a close.

In summer 1914, the tea party proceeded as normal except the tables were assembled in the motor garage thanks to the uncertain weather. This is its last recorded occurrence. The war brought the event, along with the St Thomas' Day gifts and many other traditions, to an abrupt end.

The women's tea party at Alscot Park, 1912. Bottom picture: Master Michael West on the left; Miss Gillian West second right. From WI collection.

James' eldest son James married lodging house-keeper's daughter Annette Guilford and didn't follow any particular career. Harry and Reginald were both Naval officers. The youngest, Algernon, didn't settle to a career and when he died in 1933, his obituary simply said that 'he gained a large circle of friends by reason of his happy and genial disposition.'

James died in 1918 and made Harry his heir.

Harry Charles John Alston-Roberts-West (1872-1931)

Harry began his career in the Royal Navy in 1887. He spent three years as a Midshipman [trainee officer] on HMS *Tour Maline* in North America, and also served on HMS *Undaunted* in China. In 1895 he was promoted to Lieutenant and commanded the destroyers HMS *Haughty* and HMS *Griffon* in Australia.

In May 1901, he returned home after four years away. He was met with a resounding reception. Over sixty people – servants, estate men and parishioners – were assembled at the park gates. When his carriage arrived, lusty cheers were given and *For He's a Jolly Good Fellow* was sung. Lieutenant West expressed his grateful thanks for the kindly welcome and exchanged personal words with most of those present. All were invited into the servants' hall for an abundance of good fare.

'It was easy to see,' the *Stratford Herald* continued, 'that everyone was delighted at the gallant officer's return, and for the opportunity to show their respect and esteem for him.'

That December, Harry's career took a blow. He was in command of the destroyer HMS *Salomon* when it collided with a steamship, causing the deaths of two men. Harry was court-martialled for negligence. He told the inquiry a month later that he considered the blame to be on the master of the other vessel. The adjudicating officers agreed and Harry was acquitted.

He later became an Inspecting Officer for HM Coastguard in Cornwall, then moved to Vernon torpedo school in Portsmouth. He inherited Alscot Estate in 1918 and retired from the Navy the following year. Financial problems led to the sale of many houses, farms and land following his inheritance, but Harry strived for his tenants despite his diminished means, and continued to support the school and fund celebrations.

His eldest son Reggie celebrated his coming-of-age in lavish style in September 1921. The farm tenants and their wives were invited for luncheon in a marquee on the lawn. The tables were decorated with flowers, hot-house plants, and gold cups and vases won by the sporting prowess of former squires. Reggie received many gifts, including a silver tray presented by Thomas Salmon Smith of Park Farm on behalf of the farm tenants. A series of sports, a tug-of-war and a Punch and Judy show followed.

Reggie went on to serve in the Grenadier Guards. His brother Michael joined the Oxford and Bucks Light Infantry, served in Burma, commanded the Commonwealth Division in Korea, and reached the rank of Major General.

When Harry died in 1931, Reggie succeeded to the estate.

William Reginald James Alston-Roberts-West (1900-1940)

Reggie attended the exclusive Uppingham School and the Royal Military Academy of Sandhurst, and was commissioned into the Grenadier Guards. He

Reggie West's coming-of-age celebrations, Alscot Park 1921

Back Row: ? ? ? George Carter; Mr Horniblow; ? Alice James; John Clift; Jessie Bishop; Arthur Ashby

Third Row: Charlie Snow; ? Frank Taylor; ? Dick Crosley; Rosa Ashby; ? Harvey Smith; Martha Smith; ?
Rev C Everett; Rev Morgan; Maggie Ashby; Fanny Ashby; Mrs Carter; ? ? ? ? ?

Second Row: Harry Gould; ? Jack Jaques; Arthur Ainley; Rev T Lewis; Rev Fortescue; Elizabeth Fortescue; Gillian West;
Reggie West; Harry West; Olive West; Elizabeth West; Henry Ashby; Mike West; John Ashby; Thomas Smith; Phoebe Smith ?

Front Row: George Taylor; Alfred Bishop; Alan James; Frank Hutchings; Fred Ashby; JC Cook married Isolde Grosvenor in 1930, was promoted to Captain then retired from the army following his father's death. He had two sons, James and George, who would both follow him into the Guards.

Reggie was courteous, friendly and developed into an ideal squire with a high concept of duty. He arranged regular cricket matches at Alscot, played for Stratford Rugby Club, was an excellent horseman and a member of the Warwickshire Hunt. He was also president of the Alderminster Shire Horse Society.

Reggie was an amateur jockey and kept racehorses at Alscot. He would train on a particularly steep part of Ilmington Hill by Larkstoke. He would often dismount and run up the hill, and expect the grooms to do the same. One groom, George Handy, could never keep up with him, so would hang onto his horse's tail and let it pull him up.

When war was declared in September 1939, Reggie rejoined his unit. He was in France within three weeks. In May 1940, his unit was positioned near Flanders when the Germans assaulted their lines. Reggie, recently promoted to Major, attempted to organise a counter-attack but the British were forced to retreat. Reggie was one of sixty men killed. He is commemorated in Dunkirk Memorial Cemetery. A friend wrote to *The Times*:

'His only thought since the war started was to remain at the front leading his own men against the enemy. This brave and kindly man died as he had lived; a superb example of an English guardsman and a country gentleman.'

Much changed following Reggie's death. The estate was managed by trustees, and the sporting traditions including the racehorses and the elaborate winter shoots came to an end.

Isolde remained at Alscot until her son James succeeded. She took an active part in village life: she became president of the Pig Club and a member of the WI; she organised school trips; and in 1945 arranged a lavish Christmas party including tea, crackers, toys and a 14-foot Christmas tree. Her brother-in-law Brigadier Michael West – he who had danced for the ladies' tea party back in 1912 – made an appearance as Father Christmas.

James William Alston-Roberts-West (1935-1988)

Reggie's eldest son James came of age in 1956. A party was held for several hundred guests, including all the estate tenants. Fred Hartwell from No.4, Preston's roadman, got rather drunk that night. The next morning he was found in his garden, asleep in his wheelbarrow.

James joined the Grenadier Guards and reached the rank of Captain. He married Camilla Bellville in October 1958 and retired from the army in 1960. He returned to Alscot shortly afterwards. His daughter Emma was born in 1968. The E-Wood was planted in the park to celebrate her birth.

James deplored the decline of village life and wanted to regain the sense of community which was once a defining feature of rural villages. Among other enterprises he established several local business opportunities to encourage younger families to remain.

He died in 1988 and the estate passed to his only child, Emma.

Emma Henrietta Holman-West (b1968)

Emma married Andrew Holman in 1995 and had three children. She continues to manage the estate as her forebears have done for over 250 years.

Three: House and Home: Domestic Life

The Rise of the Farmer

In common with most rural communities, the land has provided a living for the majority of Preston's residents. Under the Medieval feudal system, peasants or serfs worked on the lord of the manor's land in return for living there and keeping a cow or two. Monetary leases later replaced this system. Most people tilled the land for subsistence rather than profit, and a farmer would often work his land and tend his few animals with little difference in lifestyle to the landless labourers.

The population was rising by the 16th century. This was accompanied by an increase in grain prices and rents, advantageous to those who owned property or land. Lower wages and increased cost of living forced many into poverty while the wealthy prospered. The social and economic divide between the higher and lower classes grew.

Several men were able to purchase holdings in Preston as debt-ridden manor-lords sold off land. The Taylors were an established yeoman family by the mid 16th century, gaining considerable wealth from the wool trade. John Maunsell alias Alexander may have been the manor bailiff, and purchased a farm, probably The Gables, in 1592. Henry Smith purchased a farm from Thomas Taylor in the 1570s. His grandson Thomas bought Lower Farm in 1651. Allen Locke purchased Locke's Farm, previously rented by his father, in 1606. The Timbrell family were landowners by 1621. Thomas Yeats purchased a farm in the 1620s.

Most of the surviving timber-framed houses in Preston were farmhouses, built in the 16th and 17th centuries by wealthy freeholders who could afford a house of this quality and longevity. Farmers could now achieve a good standard of living and were ranked higher in the social hierarchy, determined almost exclusively by land possession. This hierarchy consisted of:

The Nobility. Dukes, Marquesses, Earls, Viscounts, Barons and Lords. These owned vast estates and often held posts in court or the government. They were armigerous: they bore a coat of arms. 'Lord of the manor' was an old feudal title: he was not necessarily a peer.

The Knight. The lower nobility, also armigerous, with the epithet 'Sir'. Originally mounted soldiers, knighthoods were now awarded for loyal service. Several of Preston's manor-lords held knighthoods.

The Esquire. Often the sons of knights or peers. Originally a knight's shield-bearer, the title was now given to officers of the Crown. Most of Preston's manor-lords without knighthoods were esquires.

The Gentleman. A man who didn't have to labour on his own land: he employed men to work for him. Of equivalent standing to army officers, barristers and other professionals. John Souch, also spelt Zouch, was the only gentleman in Preston in 1721; within fifty years many more yeomen would attain this ranking.

The Yeoman. A freehold farmer. Of equivalent standing to a skilled craftsman.

The Husbandman. A tenant farmer.

The Labourer / Peasant. These owned or leased no land, although they often kept a few animals on the common ground. In Medieval times a 'serf' or 'villein' was an unfree peasant obliged to labour for the lord of the manor.

A taxation record of 1695 illustrates the new status of farmers. Those with unknown occupations were probably craftsmen or better-off labourers.

Name	Amount	Occupation
John Marriett Esq	£2	Lord of the manor
John Coombes Esq	£2	Marriett's brother-in-law
Susanna Marriett	2s	Marriett's sister
John Mansell senior	5s	Yeoman, The Gables
Elizabeth Smith, widow	4s	Yeoman, The Old Manor
William Yeats junior	4s	Yeoman
John Smith	4s	Yeoman, Lower Farm
Thomas Locke	4s	Yeoman, Locke's Farm
Thomas Such	4s	Yeoman, Old Vicarage
Thomas Timbrell	4s	Yeoman, The Cottage
John Mansell junior	2s 6d	Yeoman, The Gables
William Cotterell	2s 6d	Husbandman, Rough Farm
Nicholas Alcock	2s 6d	Husbandman, Beecham Farm

Robert Phipps	2s 6d	Husbandman, Whitehill Farm
Thomas Smith	2s 6d	Yeoman, The Old Manor
Edward Walford	2s 6d	Husbandman, Ryland's Farm
William Yeats senior	2s 6d	Yeoman, ?Church House
William Farr	1s	Miller
Walter Simkins	1s	Husbandman
John Albright	1s	Yeoman
(Five others)	1s	Occupation unknown
Thomas Lowe	6d	Husbandman?
Thomas Mansell	6d	Husbandman?
William Salmon	6d	Carpenter
Richard Salmon	6d	Carpenter
John Garfield	6d	Carpenter
(Eighteen others)	6d	Occupation unknown
William Hartwell	4d	Weaver
(Three others)	4d	Occupation unknown
John Timms	2d	Labourer
(Two others)	2d	Occupation unknown
James Williams	£1	Clerk
TOTAL	£8 9s 10d	

Residents in 1721

A detailed terrier or survey of the village and farmland was taken in 1721, and recorded 35 dwellings. Eleven were freehold; nine of these owned by farmers, although some were leased out by their owners. The parish houses – occupied by poor families at the expense of the parish – weren't recorded.

Freehold Homestalls and Cottages

John Smith, yeoman: Lower Farm. A house, a cottage adjoining, two barns, a stable, two yards, a close [paddock], an orchard and a garden.

Thomas Mansell, yeoman: The Gables. A house, a barn, two stables, two yards, an orchard and a close. Also two cottages with gardens.

John Yeats, yeoman. A house, three barns, two stables, a yard, a garden and an orchard. Also a cottage with a garden. He also had a 'mud wall', probably a livestock pen, on the common against the churchyard. This can be seen on the 1760 map.

Thomas Lock, yeoman: Locke's Farm. A house, a yard, two barns, three stables, an orchard and garden. Also a cottage with an orchard and garden. He had pales [a fence] in front of his house on the common.

John Souch, gentleman: The Old Vicarage. A house, three barns, a stable, a yard, an orchard and garden. Also three cottages occupied by **William Kite, cordwainer; Thomas Bromley, tailor;** and **Daniel Walton.** The first had a close, yard and garden; the other two had gardens.

Thomas Smith, yeoman: The Old Manor. A house, a barn, two stables, two yards, a garden and two orchards.

Thomas Timbrell, yeoman: The Cottage. A house, two barns, a stable, two orchards and two gardens.

Thomas Yeats, yeoman: Church House? A house, barn, stable, yard and orchard.

William Hartwell, weaver. A cottage, two gardens and a shop [workshop].

John Albright, yeoman. A house, barn, stable, yard and orchard.

Widow Bury: A cottage and garden.

Homestalls belonging to Richard Marriett

Giles Smith, husbandman: Lingings Farm. A house, barn, stable, yard, orchard, close, rickyard, cart house and two gardens. Pales against his house stood on the common.

William Ryland, husbandman: Ryland's Farm. A house, barn, stable, yard, close and rickyard.

William Salmon, carpenter, and **John Simkins, husbandman: Simkins' Farm.** A house, two barns, two stables, two yards, two gardens and a close.

Thomas Farr, miller. A house, three mills, two stables and a yard.

Cottages belonging to Richard Marriett

Robert Gibbs. A house and orchard.

Widow Lowe. A house, barn, close and garden.

John Garfield, carpenter: Garfield's House. A house, shop [workshop], orchard and garden.

Thomas Bullard. A house and garden.

Samuel Smith. A house.

Widow Kilbey. A house, shop and garden.

Widow Smith: Widow Smith's House. A house.

John Beavington. A house.

Edward Marshall. A house and garden.

Thomas Abbotts. A house and garden, belonging to the rectory estate.
James Elson. A house and garden, belonging to the rectory estate.
Widow Mansell. A house and close.

Life in Preston for Better-off Families

Wealthy yeoman Henry Taylor died in 1561. He owned a vast sheep flock and lived an elaborate lifestyle. He employed several servants in his house, to whom he left legacies of two sheep apiece. Many of his legacies comprised sheep, a milch heifer or a weaning calf. He left his sword – an essential item for a man with status and assets to defend – and his best canvas doublet to his neighbour. A black coat, a pair of hose, a cap and a doublet went to his cousin. His black gown, a black taffeta doublet and a chamlet [a fine and expensive woollen cloth] jacket went to his brother John.

The doublet was an uncomfortable padded tunic, the standard dress of the Elizabethan upper classes. The law dictated the style and colour of clothing for each social class so a person's rank was easily recognisable. Black was reserved for the higher classes.

John Maunsell alias Alexander purchased a house and farmland, believed to be The Gables, from Thomas Hunckes in 1592. The house was newly built, or John may have demolished and rebuilt an earlier house. The close timber-framing is a hallmark of a wealthy builder, and John was probably one of the wealthiest men in Preston.

Surnames were more fluid in the 16th century. People could adopt a second surname as an alias, such as that of a maternal relative or step-father, especially if they were to inherit his property. This is probably what happened in John's case. The surname was very unwieldy and was soon shortened to Maunsell, later becoming Mansell.

John's will, proved in 1601, offers great insight into his life. Several clauses relating to the fate of his soul came first. After stating that he was: '*sick in body but of good and perfect memory, praising God therefore,*' his first act was to:

'*First commit my soul into the hands of almighty God my only maker, through the merits of whose only son Jesus Christ, being sanctified by the Holy Ghost, I assuredly trust and unfeignedly believe to be saved, and my body to be buried within the church of Preston.*'

John then carefully distributed his household items. His only son Robert, heir to his property, was bequeathed a fully furnished feather-bed and two brass pots, including the biggest. The children of his daughter Katherine, now wife of farmer Thomas Smith, received a sheep apiece. Katherine herself received a brass pot. John's three unmarried daughters would receive £60 on their marriages and a cow. His daughter Faith received two pairs of sheets, a pair of blankets and a coverlet.

We laugh at these bequests today. We'd never consider handing these items to the next generation. John's will illustrates the value in which all possessions were held.

John concluded by charging Robert to pay his wife Margaret £10 yearly and sufficient meat and drink for her life, providing she didn't remarry. Provisions such as this were common. Thomas Timbrell dictated in 1695 that his wife Ursula was to be allowed: *'a room or two in my now dwelling house, to inhabit according to her pleasure, with ways to water and to the garden.'*

A woman had no entitlement to her husband's property after his death. Without a marriage settlement which allowed her possession throughout her widowhood, she was supported or left destitute at the whim of his male heir.

Hannah Alcock, a widow and maybe the mother of Nicholas Alcock of Beecham Farm, died in 1693. She had once lived in comparative ease but owned little of value on her death. Her possessions were valued at only £19; her wearing apparel and ready money comprised half of this.

A looking glass and a feather-bed with bedstead and curtains indicate her former prosperity. She also owned a spit, irons and dripping pan for roasting meat, a rare treat for poorer people. But Hannah evidently had to work. She owned spinning wheels for linen and wool, probably supplying Preston's weavers. A piece of linen cloth, alone worth £1, suggests she also sewed sheets and tablecloths. This may indicate Hannah's lack of a marriage settlement.

John Timbrell (1566-1622) was a typical prosperous 17th century farmer. His domestic and agricultural assets were valued on his death at £239 (£23,000 today). His household goods comprised:

His apparel	£5
24 pairs of sheets	£12
Three dozen napkins; three pairs of pillow cases; five table cloths; five towels; other linen	£4 8s
Four feather-beds; six wool-beds; five feather bolsters; four wool bolsters	£7

Five coverlets; four pairs of blankets; two carpets	£7
Three bedsteads; four plain bedsteads	£2
Two tableboards; two cupboards; two chests; three coffers; three chairs; two forms; one round table	£5
Twenty pieces of pewter; six pewter dishes; other small pieces of pewter	£1 1s
Six brass pots; five kettles; three pans; three candlesticks; one warming pan; five dabnets	£1 1s
One maltmill; one cheese press	30s
Wooden and copper ware	£4

Beds were still a luxury; a blanket or a grass-stuffed sack was all many people had. John had ten: four stuffed with feathers and six with wool or *flock* – locks of coarse wool of no use for spinning. He had nine children, which suggests each had their own bed. His sheets, tablecloths, bolsters and carpets, all recorded individually, were also luxury items. Pewter and brass were cheap metals – the especially wealthy owned silver – but were still a cut above wooden or pottery dishes.

Thomas Such, later spelt Souch or Zouch, who owned The Old Vicarage and leased Milcote Manor was the only farmer in Preston to be ranked a gentleman in the 1700s. On his death in 1721, his legacies included portraits of himself and his son John; a silver pint mug; a pair of silver salts; and the silver spoons and tongs for the tea table.

John Smith of Lower Farm was one of the wealthier farmers of the 1720s. The house, rebuilt in the 19th century, comprised the typical parlour, hall, kitchen, buttery [pantry] and rooms above each.

John lived with his wife Muriel and their seven children. When he died in September 1729, aged 43, his possessions were valued at a very comfortable £569 (£49,000 today). The domestic items comprised:

In the parlour: two tables, ten chairs	£1
Parlour chamber: one feather-bed and bedstead with curtains and valances; one chest of drawers; one table; four chairs; one looking glass	£7 10s
Hall: one table; one clock; four chairs; six stools	£2 10s
Room over hall: one feather-bed; one flock-bed; two bedsteads; three chests; two chairs	£3 10s
Kitchen: several odd things not mentioned	10s

Servants' Room: one flock-bed and bolsters; two bedsteads; one chair; one stool	£1
Room over entry: one flock-bed and bolster; one bedstead; one feather-bed and bolster	£11
Chamber over buttery: one feather-bed and bolster; two chests of drawers; one case of drawers; one table; two chairs	£5
Wearing apparel and money in purse	£10
Copper ware	£6
Pewter	£3 15s
Brass	£3 15s
Two grates; three wedges; other ironwork	£1 5s
Linen: 21 pairs of sheets; two dozen napkins; tablecloths	£11
Eleven pairs of blankets	£3 13s
Beam scale and weights; one bell metal mortar	17s

John had a lot of money in the house. Without modern banking systems, it all had to be hidden at home. He also employed live-in servants. Farm workers and domestic servants – known as servants in husbandry – were hired on an annual basis and were provided with accommodation and meals.

The parlour chamber – the best bedroom – contained a feather-bed with curtains and valances [canopies around the frame]. The looking glass too was a prized possession. John's wife Muriel, thanks to the resident servants, was able to devote time to her appearance. The clock in the hall, no doubt positioned to impress visitors, was another rarity. But John's other domestic items were fairly comparable to that of John Timbrell a century earlier.

His family had financial difficulties after his death – the farm was mortgaged on several occasions – but the farm passed intact to his eldest son John on Muriel's death in 1761. Thanks to her marriage settlement, she had possession of the farm for her life.

Muriel bequeathed her gold wedding ring to John and a side-saddle with a silver-laced bridle to her granddaughter Muriel. She dictated that she was to be buried in an oak coffin in a bricked grave. A coffin or gravestone were unaffordable for many people. Her grave still stands in the churchyard.

It wasn't just the farmers who lived well. William Kite, a shoemaker and shopkeeper who also kept a few animals, rented a now-demolished cottage near The Old Vicarage. Despite his basic living conditions – a dwelling room and a shop/workshop, with a room over each – his possessions were valued at £252 on his death in 1729. He even built an extension, called the New Room, to his cottage with a cheese chamber above.

William owned a feather-bed complete with feather pillows, curtains, valances and bedstead, and three flock-beds with bedsteads and bolsters for his children and young apprentice. His linen comprised eleven pairs of sheets; eighteen napkins; three fine and six coarse tablecloths; and six pillow cases. The woollens comprised fifteen blankets and five coverlets.

The upper rooms were used for storage as well as sleeping; the best bedroom contained cheese, wool and lumber as well as William's bed. A second bedroom contained a barrel of vinegar, 28lbs of hops and a salt-box as well as various coffers, chairs and stools.

The New Room was where William's wife Jane kept her two spinning wheels. It was also used to store hops, a sack of cutlings [coarsely ground grain for animal food] and a pot of honey. The main dwelling room was crammed with a clock and case, the first and probably most valuable item; two iron grates, a fender jack and spit iron; two dozen pewter dishes and plates; four brass kettles; a furnace; two ladles; two saucepans; seven brass, four iron and two pewter candlesticks; a drinking copper; a warming pan; a frying pan; a pestle and mortar; two pairs of tongs; a fire shovel; a round table; six chairs; two stools; two forms; eight drinking glasses; six glass patty pans [pie dishes]; and a pair of bellows. One wonders where the people fitted in.

The Life of a Labourer and Commoner

Most working men in Preston were farm labourers who owned no land of their own. Little record remains of their lives besides the church registers. Their graves were unmarked and they left no wills – they had nothing of value to bequeath.

Servants in husbandry, who were employed from autumn hiring fairs such as The Mop in Stratford, now a funfair, had a fairly comfortable life with their employers. They were mostly young and all unmarried. As they were provided food and lodging for a lower wage, they were more economical for their employers. When wages fell during the 19th century, hiring workers on a daily basis became more common.

The annual contracts usually began in October, after harvest, in arable areas such as the Midlands. Preston's marriage registers for the mid and late 18th century show that about a third of marriages took place in October, suggesting a good number of villagers were employed as servants in husbandry, therefore were free to marry when their contracts ended.

Married men worked as day labourers – employed on a day-to-day basis wherever they could find work – and were often close to the poverty line. Thomas Gasey was a young married labourer in the 1730s. He and his wife Anne had two infant children. They cared for William Hartwell, a weaver who lived alone and was in failing health, and when William died in 1736 he bequeathed the couple half of his house.

The Gaseys had three further children, and forty years later in December 1775, Thomas, now 'an ancient labourer' was buried in Preston churchyard. He may have been only in his late sixties, but his lifetime of slog had probably given him the appearance of ancientness.

The average life expectancy of an adult in 18th century England was around fifty years, but John Wilson was buried at Preston in 1771 aged 86; John Alcock in 1776 aged 84; Richard Berry in 1780 aged 72. All three were labourers, suggesting their life wasn't too bleak.

Commoner's rights were a great boost to rural quality of life. These ancient rights granted privileges on another man's land, generally the lord of the manor's land. The most important was *common of pasture*. This entitled a commoner to graze a certain number of animals on the common grazing ground. Animals were also tethered on village greens and roadsides and turned onto the stubble after harvest, the latter known as *common of shack*.

All who could afford it, craftsmen and labourers alike, kept animals on the common pasture. Carpenter Richard Salmon (d.1704) owned three cows, a pig and some poultry. Joiner John Garfield (d.1730) owned two cows and a pig. Shoemaker William Kite (d.1729) owned three cows, seventeen sheep and a pig.

Numbers were regulated to prevent overgrazing, and common of pasture rights were included in sales and leases. A lease of land to John Smith in the 1670s included the right to graze six sheep and a cow on The Lenches, now scrub in the Lower Park.

Butter and cheese were highly profitable. Cheese-making was a skilled process restricted to farmhouses, but a simple type of curd cheese – 'cottage cheese' – was made by cottagers.

Salted ham and bacon could feed a family for several months – tradition states you can use every part of a pig except the squeak. The right to keep pigs on the common waste ground and in the manor woods was called *pannage*. *Firebote* entitled a commoner to take firewood from the common.

In 1759 Preston's farmland and common ground was enclosed into individual fields by a private act of parliament, and commoners' rights were swept away in one fell swoop. Labourers could no longer keep livestock or gather firewood, and a surge in rural poverty followed.

Life for the Poor

Poverty has always been an issue. Each parish had a duty to provide work for able-bodied paupers – those who couldn't support themselves or their families. Churchwardens and overseers of the poor were appointed from the 17th century to see to the relief and education of the poor. The churchwardens also managed parish property and finances, encouraged church attendance and ensured children were baptised. They were appointed on an annual basis from the more respectable tiers of society: in Preston almost always yeoman farmers.

Paupers were dependent on their parish for Poor Relief, the equivalent of income support today. First started in 1597, it was levied from the wealthier parishioners based on the value of their property.

Begging was approved for cripples, but sturdy beggars, vagabonds and rogues were treated harshly. An Act of 1597 stated that the petty constable of the manor should apprehend such people. They were to be stripped naked from the middle upwards and to be openly whipped 'until their bodies be bloody'.

The poor were often remembered in the wills of wealthier people. Thomas Locke (d.1602) left a peck [two gallons] of corn to every poor cottage in Preston. Eight years later his widow Isabel left 3d to every cottage. In 1558 Thomas Hunckes left 3s 4d to all poor cottagers who had no team of oxen. John Maunsell alias Alexander left a creditable 12d to each cottage in 1601. Thomas Yeats left 20s and Giles Smith £10 to the poor in 1635.

This custom died out by the late 17th century. Perhaps the poor weren't so needy, or perhaps a last good deed to ensure a favourable judgement on one's soul wasn't so necessary.

Each parish had to take responsibility for their residents if they became 'chargeable', so movement between parishes was tightly controlled. Official settlement was granted if a person was born in the parish, occupied a home of a specific value or, for women, they married a resident. The overseers could remove strangers that didn't fit these bounds.

James Wheeler, a soldier from Preston, married Ann Handy from Stratford in 1803. Their son Thomas was born there in March 1807. James left Ann a few weeks later – he may have been posted abroad – leaving her penniless and with no idea when, or if, he would return. Ann was now the burden of her home parish. As James belonged to Preston, she and Thomas were delivered to John Mansell, overseer for the poor of Preston.

Three years later, Ann returned to Stratford with Thomas. There was still no sign of James. She was living in Stratford without legal settlement and was summoned to JP John Lord Esq to answer her case. Lord deemed her an idle and disorderly person and ordered her to be committed to a House of Correction for 14 days' hard labour.

The whereabouts of James all this time is unclear. It was the height of the Napoleonic Wars and his regiment – the 7th Regiment of Foot – had been fighting in the Iberian Peninsula. James may even have fought at Waterloo. Or he may have simply grown tired of his idle and disorderly wife and gone to pastures new.

A stranger could settle in a new parish providing he had a certificate from his home parish, stating they would receive him back if he became chargeable. Alternatively the new parish could grant him settlement. Richard Salmon had been born in Preston in 1701 but wasn't officially 'settled' as his father was a stranger. He received a settlement certificate in 1734. It stated that:

> *We the churchwardens and overseers of the poor of the parish of Preston on Stour in the county of Gloucester do hereby acknowledge and own Richard Salmon, joiner, to be an inhabitant legally settled in the parish of Preston on Stour.*
>
> *In witness thereof we have set our hands and seals, the 20th day of June in the eighth year of the reign of our sovereign Lord George ye second by the grace of God of Great Britain, France and Ireland, King, defender of the faith, etc., Anno Dom 1734.*
>
> Thomas Smith, John Harris, churchwardens
>
> John Zouch, John Harris, overseers
>
> Attested by Thomas Ryland and Thomas Salmon
>
> *We, whose names are hereunto subscribed, Justices of the Peace of the County of Gloucester do allow the certificate above written. Dated 24th June, Anno Dom 1734.*
>
> John Gray
>
> R Dighland

Settlement wasn't always straightforward. William Purser was born in Whitchurch in 1791, the son of tenant farmer John Purser. When William was ten, his father rented a house in Stratford. Aged twelve, William was bound as an apprentice to Preston tailor William Franklin.

Seven years later, Franklin died. William continued to work for his widow for some time, then moved to Aston Cantlow. He married and had two children. He then returned to Preston where he became chargeable. He was removed to Stratford, but Stratford claimed he didn't belong to them. A lengthy legal debate ensued.

William's father, John Purser, had rented property in Stratford, which Preston's officers claimed to be worth £10/annum. Stratford's officers very much doubted this. £10 was the threshold which granted the occupier and his dependants legal settlement. But Stratford contended the value of the tenement was below this threshold.

They made a second point regarding the settlement of William Franklin, Purser's former master. A master could claim settlement for his apprentice in his parish, and a fierce debate ensued as to whether Franklin himself had been settled in Preston.

Franklin's father Thomas had come from Todenham, and had a certificate stating that Todenham would receive him and his family should they become chargeable. Therefore Thomas, his son William, and most importantly William's apprentice, were not settled in Preston.

Stratford spotted a legal loophole. The Todenham certificate was for Thomas Franklin 'and family'. It didn't mention his son William by name, and so couldn't be proved to apply to him. As William had married and raised his own family in Preston, he should be considered settled there. And so could his former apprentice.

Preston countered that William had always lived in his father's tenement, despite being married. This tenement was worth under £5/annum – below the threshold for settlement – and despite all the above points he wasn't independently settled.

The debate continued back and forth for several months, and eventually it was decided the Pursers were to live in Stratford. They had four more children; at least two died in childhood.

In 1841, William, now fifty, was still working as a tailor. It seems he was no longer a pauper. He died in 1853 in Stratford Workhouse. He had suffered from paralysis for nearly four months, perhaps from a stroke. His surviving sons moved to Warwick and raised families of their own.

The Workhouse

The system of Poor Relief changed dramatically following the Poor Law Amendment Act of 1834. The system was much abused. Employers would hire workers at low wages, knowing the parish would make up the difference. It was decided that outside relief would stop and paupers would receive relief in a workhouse. Preston became part of Stratford Union, and the Stratford Union Workhouse was built in 1836.

The workhouse has a fearsome reputation, enhanced by classics such as *Oliver Twist*. It was proposed that residency should be made a social stigma, a last resort which only the truly desperate would covet. While in many places inmates were subject to a brutal regime, Stratford workhouse appears to have had a positive outlook. The master had a genuine interest in the welfare of the paupers, the young were taught the value of good honest work, and all boys over the age of eight had some form of employment.

The system was slow to change and many paupers only entered the workhouse when they could no longer live independently. Barbara Day, a labourer's wife of No.32, was widowed in 1881. She received Poor Relief for fourteen years and entered the workhouse in March 1895, now aged 84. She died a fortnight later and was buried at Preston.

Louisa Whitrod, widow of gamekeeper Henry Whitrod, lived alone in No.30 for ten years before entering the workhouse in February 1905, aged 81. She died four months later.

Emma Davis, 25, a domestic servant, entered the workhouse in March 1885 when heavily pregnant. Her daughter Gertrude was born on the 31st. Emma left the child with her mother Sarah, wife of labourer John Davis of No.10, and went to work in Bourton on the Hill, twenty miles away.

In 1890 John fell from a wagon and suffered fatal head injuries. Emma married a year later and moved to Warwick. It seems she had no further children, and her daughter never went to live with her – perhaps her husband never knew of her existence. When Sarah died in 1898, Gertrude disappeared from the historical record.

The Model Village

Many labourers were housed in divided-up farmhouses and even farm buildings. No details survive of these dwellings in Preston, but the living conditions of rural workers by the 19th century were often appalling. Joseph Ashby, a self-educated farm labourer who campaigned for rural workers' rights, wrote reports of Warwickshire villages in the 1890s. No attention was paid to comfort or sanitation. Ill-fitting doors, broken windows and decayed roofs were common. The walls were broken, black and mouldy. Despite housing up to eight adults and children, there was often only one bedroom and one living room. As tenancy agreements required that if a labourer left his home he also left his job, and vice versa, there was little scope for better prospects.

Parish houses were allocated to paupers at the discretion of the churchwardens and overseers of the poor. They were nominally kept in good repair using parish funds. There were around ten in 1721, and probably many more by 1841. Several stood along the main village street, all now demolished.

In 1840, five parish houses were auctioned by the parish officers. They were dilapidated and no longer fit for purpose, and had a total estimated value of £75. They were occupied by Mary Manners, a young widow with five children; William Russell, 82, a farm labourer with five dependants; Mary Davis, a widow; Samuel Garrett, 43, a labourer with five dependants; and Thomas Saunders, 73, a labourer who lived alone.

John Mansell, the current overseer, confirmed that the cottages had been in the hands of the overseers for at least fifty years, were repaired out of the poor rates, and they or the parochial vestry had always placed in them such paupers as they saw fit. The residents paid an annual rent of two shillings. It was supposed that they had been built on the waste ground, but whether with consent of the lord of the manor couldn't now be ascertained. They were purchased by James Roberts-West.

A drive to improve workers' living conditions was gaining momentum and landlords were building quality accommodation. Many impoverished dwellings in Preston were pulled down in the 1850s at the instigation of James Roberts-West, replaced with modern, brick-built cottages which still line the main street today. Similar cottages were built in Alderminster, Wimpstone and Crimscote.

Laid out to the best available designs with five rooms each, their own pigsties, earth-closets, washhouses and bake-houses, they offered a previously unheard-of standard of living and were entered in a competition held by the Royal Agricultural Society to improve the standard of living for agricultural workers. The philanthropic nature of these projects was praised by social commentators.

The first residents were those who'd lived in Preston for ten or twenty years, many in those now-demolished buildings. All worked on the estate or its farms. Rents were 1s 2d a week – exceptionally reasonable – and tenants would be given a week's notice to leave if required.

The dramatic improvements are still in stark contrast to modern living standards. In 1881, Charles Dyer, a 41-year-old farm labourer, was living at No.2 with his wife Emma and their eight children, aged from sixteen years to three months. These houses are now considered cramped for a family of four.

The model houses c.1880. May include Ann Samman of No.3 and Elizabeth Bishop of No.4. From WI collection.

In 1893, an outbreak of diphtheria claimed the life of ten-year-old Edith Paxford, daughter of farm labourer Kendrick Paxford from No.7. Her sister Rose had died from the illness seven years earlier.

Diphtheria is a childhood infectious disease which causes general malaise before progressing to systematic organ damage and in many cases, coma and death. This is what happened to Edith. She had been ill for a fortnight before suffering a sudden fall in blood pressure. This caused her to fall into unconsciousness from which she did not recover.

Following the recent discovery that sewage-contaminated water was largely responsible for cholera outbreaks, water samples were taken from the local wells and analysed. Not one was found to be satisfactory. Dr Thompson, who conducted the analysis, believed that as the houses and wells were built on a slope below the graveyard, contamination had soaked down and fouled the drinking water. Scathing comments were made about how such a situation could arise, despite the houses being only thirty years old. Although, it was fairly pointed out, the sanitary business was not much thought of then.

It was during the 1880s that physician Robert Koch developed his 'germ theory of disease' and bacteria were discovered to be the cause of many infectious diseases. Developments in hygiene and sanitation triggered a rapid reduction in many illnesses. It was suggested that the village wells be cleaned out to prevent such a tragedy recurring, but Dr Thompson believed this would be ineffective in the long-term.

Subsequent research found diphtheria to be an airborne illness, so the conditions of the wells would in fact have had no impact on its incidence.

A Woman's Work...

Keeping a house, even of modest size, was a full-time occupation. The modern conveniences we now take for granted – light switches, piped and heated water, washing machines, electric ovens, vacuum cleaners – were luxuries for most families until the mid 20th century. Floors had to be scrubbed; woodwork polished; three meals a day prepared from scratch. With no refrigeration, food was bought and prepared daily. Water was drawn from a well. And all this with eight or more children to care for. A woman was judged by the standard of the house she kept, and girls were prepared for this duty from a young age.

Shopping and food preparation was an endless task. Preston bakery and grocery provided much of the villagers' needs. Many people had gardens or allotments; milk and butter were bought from the farms; but a weekly trip to Stratford was still required.

Laundry day was typically Monday. The left-overs from the Sunday roast provided the meals so the entire day could be left free. And it took an entire day. A fire was lit under the copper – a huge metal bowl – and buckets of water carried from the soft-water (rainwater) well. The laundry was beaten and worked in the copper until clean – a manual version of the rotating drum of a modern washing machine. It was then squeezed through a mangle and hung out to dry.

Before soap powder was available, lye – an alkaline solution made from wood ash – was used. Gloucestershire women discovered that boiling clothes with a handful of suet or dripping produced vastly better results. Heating alkali and fat is actually the process to make soap, so these women were far ahead of their time.

Laundry was an unpleasant job. Constant immersion in hot, soapy water made women's hands sore, cracked and swollen, and many better-off households employed a laundress. In 1901 Mary Job, a 52-year-old widow, was working as a laundress, as was 78-year-old Louisa Whitrod.

Annie Timms from Broad Campden (b.1866) married Josiah Hopkins in 1890 and the couple lived at Atherstone Hill Cottages. Josiah spent 48 years as a carter for George Brookes at Atherstone Hill Farm. Annie recalled in 1940 that she had to go out washing each day, from eight to five, earning a shilling a day, and this with two young children to care for. She would get up at 4am to ensure they were clean and tidy for school.

She was scathing about the younger generations. The two cottages next to theirs were empty, and in the familiar lament of the elderly she said; 'Nobody wants to live here, so far from the bus route. They should have lived here in the old days, when there wasn't even a carrier's cart. The young aren't happy and won't stay, even with bicycles and the bus. They won't work on the land, they all want to work in the towns.'

Strange to think those young people are the elderly of today, who make similar comments about the present young generations!

The well outside Priest's Cottage c.1911. Park Farm is on the left. From WI collection.

Food was cooked on a coal-fired range, a stove set into the fireplace, or over an open fire. Pots stood on trivets and the kettle hung on a hook. Joe Newland of Radbrook Cottages (1901-1993) remembered his mother cooking meals in a pot over the fire – rabbit, vegetables and jam roly poly pudding all simmered up together.

Child-minding was a task for older girls. Valerie Bliss, nee Jaques, and her younger sister Barbara lived at Atherstone Hill Farm in the 1940s. They were often left in charge of their baby brother Robert. They had great fun rolling him down the flagstone path in his pram. When they were bored with that, they would put the cat in the pram and do the same.

When Robert was new-born, he was put in a drawer to sleep. He then graduated to the washing basket. When he was a few months old, he moved into the bath. With no mains water the bath was never used, so their mother filled it with clothes to make him a bed.

Any new baby was inevitably the subject of much cooing by the other women. When Chris Daniell's son Mark was born in 1970, she was complimented on what a lovely baby he was.

'Hitler was a lovely baby too, once,' teacher Molly Ashby remarked.

Fred and Emily Dyde of The Old Manor with their first child Elsie, c.1908. A family photograph was a rare event: they are in their best clothes. Courtesy of Geoff Vickers.

Life in the Sticks

Marjorie Dyde (1909-1985) the daughter of Fred and Emily Dyde, married George Vickers, a Birmingham mechanic. She often came back to Preston with her sons, Geoff, Robert and Dennis.

The boys loved Preston. The freedom and space was unreal and they were soon friends with all the local children. They always cried when it was time to go home – the long bus journey back to Birmingham made Preston seem impossibly far away.

Life was very different here. They were used to hot water, flush toilets, mains electricity and dozens of shops. In Preston, light came from oil lamps and candles. Groping one's way down the garden in the cold and the dark to the privy was an experience for anyone not used to it. Squares of newspaper were used as toilet roll. At night, a chamberpot under the bed was used. Stone hot water bottles and warming pans – long-handled pans filled with coals – warmed beds, as did hot bricks.

The difficulty of fetching and heating water meant bath-night was a weekly affair. It was conveniently considered healthy for Victorian children to have a cold bath in summer and a tepid bath in winter. A tin bath in front of the fire was shared by everyone. The Jaques children at Atherstone Hill Farm had a bath in the copper when the laundry was finished.

George Vickers, city-born and bred, didn't like Preston and soon stopped coming to visit. And when Fred went to stay in Birmingham, he couldn't wait to get back home. Although Marjorie was a country girl, she liked Birmingham and was proud of where she lived, so was happy in both worlds.

During the Second World War, several families moved to Preston. George and Elsie Harding moved from London in 1940. Bill and Lillian Walton also moved, as did Bob and Doreen Stredder. Queenie Coomber came with her children Ralph and Beryl, while her husband Ted, a member of the National Fire Service, remained in London. Their son Roger was born in Preston in 1943. All four families would settle in Preston for good.

Arthur and Marian Jaques lived on a farm in Essex. When bombs started falling only a few miles away, the family moved to Atherstone Hill Farm.

Reg and Nell Stoppard lived in Birmingham with their children. In 1940 a bomb fell just outside their house, and Reg told his wife she had to leave. So Nell packed everything she could into a pram, gathered the children and caught a train to Stratford. She also moved into Atherstone Hill Farm.

Despite having no electricity, mains water or inside toilet, both families enjoyed their time at the farm, the children especially so. When the Stoppards returned home after the war, they missed Atherstone so much they moved back. They eventually emigrated to New Zealand, but both families have remained solid friends ever since and still visit the place that provided the happiest days of their lives.

Nine-year-old Joan Hulbert, nee Knight, was evacuated from Dagenham in Essex in 1939. Four of her siblings, 12-year-old Violet, 11-year-old Harry, 8-year-old Doris and 6-year-old Mary, accompanied her. In June 1940, the children were moved to Preston.

It was a shock to find no electricity, running water, bathroom or inside toilet. The expedition to the outside toilet at the top of the garden, in the dark and with a pig grunting in the sty next door, was terrifying. Joan never got used to this, although the children quickly adapted to oil lamps and had fun with the water pump.

Joan and Doris were taken in by Charlie and Rose Horseman of No.8. Mary and Violet went to Gladys Gibbins of No.6, and Harry went to Elizabeth Walton of No.36. Mrs Walton could be very strict with children. When they climbed the tree outside her cottage she would come out with her stick and chase them away. Harry could be a bit naughty, which didn't suit Mrs Walton's temperament. He tried to run away and was eventually moved to another home.

Many families in Preston took in evacuees. These women who opened their homes for uprooted and frightened children were, in Joan's opinion, the forgotten heroes of the evacuation process. Rose Horseman was strict but always fair and treated them no differently to her own son John. She wasn't one for idleness and taught the girls to cook, darn and sew – their work was always thoroughly inspected – as well as providing the love and stability they needed. Her husband Charlie was also wonderfully kind to them; Joan remembers him putting a hot brick in her bed to warm it.

In their five years away, Joan and her siblings only saw their parents a couple of times. Returning to Dagenham after the war was almost as traumatic as leaving. Joan had left Dagenham a child; she was now a young woman. Even the youngest girl was almost a teenager. Their parents had become near strangers, and they had to say goodbye the new family they'd found.

Joan and her family remained in constant touch with the Horsemans and they often came to Preston for holidays. Seventy years after she returned to Dagenham, Joan still looks back on her years in Preston with fondness, and acknowledges the enormous influence – all for the good – her experience has had on her life and the person she became.

The Modern World Arrives

Electricity

Alscot Park was the first house in Preston to gain electricity when a hydro-electric pumping station was installed in the 1890s.

The first electrically-lit house had been engineered in 1880. A hydro-plant comprising a dam and sluice directed water against a series of turbines which spun a generator. A similar system was designed for Alscot. The now-derelict pumping station is by the Stour on the Atherstone boundary; a generator was installed in a building in the grounds.

This provided enough power for lights, a single-bar fire and later on a wireless, along with a full-time job for the estate's electrical engineer. Albert Jackson held this position in 1901. Albert had been a grocer's assistant in Yorkshire; moved to London where he worked as an engine driver; then moved to Preston in the 1890s.

One Saturday evening in December 1901, he had a tragic accident. He walked home across the deer park while the river was in flood, lost his footing in the dark and fell. His body was found the next morning. His wife and young daughter left Preston soon afterwards and their house was occupied by Albert's successor, electrical engineer Percy Dove from Hampshire.

Mains electricity was installed in a few houses in 1933. The Gables, now owned by wealthy former mayor Robert Mansell Smith, was undergoing drastic modernisation. Chromium taps were installed in the scullery. Electric bell-pulls, lights, fires and a cooker were added. Hot water pipes heated the rooms. As a feature in the *Stratford Herald* enthused, it might well be a display in an ideal homes exhibition. Park Farm had electricity installed at a similar time.

The majority of Preston, along with Alscot Park, was connected to the mains in the 1950s. Not everyone was impressed. Fred Dyde of The Old Manor, now in his seventies, wanted to keep the oil lamps he'd always used. As his house was owned by Alscot Estate, electricity was installed anyway.

Mains Water

The Warwickshire Agricultural Show was hosted by Alscot Park in June 1949. The arrangements went well until the committee asked for the mains water supply. There wasn't one. The show cattle were all tuberculosis-free so couldn't have well or river water. A line had to be put in before the show could proceed. A pipe was run from this into the house. Then in 1953 pipes were laid into the village, the work completed in January 1955.

In July 1954, John Ward from Stratford, who had been working on the installation, stole 400lbs of lead from the site. He called a taxi and loaded the lead into the back. He informed the driver he was the site foreman, and the taxi took him to a dealership in Coventry where he sold it.

It transpired that Ward, a Dunkirk veteran, had 23 previous convictions. In his defence, a letter from a woman in Stratford was produced.

I will still marry you when you come out to show I love you.

This didn't sway the court, and Ward was imprisoned for two years. Whether the unknown lady kept her promise is lost to history.

Bathrooms were soon installed. The bigger houses converted a spare bedroom, but a separate room was built on the smaller cottages. Taps and flush toilets were now found in every house. The tin bath in front of the fire and the expedition to the privy became a thing of the past.

Laying water pipes under the Stour, 1954. From WI collection.

Transport

Until the 20th century most people had to travel on foot, no matter the distance. Annie Hopkins of Atherstone Hill Cottages remembered in 1940 that when she first married she'd walk four miles to Stratford and carry a week's worth of food back. John Leese (b.1931) lived at Beecham Farm. His mother Margaret would walk along the railway line to Stratford to save the few pence bus fare. The children had to walk nearly two miles to school, and when they got home, John's eldest sister Valerie, aged eight, would often be sent back again to the village shop.

Horses and traps were limited to farms and bigger households, but the carrier's cart provided a reasonably-priced conveyance from the 1900s. Very few people left the village except for necessity, and days out were unknown.

Land agent Robert Burra outside The Cottage c.1900. Courtesy of Bridget Loader.

Most farmworkers could afford a bicycle by the 1930s. Dozens of bikes went through the village at midday as the men went home for dinner. Farmer Reg Ashby from The Old Vicarage owned a motorbike, complete with a sidecar for his wife to ride in.

A regular bus service from Stratford started in the 1930s, run by Stratford Blue Motors Ltd. George Harding, who moved from London in 1940, spent most of his working life with the company. In 1961 he received an award for 21 years service, all accident-free and with no driving convictions. By this point he had driven the equivalent of one and a half times around the world.

He had, in fact, received one conviction. In 1947 he was charged with stealing a gallon of petrol from a bus. He said he needed it to get to work. As he had an unblemished record, the case was dismissed.

Motor cars were owned at Alscot Park from the 1890s, but even in the 1950s, if a car or taxi came into Preston, everybody would rush to their windows to look.

Many people owned cars by the 1970s. Council worker Monty Preston parked his by the church. If it wouldn't start, he'd roll it down the road beside the church to get it going. If that didn't work, he'd go down the main street. If that didn't work, he'd go down the Cow Lane. If it still wasn't going, he'd ask Harry Smith to tow him back up for another go.

Bob Spencer of Park Farm bought a pick-up truck in the 1960s. When he went on holiday it disappeared. His mother Elsie, known for her formidable personality, noticed. She collared Monty Preston who parked his tractor on the farm.

'Where's the truck, Monty?'

'I don't know, Mrs Spencer.'

'Where's the truck, Monty.'

'Down at Fred Dale's, Mrs Spencer!'

Fred had borrowed it thinking nobody would know.

Medical Care

The array of medical facilities we take for granted today was unknown before the 20th century. The first port of call for medical treatment was the home and the natural world. Plant-based remedies were widely known and household items were used for myriad ailments. Raw onions were used for wasp stings; the ubiquitous vinegar and brown paper for toothache, sprains and bruises. Everybody knows dock leaves for nettle stings; some remember using cobwebs to staunch bleeding.

A doctor's visit was expensive, but the poor could get permission to send for a doctor at the Union's expense. In 1873, Elizabeth West of Alscot Park wrote a complaint that the Relieving Officer, from whom permission had to be obtained, now lived in Wellesbourne, over eight miles away. A man had to lose a day's work to walk there and back. Mrs West requested that the Officer should live at Stratford near the parish doctor, as he had previously done.

The all-too-familiar response stated that due to cost-cutting, the Relieving Officers now coped with many extra duties, and covered much larger areas. A local officer was no longer possible.

Nursing and midwifery care was performed by local women. When Sarah Smith of Park Farm fell ill in November 1870, suffering from phthisis [tuberculosis] and exhaustion from her fourth pregnancy, she was nursed by labourer's wife Barbara Day. Sarah deteriorated and she died with Barbara at her side. She was 35, and her youngest child was four years old.

Her grave is today a mass of snowdrops in spring. They became widely popular in the mid 19th century; perhaps her husband Giles or her children planted the first bulbs there.

Sarah Smith's grave

Thirteen-year-old Mary Currier came to Preston from Quinton in 1837 to work as a nursemaid at Locke's Farm. She later married farm labourer Giles Horseman, moved to No.1 and had eight children. Their son Giles became the Sub Postmaster.

Mary became the village midwife and also provided nursing care for poorer families. She had no professional training and learnt her skills entirely through patient experience. She loved her work, had a quiet and confident demeanour, and successfully delivered dozens of local babies. She retired to Locke's Farm after being widowed and died in 1916, aged 92.

Mary Horseman with her husband Giles, outside No.1 c.1900. From WI collection.

District nurses, usually single women who had attended nursing school, were funded from the 1860s for those who couldn't afford medical care. Revd Harvey Bloom of Whitchurch petitioned for a district nurse for the Alscot villages in the 1900s. He was duty-bound to provide a nurse from his own funds if one of his flock fell sick, and this nurse had to be summoned from Stratford, a long and lonely walk in the middle of the night.

Henrietta (Hetty) Hawkins from Middlesex took the job *c.*1905. She lived at No.9 Preston – next to the Post Office, which had a telephone – with her widowed mother Fanny. She would go about her duties on a bicycle, usually with a spaniel in the basket for company. This was provided to guard the bicycle while she was visiting.

Nurse Ballard was the district nurse in the 1930s. The nurse's house was now No.3. A wooden outbuilding beside the house was installed as a surgery.

The next nurse was Margaret Hayward. Margaret was born in Gloucester in 1907 and trained as a nurse and a midwife. She worked at various hospitals before moving to Preston *c.*1938. Like her predecessors, she went about by bicycle, but in later years she was provided with a car.

Margaret delivered many local babies. Doreen Smith of Lower Farm was one of her first. Marjorie Vickers, nee Dyde, now living in Birmingham, returned to Preston for the birth of her first child in 1939. Dennis was safely delivered by Margaret in the same room where his mother had been born. Ethel Davies, nee Newland, born in Cutlin Mill in 1944, was Margaret's last. One of the good things about being a village midwife was that she got to see 'her' babies growing up, a rarity for a hospital midwife.

One of Margaret's long-term patients was baker Richard Beavington, who'd suffered a stroke in 1919. She became friendly with his son Dick, and they would chat when Dick passed her house on his delivery round. The couple were married in 1942. Margaret gave up nursing when her daughter Elizabeth was born in 1945, but she remained 'Nurse Beavington' and people long continued to seek her advice on medical matters.

Margaret was followed by Nurse Harris, who again lived at No.3. She was a small woman who walked with a limp and drove an Austin 7 car. She was the last district nurse to live in Preston, and left around 1956.

Mary and Daisy Porter of No.8. By 1911, Mary was working as a sick nurse at a women's convalescent home in Woking. Daisy also followed a nursing career. Courtesy of Maurice Porter.

Crime and Punishment

The Middle Ages

During the Middle Ages, minor crimes were dealt with by the lord of the manor. A Court Leet was held twice yearly, which all adult males were obliged to attend. This dealt with minor offences and issues such as repairing fences and highways.

It was obligatory to practice archery on Sundays and Holy Days, and this was brought up a few times at the Preston Court Leet. In 1593, yeoman John Maunsell alias Alexander was exempted from this.

More serious crimes were judged by appointed officials. In October 1553, Thomas Taylor, a wealthy Preston yeoman, had an altercation with yeoman John Amaundesley of Nether Ettington. Thomas attacked Amaundesley with a piked staff and chased him along a road, probably Shakersway, as far as the Atherstone gate. Amaundesley couldn't flee further so he drew his sword and struck Taylor in self-defence. Taylor's left arm was badly cut. The wound became infected and he died a week later.

An inquest was held. Amaundesley surrendered to Marshalsea Prison and the coroner and Chief Justice granted him a pardon for the death.

The Stocks

The stocks were a common punishment until the early 19th century. A law passed in 1405 decreed that every community must have its own stocks to punish minor crimes such as blasphemy, drunkenness and playing sports on a Sunday. They were erected in a public place – the village green or the market place – and passers-by were free to mock offenders or throw the proverbial rotting vegetables at them.

Preston's stocks stood on the green under a lime tree called the Stocks Tree, which blew down in 1958. Fanny Garrett, nee Winter (1873-1953) recalled to Dorothy Unett that she remembered the stocks still in position. Rumour had it they were last used in 1840 to punish boys for trampling the corn.

Condemned with Book, Bell and Candle

When religion and government were closely linked, the Church was often responsible for meting out punishments. For more severe cases, this could mean excommunication. This involved exclusion from Christian society, which at the time included all aspects of normal daily life and therefore meant general ostracism. It wasn't equivalent to eternal damnation as is commonly supposed. A public ceremony would take place where a bell was tolled, the Book of Gospels ceremonially closed and a candle snuffed out. Repentance and confession could usually secure a reversal.

In November 1403, robbers broke into the house of John Smith in Preston, and John was killed in the struggle. His wife Joan was later maliciously defamed by several people who said she'd aided the robbers.

Word reached Richard Clifford, the Bishop of Worcester, and he sent a mandate to the chaplain of Preston that all those who had defamed Joan were to incur excommunication. He wrote that:

It is to be done in the presence of the people and in the solemnities of the mass, with cross erect in their hands, bells tolling and candle lighted, and then these are to be extinguished and cast to the ground as the denunciation is uttered.

Whether the robbers were caught, whether Joan had indeed aided them, and whether those excommunicated ever repented their crime will probably never be known.

The Nineteenth Century

Offences were now judged in regular sessions by Justices of the Peace and magistrates, or in quarterly county Assizes for more serious crimes. The Metropolitan Police was formed in 1830 and other counties established police forces soon afterwards. By the 19th century the lord of the manor had minimal judicial authority.

One of the commonest crimes of the Victorian era was drunkenness. The Licensing Act of 1872 decreed that any person found drunk in the highway or in a public place was liable to a fine of forty shillings or a month's imprisonment.

In September 1872, William Bishop, 21, who lived with his parents in Silvester's Row, became the first person charged under this Act in Stratford. He was found drunk and noisy in Stratford at 11.30pm by Police Sergeant Cross. Bishop had 'evidently been a disciple of Bacchus' [the Roman God of wine] and was desirous of a fight with anyone who would stand before him. He then smashed a window.

William was given the choice of a 10s fine with 13s costs, or 21 days' imprisonment with hard labour. He chose the fine but didn't learn his lesson. In 1879, now 28 and still living with his parents, he was again found drunk, and this time was fined £1 6s.

In 1889, Richard Osbourne, a Preston labourer in his fifties, was charged with being drunk and incapable in Alderminster. When he appeared in court he said he had nothing to say in his defence and he hoped the magistrates would not say much either.

They said he was fined ten shillings.

Who's the Daddy?

An indelible stigma was for centuries associated with unmarried mothers, but nevertheless the church registers abound with the baptisms of illegitimate – base-born or bastard – babies. The child almost always took its mother's surname.

In rare cases, the father was acknowledged. In 1762 was the baptism of: *William, the son of William Jilks and Elizabeth Forster.* Elizabeth already had an illegitimate son John, baptised a year earlier.

Over a decade later in 1774 was the marriage of: *William Jilks and Elizabeth Forster, old acquaintances.* It seems the couple were in an accepted extra-marital relationship.

In August 1777, her son John, presumably he who was baptised in 1761, was buried. He was recorded as: *the base-born son of John Watts of Stratford and Elizabeth Forster.* It seems Elizabeth had a relationship with more than one man.

More often, young women, seduced with promises of marriage, found themselves pregnant with no wedding forthcoming. This happened to 17-year-old Sarah Rouse in 1867.

Sarah, a labourer's daughter from Alderminster, was a plain girl: short, stout, with light brown hair and a red birthmark on the side of her nose. She went into service aged 14, working for Frederick and Jane Silvester at The Cottage. She worked without fault for three years.

Then she fell pregnant. She told nobody, and on 1st February 1867 she went into labour. Ellen Price, the Silvesters' nursemaid, later deposed that Sarah had become very ill that morning and couldn't leave their bedroom. When Sarah managed to go downstairs, Ellen found a dreadful mess on the floor. Sarah's box was, unusually, locked.

Ellen found the key on the floor – Sarah must have dropped it. She opened the box. Inside, she found the body of a female baby.

Ellen didn't know what to do. She closed the box and waited until her mistress returned home the next morning. 'Sarah had a child yesterday,' she said.

Jane was shocked. She'd had no suspicion at all that Sarah was in the family way, and the girl had been of entirely good character for the past three years. She sent for Sarah at once.

'Is anything the matter?'

Sarah said nothing.

'Where is your child, Sarah?'

Sarah started to cry. Jane saw she was looking very ill and ought to be put to bed. She sent for her mother and for surgeon Thomas Barman, who examined the baby. It was fully grown and he could find no marks of violence. He conducted a post mortem but couldn't say whether the child been born alive. Considering the circumstances, its death was probably unsurprising. Sarah couldn't be charged with murder, but she stood trial for concealing the birth.

Mr Harrington, conducting her defence, asked of the jury; 'Could you hold this poor young girl, seduced by some scoundrel and utterly inexperienced, responsible in a case where it is perfectly uncertain if she intended concealment?'

'The objective of punishing concealment of dead babies is to prevent unfair play to living children,' the judge pointed out. 'Why did she not disclose her condition, and make preparations for her confinement?'

Sarah had in fact told Barman she'd intended to tell her mistress, and she believed the baby was premature. The jury found her guilty, but recommended her to mercy. She was sentenced to six weeks imprisonment with hard labour.

Sarah never went on to marry. She moved to Milverton, twenty miles away, perhaps where nobody would know of her past, and worked as a cook for fifteen years. In 1891, now unemployed, she was living with her brother Henry in Leamington Spa.

Her life then took a turn for the better. In 1911, now aged 60, she was living in a sizeable house in Leamington Spa and was running her own business as a wardrobe dealer. Her niece Evelyn worked as her assistant. She died in 1936 aged 87. The scoundrel who fathered her child was never identified.

If an unmarried mother disclosed the name of the father, he could be bound to pay maintenance for the child's upbringing, especially if he was of means and the child would likely become chargeable to the mother's parish.

In 1807, Mary Spencer, an unmarried charwoman from Chesterton in Warwickshire, declared herself with child. She disclosed that the father was Robert Smith, 23, the younger son of John Smith from Lower Farm in Preston. The churchwardens and overseers of Chesterton bound Robert to pay:

All manner of costs, payments, and charges whatsoever, for or by reason of the pregnancy and lying in of the said Mary Spencer of which she is now envient, or the clothing, maintenance or bringing up of said child/children, and also of all other charges taxing or concerning the same.

Robert's brother-in-law Charles Ward, a farmer at Wincote, was bound to pay if Robert did not.

Mary was delivered of a healthy baby boy, George, who was baptised as her illegitimate son in March 1808. Robert married later that year and went on to have eight legitimate children. Mary's future is unclear, but George Spencer moved to Bidford on Avon and became an innkeeper.

A Case of Lunacy

Richard George (b.1832) was the eldest son of wheelwright William George and went into the family trade in his teens. He never married, but remained living with his father in Silvester's Row. It appears he suffered from a mental illness.

In May 1879, now aged 47, Richard was admitted into Stratford Workhouse suffering from an 'affliction of the brain'. He showed some disposition towards violence – it took six men to convey him to Stratford – but officials had no reason to suppose him a lunatic, and didn't consider it necessary to certify him for an asylum.

After a few days, Richard became troubled with hallucinations. His behaviour became erratic and delusional. He refused to adhere to workhouse discipline and became violent.

After few weeks he managed to escape. A search was mounted but no sign of him was found. Then his father contacted the workhouse. Richard had turned up at his home and was threatening to kill him. Charles Collingwood, the master of the workhouse, set out for Preston with a police constable at once. They found Richard armed with a poker. 'Don't come near me!' he shouted.

He couldn't be reasoned with. They tackled him and disarmed him. He was returned to the workhouse where he was placed under secure guard.

The following day, despite his guard, Richard managed to steal a table fork and conceal it on his person. He was becoming increasingly violent and was convinced his father had bribed Mr Collingwood to cut his throat. Collingwood called for police assistance. Inspector Brindley of the Warwickshire Constabulary arrived with another constable and the three men entered the infirmary.

Richard retreated into the narrow space between two beds, preventing the men from surrounding him. He was brandishing the stolen fork. Brindley tackled Richard and a struggle ensued. Both men fell. Brindley tried to pin Richard's arms, but Richard got a hand free. He stabbed Brindley in the face with the fork. The prongs entered his eye. The other two men managed to drag Richard away. A surgeon was called.

Richard was taken to the county magistrates' court on a charge of grievous bodily harm. He now appeared harmless and dejected. The charges were read out to him.

'Do you understand what is said to you?'

'No, sir.'

'You are charged with stabbing Inspector Brindley.'

'I never wished to do that, not half as much as they wanted to do something to me. I wouldn't have done it if they hadn't started pulling me about.'

The proceeding concluded that Richard should be certified insane, and within a week he was conveyed to an asylum.

The damage to Brindley's eye turned out to be minimal. The prongs had just grazed the eyeball and the surgeon believed he would make a full recovery.

Richard spent the rest of his life in an asylum. In the 1891 census, twelve years after his detainment, he was an inmate of Gloucester County Lunatic Asylum. In the disability column was written 'lunatic'. The asylum had around 500 inmates. Most were 'lunatics'; some were 'imbeciles'; a few children were 'idiots'.

Life in the asylum was calm and orderly. It was believed that lunatics should be kept occupied and calm; many worked on asylum farms or gardens. The brutal practices such as electro-convulsive therapy, insulin shock and lobotomy date from the early 20th century when the term 'mental illness' was coined and linked to an imbalance in the brain.

In February 1892, Richard contracted erysipelas, a deep skin infection which developed into pneumonia. He died shortly afterwards.

Four: A Child's Life

Dozens of generations of children have grown up within the bounds of Preston parish. Childhood has always followed a similar pattern: playing, learning, making friends, pushing the boundaries and hoping nobody will ever find out!

There was no formal education system in Preston until the 19th century. Family members and hired tutors – farmer's son Thomas Simkins was a writing master until his death in 1769 aged 68 – provided education for children if advantageous and means allowed. Schools were mainly located in towns, although clergy and charitable initiatives often provided education on a local level.

Literacy rates among the lower classes were low, but men of higher social standing would arrange education for their sons, and less often, their daughters. By the 18th century, many occupations including agriculture were fast becoming business enterprises. A good standard of literacy was near essential.

From 1753, newly-weds had to sign the church marriage register: with their name if literate; their mark, usually a cross, if not. This gives a good indication of changing literacy levels.

From 1753-65, 53% of men and 33% of women married in Preston could write their name. There is an obvious division by social class. Farmers and craftsmen could write their names; the labourers could not. Farmer Thomas Heydon and shoemaker Charles Stanley had notably arranged lessons for their daughters as well as their sons.

In 1818, a Dame School – a school run by a woman – opened, run by 25-year-old spinster Elizabeth Salmon, a descendent of the long-standing carpenter family. She lived in No.36 with her father Thomas. On his death in 1844, she moved to a dilapidated dwelling behind No.40. She taught around a dozen children to read and write, as well as minding younger children while their mothers worked. Her first pupils would have begun to marry in the 1830s, and an increase in literacy levels in Preston is seen from this point.

In 1848, Elizabeth's career ended. A new purpose-built school opened in the village, and within three years she was a pauper. She remained alone in her impoverished dwelling until 1864, when she died aged 72.

The Village School

The school was built by James Roberts-West in 1848 for Preston and the neighbouring villages, at a cost of £1500 (£90,000 today). It was originally two schools, one for boys and one for girls, which were later combined.

The building comprised a central school with teacher's houses at either end. A succession of teachers lived in No.19, but no teacher is recorded as living in No.20. The schoolroom was divided by partitions, still in place today. The playground behind the school was also segregated, and remained so long after the classes were mixed. Privies for teachers, boys and girls were at the bottom of the playground.

The school could take 120 children, and in the 1851 census, 31 Preston children aged from 4-12 years were scholars. In 1861 it was 78. More would have attended from other villages.

Very few children were now at home or in employment. One of the few cases of non-attendance was the family of William Garrett, a garden labourer who lived in a dilapidated dwelling behind the new model cottages with his wife and five children. His sons George, 11, and Thomas, 8, were working as plough-boys.

Literacy levels were now soaring. By the 1860s, 80% of men and 90% of women signed the marriage registers. Interestingly, most of those illiterate were now male. Boys, especially from poorer families like George and Thomas Garrett, began their working life at a young age and had no opportunity to attend school. And the cost of education – 1½d per week for one child and ½d for siblings – was unaffordable. Fees were paid until 1891.

Education became compulsory for 5-to 10-year-olds in 1880, a burden for those who lost several bread-winners and their desperately needed pennies. In 1893 the leaving age was raised to eleven; in 1899 to twelve; and in 1918 to fourteen. In 1944 it was raised to fifteen and children now had to attend a secondary school – either a secondary modern or a grammar school – although it was several years before this was fully in place.

Thomas Vincent

The first master of Preston school was Thomas Vincent, a basket-maker's son in his twenties from Tiddington. Elizabeth Hyatt, a gardener's daughter, taught the girls. In 1850, Thomas and Elizabeth were married. They remained at Preston for three further years then moved to a school in Wiltshire.

Joseph and Mary Ann Webb

In 1853, 20-year-old Joseph Webb from Bristol became headmaster. Two years later he married Mary Ann Pearson, headmistress of the Alcester Road School in Stratford, and she took over the girls' school.

Joseph's teaching was strict but also practical and useful. Josiah Hopkins (1869-1942) attended school until aged ten. He recalled in 1940 that Mr Webb was 'a nice old blue pencil, but an excellent school gaffer.'

Another anonymous former pupil wrote shortly afterwards to the *Stratford Herald*:

> 'Mr Webb was without doubt one of the best, although I am afraid we did not always think so at the time. He was very strict in school, but also tried to make us happy in our playtimes, and on frosty nights he would pour buckets of water down the playground so that in the morning we had a grand slide, on which he would join us and see that everyone had fair play. I realise that it was to a great extent his teaching that enabled me to obtain and hold a position for 45 years.'

These sentiments were reflected by the consistently glowing reports given by the school inspectors after the children's annual examination. In 1890 the inspector reported:

> 'I have nothing but praise for the admirable manner in which the boys do their work. The girls too do their work in admirable style, and I am much pleased with the general condition of the school. The infants are well taught and instruction is properly varied. Both departments received the award excellent again.'

In 1893, a diphtheria outbreak forced the school to close for two months but the results were still commendable. The inspector reported:

> 'Geography in particular deserved a word of praise; grammar was also well done; and the needlework of the girls was of the highest merit.'

The school now taught a hundred pupils and help was needed. Teaching was now an accepted career option for young women, with requirements based on ability rather than social class. Fanny Winter, the blacksmith's daughter, became a 'pupil-teacher' in the 1880s. These children finished their statutory education aged twelve, then taught younger pupils and received after-hours tuition themselves. After three years they would complete a formal college course.

Fanny taught until she was fifteen but never went to college. Instead she became a kitchen maid in the large household of magistrate Bevil Granville in Herefordshire. Her extra education may have secured this lowly but still lucrative position.

In 1894, Mary Ann Webb resigned. She was 66 and had been thinking about retiring for some time. Joseph was prepared to continue, but was politely informed that his services could be dispensed with. Younger blood was now wanted. The couple then left Preston for Birmingham.

George and Mabel Clarke

George Clarke, 33, took over the boys' school in October 1894. His wife Mabel took the girls.

The desired younger blood brought in several changes. Girls and boys were taught together although seated separately and with separate playgrounds. It seems George also instigated the annual prize-giving, the first record being Christmas 1896. The prizes were awarded by Mrs West, who also gave each child a Christmas card and an orange.

Dick Beavington (1893-1991) recalled that Mr Clarke was strict but fair. Joe Newland (1901-1993) was also taught by 'Old Clarke', whom he thought rather gruff, especially when he'd had a haircut. In 1902 the school inspector reported that:

'The children are clean, orderly and industrious, and attainment does credit to the hard-working teachers. The reading and recitation being done in better style. Needlework is a strong point; the new light in the senior room is a great improvement; and the infants are carefully taught.'

The main focus was the Three Rs: reading, writing and arithmetic. Dick Beavington's daughter Elizabeth Lyne recalls that Dick, aged ninety, could add up a column of figures with greater speed and accuracy than herself.

Joe Newland's favourite day was Friday when they did reading and drawing. Dick Beavington also enjoyed the weekly drawing classes. Boys learned geometry; girls knitting and needlework. Dick Beavington's sister Millie was awarded a silver thimble for her sewing.

The children had to be annually examined in religious knowledge by diocesan officials. The glowing reports matched their secular work. Revd WA Douglas reported in 1902:

'I was exceedingly pleased with the results of the examination of this school, which is one of the best in my district. The unusually ready and correct answers indicated a most painstaking and efficient teaching, and the written work was faultless. I found these children admirably taught, and their tone and order excellent.'

Gamekeeper's daughter Mary 'Polly' Noyce started as an assistant teacher for George Clarke in her teens in the 1900s. She had no formal training and taught the infants only. She taught until the 1920s when she married postman Frank Goodall.

Older pupils were also called on to assist if necessary. Ivy Ashby, nee Noyce (1911-2008) recalled that she was taking the infants' class when John Smith of Lower Farm asked to go to the lavatory, 'and be quick or I'll fill my breeches!'

Hilda Kedward pursued a teaching career at Preston. Hilda was born in London in 1889, the daughter of horse-keeper Charles Kedward. The family settled in Halford and Hilda began to teach at Halford School before moving to Preston in 1912. She lodged with Thomas Smith at Park Farm. Thomas died in June 1927 and Hilda returned to London a month later.

George and Mabel Clarke retired in 1922 and moved to Malvern. They retained fond memories of Preston and in 1948, now in their eighties, they returned to attend the school's centenary celebrations.

Preston school pupils, 1922

Back: Harry Lord (headmaster); Walter Morris; Kath Ashby; Gladys Robbins;
Doris Morris; Emily Morris; Cyril George

Middle: Tom Lancashire; Violet Townsend; Louisa Noyce; Nancy Miller;
Ivy Noyce; Muriel Morris; Joan Bishop; Jim Lancashire

Front: Maurice Porter; Elsie Noyce; Barbara Bishop; Nellie Miller;
Joan Ashby; Betty Collicot; Mary Ashby; Bill Morris

Harry Lord

The next headmaster was 37-year-old Harry Lord. Harry had completed his teacher
training at St Luke's College in Exeter before serving in the First World War – he had
parts of his fingers missing as a consequence – and came to Preston in 1922.

Ray Francis (b.1924) attended the school until aged ten. He remembers
that everyone liked Mr Lord: he was rather a softie and maintained discipline in
a gentle way, although Vera Watson, nee Noyce (b1925) recalls he could be very
hard on the older boys who were often caned.

Preston was becoming a gentrified village, and pupil numbers were falling
despite the raised leaving age. The children were taught in three classes divided
by age, with the headmaster taking the top class. The school still received high
ratings and Ronald George from Wimpstone, aged 11, won a scholarship to
Stratford Grammar School in 1923. His brother Cyril followed a year later.

Several other teachers – still predominantly women – taught at Preston. They were now required to complete secondary education and college training. Gladys 'Molly' Hand came from Kidderminster *c*.1930. She took the infants' class and was very strict. She married Wimpstone farmer Reg Ashby in 1935 and the couple lived in The Old Vicarage.

Ada Cale, a coal miner's daughter from Gloucester, began teaching in 1922, aged eighteen. She took the middle class. Miss Cale was never one for harsh words, Ray Francis remembers, and the cane was rarely seen in her lessons. She lodged at Priest's Cottage and also gave piano lessons. She married gamekeeper Bill Noyce in 1931 and taught for another two years until she left to raise a family.

Lilian Wilson began teaching in Preston in November 1937 and lodged at Park Farm.

Preston school pupils, 1935

Back: Bertie James; Norman Hartwell; John Garrett; John Ashfield;
            ? Michael Swainston; Hedley Ashby; ?

Second Row: Frances Sparrow; N Thomas; ? Olive Handy; Vera Noyce;
                  Doris Maton; Annie Hartwell; Lily Maton; Natalie Bishop

Third Row: Janet Smith; Marjorie Robbins; Betty Dale; Barbara Yates;
             Marian Bishop; Audrey Jobe; Eileen Ashfield; ?

Front: ? ? Eric James; Martin Sumners

Lessons still followed the traditional format: reading, writing and arithmetic; needlework for the girls; carpentry and gardening for the boys – the schoolmaster had his garden dug and tended under the auspices of education. The top class girls went by bus to Broad Street School in Stratford each week for cookery lessons. The highlight of the week, Vera Watson remembers.

Harry Lord was very keen on singing, literature and poetry, and the children had to learn poems by heart, including Henry Longfellow's 94-line *Song of Hiawatha*. Regular concerts were given. In October 1924 this included solos of national songs such as *Land of my Fathers*, along with the popular song *Sing Along Sambo*, which would no doubt attract much controversy today.

Ray Francis has fond memories of the Christmas plays. These were always extremely popular with parents scrambling for front-row seats. One performance was *Little Miss Muffet*, with six-year-old Marjorie Taylor from Whitehill Farm as Miss Muffet and Ray as the spider. Ada Cale and Harry Lord's wife Emily designed and made the costumes. Another play was *Sweeney Todd the Barber*, in which the lead was played by 14-year-old Andrew Bishop from Beecham Farm. Andrew was a first-rate actor, and Ray still remembers him leering at his intended victims as he stropped his razor.

Religious education was still important. The vicar came once a week for prayers and hymns. The children had to learn the Collect for each Sunday and were tested on Monday mornings. Woe betide if they couldn't repeat it! Dick Beavington could remember many of these into his old age.

Most children walked to school. Those from the surrounding villages had a journey of over a mile. One wonders how many five-year-olds could manage this today. John Leese and Eric James remember toasting cheese sandwiches over the school fire, using a forked stick from the hedge as a toasting fork.

Mrs West still gave each child a Christmas card and an orange and awarded the annual prizes. Ray Francis, aged six, received a copy of *The Rosy Cheeks Story Book* in 1930. Vera Noyce, aged 13, was awarded Rudyard Kipling's *Selected Stories* as the literature prize in 1938.

Harry Lord taught until December 1942, when he was taken suddenly ill. He died the same day. He was 57 years old.

From the Stratford Herald, December 1933

Miss Lilian Bailey

Harry Lord was replaced by Preston's first female headteacher, Lilian Bailey, who taught from 1942-46. Miss Bailey, John Horseman (b.1936) remembers, was a small woman and was extremely strict. She would march and bustle about, and stood no nonsense at all. But when John met her after he'd left the school, she was very pleasant and enquired with interest into his progress.

Dagenham evacuee Joan Hulbert, nee Knight remembers she had a modern approach and taught music, drama and dancing. The children all knitted dance slippers and held demonstrations at Alscot Park.

Mrs Joan Bretherton

Lilian was followed by Joan Bretherton, who taught for a year from 1946-1947.

Mrs Dorothy Unett

Dorothy Unett, whose late husband's family had come from the village, took over in 1947. It was her last position before retiring. Dorothy was a good teacher, liked by her pupils, and loved rural life and history. She collected a vast array of pictures, memories and cuttings of Preston, invaluable to this book.

Miss Bullard from Stratford now took the infants. Elizabeth Lyne, nee

Beavington, remembers she was a lovely teacher. Elizabeth cried for her first few days, but Miss Bullard got her settled down and she enjoyed the rest of her school days.

Tom Hoyle, who lived at The Steps, took the middle class. He was young, enthusiastic and very inspiring. He was also a very good shot with a piece of chalk if anyone wasn't paying attention. He arranged sports days and fancy dress parades which he led with his accordion.

A head boy and girl were now elected and crowned king and queen of the summer festival. In 1949-50 these were Arthur Wood of No.51 and Monica Felton of the Atherstone aerodrome. They were given illustrated Bibles for their achievement.

The annual prize-giving was still held at Christmas, now incorporating carol concerts, Christmas parties, and in 1948, a film show. School trips were growing more frequent. Mrs West took the children to the theatre to see *Alice in Wonderland*; they also went to Warwick Castle.

In April 1948, the school marked its hundredth anniversary with a tea party attended by over a hundred former scholars. These included John Horseman, 83, who was schooled by Joseph Webb in the 1870s. John had worked as a shepherd before moving to the industrial town of Bilston to work on the railways.

Dorothy Unett, former head mistress and local historian, outside Locke's Farm c.1955.
From WI collection.

Mrs Lucy Bartlett

Dorothy retired in 1949 and moved to No.46. She was replaced by Lucy Bartlett. Lucy, a very strict teacher, was keen on amateur dramatics. She and her husband would arrange performances by both children and adults. A performance in April 1950 included a hilarious burlesque version of *Cinderella*. This starred E. Cook as Cinderella; C. Robbins as the fairy queen; Harvey Smith's daughter Ruth as the prince; and George Nason and Ted Coomber as the ugly sisters. The show was held over two nights and the money raised was put towards the school residential trip to Bexhill-on-Sea, held that summer.

Lucy left for a post in Ipswich in summer 1951, to be replaced by Miss Nellie Bulbick.

Drama production, The Wind and the Sun, c.1950. Back row: Ray Beauchamp; David Wood; Roy Cook; Bill Bowie. Middle: Jennifer Spires; Milly Dale; James Stredder; Pauline Reason. Front: Elizabeth Beavington. Courtesy of Elizabeth Lyne, nee Beavington.

Miss Nellie Bulbick

Miss Bulbick was overly strict and universally disliked, although many pupils now acknowledge she was a very good teacher. She was heavy handed with punishments and boys were often caned. Swearing was punished with a mouthwash of soapy water.

'I hated her and she hated me,' Fred Dale remembers. Chris Daniell, nee Reason was terrified of her and hung onto the railings as her mum forced her into school.

There were now only two classes, as the older pupils went to secondary schools. Numbers were rapidly falling, although the 'aerodrome kids' – living on the former Atherstone airfield – swelled the numbers until the site was abandoned in the 1950s. Mrs Doreen Hathaway from Alderminster replaced Miss Bullard in 1962 as the infants' teacher, while Nellie took the older class.

Lessons took advantage of the rural setting. The children went on nature walks and learnt to identify flowers and trees. A pressed-flower competition was held each year. Miss Bulbick loved handicrafts and taught the children to stitch books, make cane baskets, knit and darn – this now involved boys as well as girls. The girls made their own blouses and skirts. The children would listen to *Story Time* on the wireless in the school hall, with the famous words, 'Are you sitting comfortably, then I shall begin.' The toy cupboard was opened on Friday afternoons and plasticine issued. Every child had to bring a tin in which to play with it.

The school gardens were still tended by the pupils. David Hall from Sweet Knowle Cottages remembers Bernard Felton from the aerodrome pushing him into the vegetable patch – Miss Bulbick caught David and gave him a hiding for it.

Nellie remained at Preston until 1966, then Mary Rickards took over.

Mrs Mary Rickards

Mary Rickards was the last headteacher. The school had been marked for closure as early as 1947, and by the 1970s there were only twenty pupils, less than half the number needed to make it viable.

The teachers were proud of the individual attention they could give their pupils. They arranged country dancing displays for the village – Marianne Newitt, nee Boyd (b.1967) was often partnered with David Howes, a very strong boy from Alderminster, and she often ended up in a heap on the floor. Marianne was left-handed, and Mrs Hathaway tied her hand behind her back to force her to use her right hand. It didn't work: Marianne is still left-handed today.

Margaret Boyd dished out the dinners, which were brought in on large trays. If the children didn't eat their dinner, they had to sit there until they did.

The children were taught to read using the ITA [Initial Teaching Alphabet] method, based on a simple phonetic system: they would learn 'sed' rather than 'said'. Older pupils were taught the correct spelling. When the children were moved to Bridgetown School in Stratford, these errors got them teased and it was a while before they caught up with their peers.

In 1974, the closure was finalised. Doreen Hathaway stated: 'We've fought tooth and nail to save the school, to no avail. It's now fashionable to teach in schools with large numbers.'

The school then became the village shop.

Youth Spent and Misspent

Preston's fields, hedges, streets and woodlands have entertained dozens of generations of children, and almost everybody who grew up here has fond memories of their childhood. 'The happiest days of our lives,' many recall.

The amusements we take for granted – televisions, stereos, Xbox, computers – were unknown until a generation ago. John Horseman went carol singing at Preston Pastures in the 1940s. The farmer, JC Gamble, had a television set. It was the first time John and his friends had seen one, and the carols were forgotten as fascination with a screening of *Cinderella* took over.

There was little scope for trips outside Preston. Joan Hulbert, nee Knight, evacuated to Preston aged nine, remembers their twice-yearly treat was a visit to Stratford. They would walk four miles there, have a picnic by the river, look around the town then walk home again.

Fishing, building dens, searching for birds' nests, building rafts and playing sports were the immortal pastimes for Preston's youth. John Smith of Lower Farm was rarely allowed to be indoors except for meal times. Fred Dale and John Horseman remember a similar attitude. Children enjoyed total freedom. With no traffic or television to betray bad news, there was no reason to worry.

Accidents and injuries were considered part of growing up. In the 1930s, 12-year-old Robert Collicott from Wimpstone was hit by Mrs West's car when he ran into the road and suffered considerable facial injuries. Eric James cut his head badly when he raced down the green, lost his balance and crashed into the school railings. Neither incident was considered an issue.

Susan and Bridget Burra, daughters of Robert and Susan Burra of The Cottage, 1911. Courtesy of Bridget Loader.

The boys formed two rival gangs in the 1940s, one led by Derrick 'The Duke' Ashfield of No.9 and the other by Martin Knapp from Preston Pastures. The Duke's speciality was stuffing people into a hollow tree and throwing cowpats in after them. His gang would march to battle singing '*Whistle while you work, Martin Knapp's a twerp...*' before commencing their fight with homemade wooden swords. The Duke was idolised by the younger boys, but he eventually gave up gang leadership for a staid career in accountancy.

Tony Ashfield, Derrick's brother, also had his moments. When he wasn't allowed into Wimpstone village hall, which held regular film nights, he climbed onto the roof and stuffed up the chimney so the hall filled with smoke.

The children at Alscot Park had a treehouse in a cedar on the lawn, the perfect hiding place from the grown-ups. It was probably built in the 1910s by the young Reggie and Michael West, and even had its own electric lighting.

Cricket was the most popular sport. The boys played in the street, using John Horseman's gateposts as the stumps. Once John sent the ball through George Handy's window. Mrs Handy was very angry and wouldn't give them their ball back. They also played rounders, zigzagging across the street between gateposts. Sid Garrett from Silvester's Cottages was discussing a recent cricket match with Fred Dyde from The Old Manor. A lot of swearing was involved. Fred later said to his grandchildren Dennis and Geoff Vickers, 'don't you repeat any of the words he said!'

Knock up Charlie was a popular game. The boys would tie a string between opposite door knockers, knock on one door then run away. When the door was opened, it would sound the opposite knocker. This usually caused them more trouble than amusement.

The river provided much entertainment in summer. Many children learnt to swim there, John Horseman and George West included. The spot by the White Bridge was particularly popular. Picnics on the banks were common, and regular excursions were taken to Wimpstone Bridge.

Will Spencer and John Smith built rafts which they would punt upstream towards Wimpstone. They discovered a shallow gravelly stretch which was perfect for swimming. The roots of four ancient willow trees even formed steps. A decade later, when working at bale-cart in the nearby fields, they would come to the same spot to cool off after a hard day's work.

The winter months were no less entertaining. John Horseman remembers sledging down the green to come to a crashing halt at the school railings. The bank above Park Farm was particularly good for tobogganing. John Stoppard from Atherstone Hill Farm made his own sledge, as did most of the boys, which slid well providing someone towed it. The West brothers had a fancy sledge which had no trouble flying down the hills.

The children would also play on the frozen ponds. George West from Alscot Park, aged 3, learnt to skate on the ice in 1940, holding onto a chair for balance. Fred Dale, who lived at Atherstone Hill Cottages, had just started school in 1947 when snowdrifts blocked the roads. He was thrilled at the thought of time off, but his dad walked him down into the village to stay at his grandmother's house. They had to walk along the tops of the hedges as the narrow road had drifted full of snow, and it was three weeks before Fred could return home.

David, Anne and John Smith; James Stredder with Revel; and Robert Stredder, on the frozen Stour, January 1963. Courtesy of John Smith.

Running battles with the 'Wimpstonites' were regularly held, with water-bombs, mud pies and specially-hoarded rotten eggs as ammunition. A few more-than-disgruntled mothers then had to be faced.

Stephen 'Monkey' Monks was by the bridge with some other boys when a lorry drove past. Stephen screamed like he'd been run over, then ran away. The driver slammed on his brakes and leapt down. 'What's happened?'

'It wasn't us, it was Stephen!'

'I'll give him Stephen!' the angry driver retorted.

John Horseman and his friends discovered where the key to the church tower was hidden, and sometimes sneaked up there. One day they found a fountain pen in the street. They thought; 'what would happen if we threw it off the top of the church tower?'

They duly crept up there. A moment later the pen exploded into fragments of glass and spatters of ink.

Later that day, a message went around the village. Mr Hunt, the vicar, had lost his fountain pen. They never dared confess what they'd done.

Terence Ashfield from No.9 found some mushrooms in a field along the Radbrook Road. He and Dennis Vickers went on their bikes to pick them. Terence's mother Phyllis worked for Joe Spencer at Whitehill Farm, and Joe later mentioned that someone had been stealing his mushrooms. Both boys managed to feign surprise.

During the 1950s, PC Gibson from Alderminster police station would ride through the village a few times a week on his bicycle. He would keep a slipper in his back pocket in case he had to punish any wrong-doing, but more often he would stop and chat and play a bit of cricket with the boys.

Somebody once dumped some old apples on the allotments, so Fred Dale and his friends decided to throw them over the top of the houses into the street. An apple went through somebody's bedroom window. A few days later, PC Gibson was waiting for Fred as he came out of school.

'You're in a bit of trouble,' he said. 'What's this about you breaking people's windows?'

'It wasn't me, Mr Gibson!'

'Well, I've heard different.' And he gave him a clip round the ear.

'Now go home and tell your dad.'

Fred went home and told his dad. His dad gave him another clip round the ear. Lesson learnt.

Tom Hiatt, a friend of Captain Reggie West, made his own cider. When he was working at Alscot Park in 1945, he offered some to James and George West, aged ten and eight.

'Are you allowed cider?' he added.

'Oh yes, Mr Hiatt. We're allowed it on Sundays.'

They were duly given a drink. George handled it fairly well. James was very much the worse for it, and was sent to bed in disgrace.

For the farm children, an extra dimension was added to childhood. In the 1960s, John Smith, aged twelve, was at Bird's Scrap Yard in Long Marston with his dad when he saw a younger boy driving an old Ford Popular around the yard. The boy took John for a ride.

'Want to sell it?' John asked.

His dad pointed out a problem. 'How are you going to get it home, John?'

They eventually settled on towing it – a driving licence wasn't needed to steer a towed vehicle – and John was soon driving it around the fields.

Will Spencer was jealous and soon got one of his own, as did Roger Hawkins from Ailstone Farm. Once they went a mile up the old railway line to Goldicote Bridge.

When not driving them around, they had them in the farm workshops. John and Will stripped the bodies off then welded lorry hoops to make a roll bar, using Harry Smith's new electric welder. They used tin sheets for the sides and balanced the seat back on the chassis. They also took the silencers off. Improving the speed was a major concern, so they reduced the weight and added bigger wheels.

As they weren't allowed to drive on the roads, a bit of ingenuity was needed to move them about. Often they got a gang of boys to pretend to push it. They would switch the engine off if anybody came near. On Sunday afternoons, if Will's dad wasn't at home, they would drive up the Atherstone Road to the fields around Park Farm. Barbara Ayerst of Top Lodge would soon be on the phone to Harry Smith. 'Those boys are driving on the road again!'

It was forty years before Harry mentioned any of this to John.

Five: The Farming Landscape

Agriculture is that greatest of all manufactures, and beyond doubt the foundation of every art, business and profession. King George III

In 1721 there were twelve working farms in Preston, held by members of ten families and all located within the village itself. Each farmer would bring wagons, horses and droves of livestock along the unpaved roads on a regular basis, and it is no wonder that the village, until the end of the 19th century, was proverbial for its mud.

The age-old scene, c.1960. Locke's Farm is behind. From WI collection.

The village once comprised two separate manors, Preston and Alscot, their farmland divided by the Stour. In the 18th century Preston Field was managed by the open field system, and Alscot Field by the enclosed system of individual fields which now dominates British agriculture.

The open field system was a communal system, a relic of piecemeal clearance of land between Anglo-Saxon and Tudor times. The result was a single huge area of land, a thousand acres or more, belonging to and worked by the village as a whole. This was called *the field*. What is called a field today – an area of land enclosed by hedges or fences – was previously termed a close; en-*close*-d land. Parliament ordered the enclosure of Preston Field in the 1750s.

The basic unit of farmland until the 18th century was the *yardland*. This had no standard value, but increased as more land was cleared for cultivation. A yardland in Preston was 23 acres in 1540; 27½ acres in 1615; and 42 acres in 1721, when a detailed terrier or land survey was taken.

Preston Field was 1087 acres in 1721, comprising 25 ¾ yardlands shared between fourteen men. Alscot Field comprised 651 acres or 15½ yardlands, shared between three individual farms.

Around half of Preston Field was owned by freeholders. The land held by the lord of the manor – the *demesne* or *the farm* – comprised 6½ yardlands, originally a single unit but now divided and leased to various farmers: a *yardland of farm*. The term 'farm' meaning a consolidated holding of land, as we define it today, originated after the enclosures.

The Farmers of 1721

Mr Marriett (Alscot Park): held 1 yardland of farm.
Richard Marriett, current lord of the manor, is the only man to have the title 'Mr', meaning master. This was reserved for men of high social rank, usually a manor-lord without a knighthood.

Thomas Smith (The Old Manor): 1½ yardlands of his own.
Thomas had inherited The Old Manor in 1687 from his father Thomas, who'd purchased it from Richard Marriett. Thomas and his mother Elizabeth were high taxpayers in 1695 (see chapter 3).

Giles Smith (Lingings Farm): 1 yardland of farm; 2½ yardlands of Lingings Farm.
Giles was the younger brother of Thomas Smith. Lingings Farm was probably once owned by the Lingen family of Radbrook Manor. By 1721 it was owned by Richard Marriett. It may have been where Numbers 3 and 4 now stand.

John Smith (Lower Farm): 1 yardland of farm; 1½ yardlands of his own; $1^1/_3$ yardlands of Taylor's farm with a barn, yard and orchard; 1 yardland of parsonage land with a barn, yard and close.

John, the cousin of Thomas and Giles, had inherited Lower Farm in 1709 from his father John. The family had owned the farm since the 1650s.

Taylor's farm had belonged to a wealthy freehold family, now fallen from prosperity. It was leased by Thomas Marriett to John's father and uncle in 1671; the lease eventually transferred to John.

The parsonage land or rectory estate was owned by the lord of the manor subject to a payment to the Dean of Christ Church in Oxford.

William Ryland (Ryland's Farm): 1 yardland of farm; 1 yardland of copyhold land.

Copyhold tenancies were a lease for life, or a number of lives, providing for the holder's heirs. They were agreed at the manor courts and recorded on court rolls. A copy of this document was held by the tenant.

William's father Joseph, of Wimpstone Farm, held this copyhold land until his death in 1709. It then passed to William. It seems neither lived in Preston and the farm was sublet to Edward Walford, a substantial taxpayer in 1695.

John Souch (The Old Vicarage): 1 yardland of farm; 1½ yardlands of his own.

John Souch, also spelt Zouch or Such, was the son of Thomas Such (d.1721.) Thomas, who leased Milcote manor house, was one of the higher taxpayers in 1695. John was the only gentleman in Preston in 1721 and also lived at Milcote. The Old Vicarage was either leased out or managed by a steward.

John Simkins (Simkins' Farm): 1 yardland of farm; 1 yardland of parsonage land.

John, who shared a farm with William Salmon, was the eldest son of husbandman Walter Simkins, who had moved to Preston from Alderminster. Walter paid 1s tax in 1695; he was a small-scale farmer. The lease probably passed to John on Walter's death in 1702.

William Salmon (Simkins' Farm): ½ yardland of farm.

William Salmon was a carpenter. This small lease of land proved to be the first step of the family's rise to considerable prosperity.

Thomas Mansell (The Gables): 2½ yardlands of his own, including ¼ yardland called Worralls.

Thomas inherited The Gables, believed to have been owned by the family since 1592, when his elder brother John died in 1699. Worralls, recently purchased by Thomas, probably once belonged to the Worrall family who farmed in Preston until the 17th century.

John Yeats: 1½ yardlands of his own.

The Yeats family, also spelled Yate or Yeate, was one of the oldest in Preston. John de Yate was a taxpayer in 1327; Thomas Yate was mentioned on court rolls in 1478 and 1499; Thomas Yeats was the blacksmith in the 1580s.

The family farm, purchased in the 1620s, had been divided between brothers Thomas and John Yeats in 1634; on Thomas' death it was shared between John and their brother William. John's son, another William, was a high taxpayer in 1695. His land and house, maybe Park Farm or Rosehip Cottage, passed to John Yeats, of unclear family relationship.

Thomas Yeats (Church House?): ½ yardland of his own.

William Yeats, who also inherited a share of the family farm, was a relatively high taxpayer in 1695. His house and land passed to Thomas Yeats, of unclear relationship.

Thomas Timbrell (The Cottage): $1^1/_3$ yardlands of his own.

Thomas Timbrell inherited The Cottage from his father Thomas in 1695. He married Thomas Smith's daughter Elizabeth and became very wealthy. He had moved to Bretforton c.1698 and the farm was leased out. It's unclear how long The Cottage had been in the family's hands.

Thomas Locke (Locke's Farm): 1½ yardlands of his own.

The first record of this family in Preston is a lease of land by one William Locke in 1499. Locke's Farm was purchased in 1606 and leased for some time before that. Thomas Locke inherited the farm in 1697 from his father Thomas, one of the highest taxpayers in 1695. He also leased a farm at Milcote.

John Albright: ¼ yardland of his own.

John's farm may have been Park Farm or Rosehip Cottage, inherited from his father John in 1702. John senior was the first recorded member of the family in Preston. He paid 1s tax in 1695, suggesting he was a small-scale farmer.

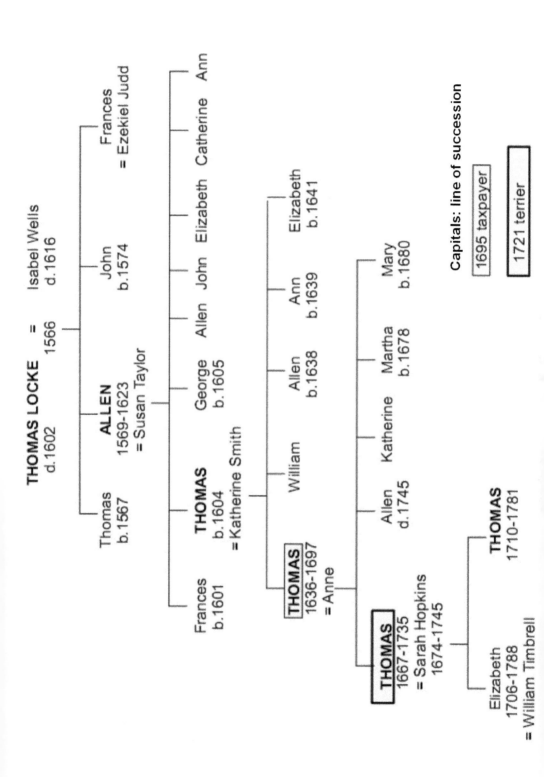

THOMAS LOCKE = Isabel Wells
d.1602   1566   d.1616

Thomas b.1567

ALLEN 1569-1623 = Susan Taylor

John b.1574

Frances = Ezekiel Judd

Frances b.1601

THOMAS b.1604 = Katherine Smith

George b.1605   Allen   John   Elizabeth   Catherine   Ann

William

THOMAS 1636-1697 = Anne

Allen b.1638   Ann b.1639   Elizabeth b.1641

THOMAS 1667-1735 = Sarah Hopkins 1674-1745

Allen d.1745   Katherine   Martha b.1678   Mary b.1680

Elizabeth 1706-1788 = William Timbrell

THOMAS 1710-1781

Capitals: line of succession

1695 taxpayer

1721 terrier

115

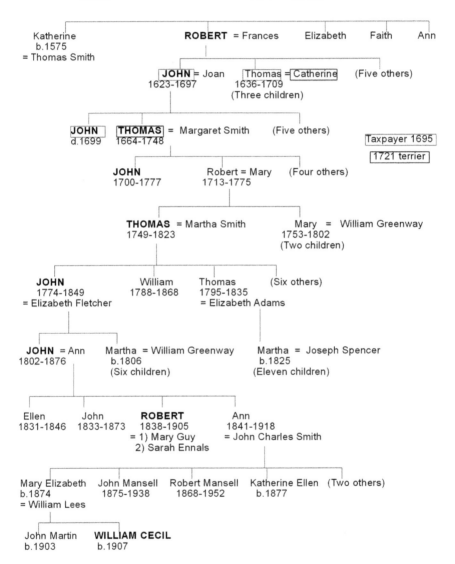

JOHN MAUNSELL ALIAS ALEXANDER = Margaret Jeffes
d.1601   1574   d.1605

Katherine   ROBERT = Frances   Elizabeth   Faith   Ann
b.1575
= Thomas Smith

JOHN = Joan   Thomas = Catherine   (Five others)
1623-1697   1636-1709
(Three children)

JOHN   THOMAS = Margaret Smith   (Five others)
d.1699   1664-1748

Taxpayer 1695

1721 terrier

JOHN   Robert = Mary   (Four others)
1700-1777   1713-1775

THOMAS = Martha Smith   Mary = William Greenway
1749-1823   1753-1802
                                        (Two children)

JOHN   William   Thomas   (Six others)
1774-1849   1788-1868   1795-1835
= Elizabeth Fletcher   = Elizabeth Adams

JOHN = Ann   Martha = William Greenway   Martha = Joseph Spencer
1802-1876   b.1806   b.1825
                      (Six children)   (Eleven children)

Ellen   John   ROBERT   Ann
1831-1846   1833-1873   1838-1905   1841-1918
                                  = 1) Mary Guy   = John Charles Smith
                                     2) Sarah Ennals

Mary Elizabeth   John Mansell   Robert Mansell   Katherine Ellen   (Two others)
b.1874   1875-1938   1868-1952   b.1877
= William Lees

John Martin   WILLIAM CECIL
b.1903   b.1907

116

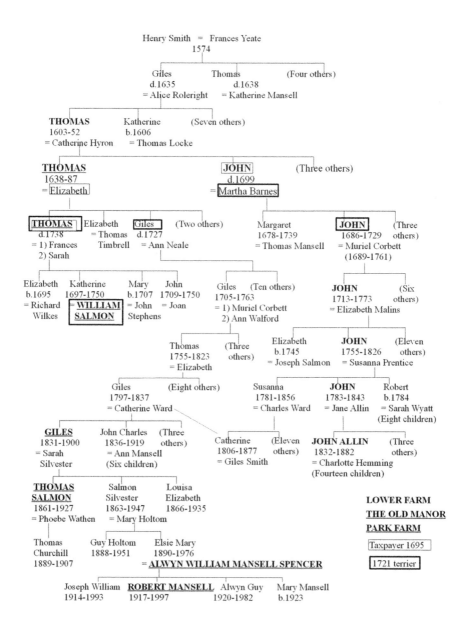

Henry Smith = Frances Yeate
1574

Giles
d.1635
= Alice Roleright

Thomas
d.1638
= Katherine Mansell

(Four others)

THOMAS
1603-52
= Catherine Hyron

Katherine
b.1606
= Thomas Locke

(Seven others)

THOMAS
1638-87
= Elizabeth

JOHN
d.1699
= Martha Barnes

(Three others)

THOMAS
d.1738
= 1) Frances
2) Sarah

Elizabeth
= Thomas
Timbrell

Giles
d.1727
= Ann Neale

(Two others)

Margaret
1678-1739
= Thomas Mansell

JOHN
1686-1729
= Muriel Corbett
(1689-1761)

(Three others)

Elizabeth
b.1695
= Richard
Wilkes

Katherine
1697-1750
= WILLIAM
SALMON

Mary
b.1707
= John
Stephens

John
1709-1750
= Joan

Giles
1705-1763
= 1) Muriel Corbett
2) Ann Walford

(Ten others)

JOHN
1713-1773
= Elizabeth Malins

(Six others)

Thomas
1755-1823
= Elizabeth

(Three others)

Elizabeth
b.1745
= Joseph Salmon

JOHN
1755-1826
= Susanna Prentice

(Eleven others)

Giles
1797-1837
= Catherine Ward

(Eight others)

Susanna
1781-1856
= Charles Ward

JOHN
1783-1843
= Jane Allin

Robert
b.1784
= Sarah Wyatt
(Eight children)

GILES
1831-1900
= Sarah
Silvester

John Charles
1836-1919
= Ann Mansell
(Six children)

(Three others)

Catherine
1806-1877
= Giles Smith

(Eleven others)

JOHN ALLIN
1832-1882
= Charlotte Hemming
(Fourteen children)

(Three others)

THOMAS
SALMON
1861-1927
= Phoebe Wathen

Salmon
Silvester
1863-1947
= Mary Holtom

Louisa
Elizabeth
1866-1935

LOWER FARM
THE OLD MANOR
PARK FARM

Taxpayer 1695

1721 terrier

Thomas
Churchill
1889-1907

Guy Holtom
1888-1951

Elsie Mary
1890-1976
= ALWYN WILLIAM MANSELL SPENCER

Joseph William
1914-1993

ROBERT MANSELL
1917-1997

Alwyn Guy
1920-1982

Mary Mansell
b.1923

117

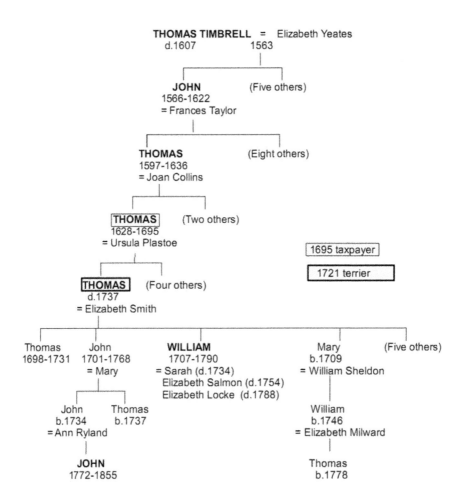

THOMAS TIMBRELL = Elizabeth Yeates
d.1607   1563

JOHN   (Five others)
1566-1622
= Frances Taylor

THOMAS   (Eight others)
1597-1636
= Joan Collins

THOMAS   (Two others)
1628-1695
= Ursula Plastoe

1695 taxpayer

1721 terrier

THOMAS   (Four others)
d.1737
= Elizabeth Smith

Thomas   John   WILLIAM   Mary   (Five others)
1698-1731   1701-1768   1707-1790   b.1709
            = Mary   = Sarah (d.1734)   = William Sheldon
                           Elizabeth Salmon (d.1754)
                           Elizabeth Locke (d.1788)

            John   Thomas   William
            b.1734   b.1737   b.1746
            = Ann Ryland   = Elizabeth Milward

            JOHN   Thomas
            1772-1855   b.1778

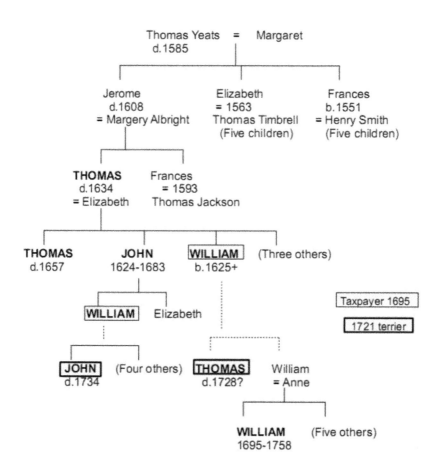

Thomas Yeats = Margaret
d.1585

Jerome
d.1608
= Margery Albright

Elizabeth
= 1563
Thomas Timbrell
(Five children)

Frances
b.1551
= Henry Smith
(Five children)

THOMAS
d.1634
= Elizabeth

Frances
= 1593
Thomas Jackson

THOMAS
d.1657

JOHN
1624-1683

WILLIAM
b.1625+

(Three others)

Taxpayer 1695

1721 terrier

WILLIAM   Elizabeth

JOHN   (Four others)
d.1734

THOMAS   William
d.1728?   = Anne

WILLIAM   (Five others)
1695-1758

119

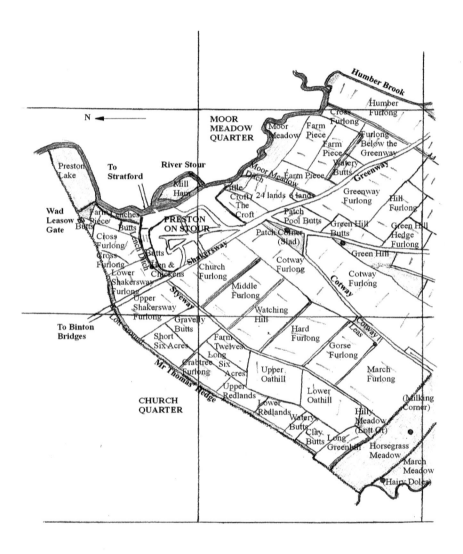

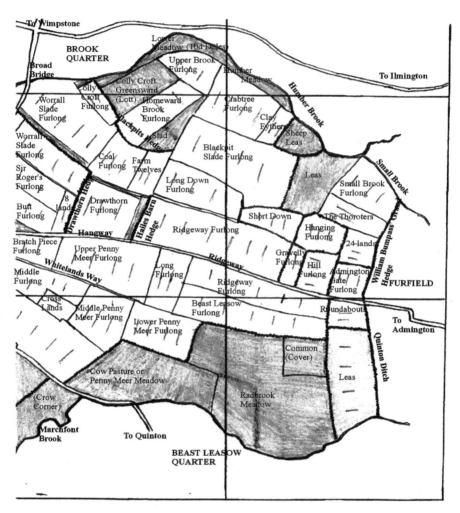

To Wimpstone

BROOK QUARTER

Lower Meadow (10d Doles)

Upper Brook Furlong

Broad Bridge

Humber Meadow

To Ilmington

Colly Croft Greensward

Colly Croft

Colly Croft Furlong

(Lott)

Homeward Brook Furlong

Crabtree Furlong

Humber Brook

Worrall Slade Furlong

Blackpits Hedge

Clay Fethers

Slad

Sheep Leas

Worrall Slade Furlong

Coal Furlong

Farm Twelves

Blackpit Slade Furlong

Leas

Small Brook

Sir Roger's Furlong

Long Down Furlong

Small Brook Furlong

Butt Furlong

8 lands

Drawthorn Furlong

Drawthorn Hedge

Short Down

The Thoroters

Hanging Furlong

24 lands

William Bumpass Hedge

Bratch Piece Furlong

Hangway

Hailes Barn Hedge

Ridgeway Furlong

Gravelly Furlong

Hill Furlong

Admington Gate Furlong

FURFIELD

Upper Penny Meer Furlong

Long Furlong

Ridgeway

Middle Furlong

Whitelands Way

Ridgeway Furlong

Cross Lands

Middle Penny Meer Furlong

Beast Leasow Furlong

Roundabouts

To Admington

Lower Penny Meer Furlong

Common (Cover)

Quinton Ditch

Cow Pasture or Penny Meer Meadow

Leas

(Crow Corner)

Radbrook Meadow

Marchfont Brook

To Quinton

BEAST LEASOW QUARTER

Preston Field in 1721. Directions of the lands are indicated. Ponds, headlands and access tracks are marked. Shaded areas indicate grassland. Known hedges are indicated as zigzags.

Preston Field

Preston Field was divided into long, narrow strips called *lands* or *selions*. They were nominally a furlong (220 yards) long and around ten yards wide – roughly half an acre – but could vary wildly. The lands were grouped into units called furlongs, so-called because of their notational length. A farmer could have hundreds of lands scattered around the field: everyone had an equal share of good and poor land. The lands were sown and harvested individually, but each man had to keep to a rigid timetable.

All furlongs had names, which give a wealth of information about their history and characteristics. The names were often transferred to the new fields after the enclosures; many are still in use today.

The distinctive ridge and furrow pattern, now 'fossilised' in permanent grassland, is a result of ploughing each land individually. The soil was turned into the centre with each bout up and down, which left a ridge in the middle and empty furrows on the edges. With passing decades and centuries, the ridges and furrows grew ever more prominent.

Some lands have a reversed 'S'-shape. These were originally ploughed by oxen, which were less nimble so turning the plough had to begin early. Straight lands, ploughed only by horses, indicate ground first cultivated when oxen had disappeared from farms.

The headlands, hadlands, or hades were strips running perpendicular to their furlong, used to turn the plough and access other furlongs. They were dug by hand after the ploughing was completed. Grassed tracks or *balks* – Styeway and Whitelands Way – also provided access.

A great deal of ridge and furrow in the Midlands remained after the fields were enclosed, and can be seen on aerial and satellite photographs such as those available at https://earth.google.co.uk. Despite regular fallowing, the soil was becoming exhausted, having been under cultivation for several hundred years. Encouraged by the soaring prices of mutton and beef in the late 18th century, farmers turned poor-yielding fields into pasture, which it has remained ever since.

The furlong layout is often preserved in the post-enclosure field boundaries. A straight hedge with a sudden kink in it, for example, indicates a boundary between two furlongs. The hedge was planted along a ridge. Where the ridges of the next furlong were not quite in line with the first, the hedge had to be shifted slightly.

Roads can also betray their layout. The road from Preston to Admington, just after it crosses the boundary into Admington Field by Harbour Hill, takes two rapid 90° bends. This was to skirt around the old furlongs, still visible in the adjacent pasture.

Ridge and furrow can be seen in coppices and woodland, and as crop marks in cultivated fields. The ridges were levelled into the furrows, which therefore contained a good depth of topsoil. The former ridges were were left with poorer, less fertile subsoil. In spring, parallel strips of dark green plants are alternated with shorter, paler crops.

Ridge and furrow in The Little Churchground

Furfield (The Further Field) lay near the boundary with Admington manor. It was probably the last land to be cleared for cultivation and was enclosed by private agreement in 1721. Landowners were now arranging the enclosures of open fields to enhance efficiency. The lands were grouped into parts lying together, instead of lying 'interspersed and intermixed one with another' and cast for by lot between Richard Marriett and six of his tenants:

Richard Marriett Esq	Short Down; 35 lands
Giles Smith	Roundabouts; 13 lands
John Simkins	Hill Furlong; 24 lands
John Souch	Gravelly Furlong; 19 lands
William Ryland	Hanging Furlong; 22 lands
John Smith	Admington Gate Furlong; 19 lands
William Salmon	A part of Small Brook Furlong, interspersed with the freeholders and unenclosed; 15 lands

Areas of common grazing called leas, slads or lott ground were interspersed through the furlongs. They were usually poorer areas or awkward corners of no use for ploughing. Lott ground was al-*lott*-ed by rotation; slads were held by particular farmers; leas were larger areas divided into selions, and were cultivated then grassed in rotation.

Other areas were designated for meadows or pasture. A meadow was mown for hay; pasture was not. These were usually the furthest areas of the field. It is easier to drove animals long distances than to move ploughs and wagons; and the village boundaries were often demarked by water courses which supply water for the livestock.

Meadows were divided between the holdings in a similar manner to the furlongs. The allocations or *doles* were marked by hurdles. March Meadow contained an area called the Hairy Doles, which perhaps refers to a species of grass. Seven lands of the meadow by the Humber Brook were called the 10d Doles, implying their worth. Three doles in March Meadow were called Crow Corner. Part of the Horsegrass Meadow was called the Milking Corner: this perhaps had the richest grass, or maybe had a building used for milking.

Much grassland was ploughed up during the 17th century when grain became highly profitable. There was pasture for 905 sheep and 193 cattle in 1540; a hundred years later much less. This was presented to the manor court on several occasions, and in 1658 it was decreed there should be no further ploughing of the greensward.

Hedges were relatively rare in the open field system, mainly used to stock-proof pastures or denote boundaries between manors. Mr Thomas' Hedge marked the Preston-Atherstone boundary: William Thomas was an 18th century clergyman and historian who owned Atherstone Hill Farm. William Bumpass' Grand Hedge separated Preston and Admington Field. The Bumpass family were wealthy yeoman farmers in Admington.

Drawthorn Hedge divided Brook Quarter and Moor Meadow Quarter. Blackpits Hedge and Hailes Barn Hedge may have once enclosed pasture ground. These three are of obscure meaning, but the latter may link to the Medieval word *haye*, meaning hedge.

Furlong Names in Preston Field

Admington Gate Furlong Adjacent to the gate dividing Preston and Admington manors.

Beast Leasow Furlong Probably refers to the quarter in which it is found. Alternatively it may have been grassed at some point and used to pasture cattle or oxen. *Leasow,* pronounced *lezzer,* means 'grazing land'. Exhausted soil was often remedied this way.

Blackpit Slade Furlong *Slade* refers to a marshy valley; *slad* to grazing land. It may have been recently-ploughed grassland. *Blackpit* may refer to the colour of the soil, or to large-scale burning. Scrub was often burnt off as land was cleared for cultivation.

Bratch Piece Furlong *Bratch* or *breech* refers to newly-broken land. It intrudes into the common grazing area of Greenhill.

Butt Furlong An odd piece of land between larger furlongs. See Watery Butts.

Church Furlong Next to the church.

Clay Fythers Clay-rich soil, maybe with a texture akin to feathers, i.e. very soft. Alternatively it may derive from *fother*: an odd piece of land. The latter suits its location.

Coal Furlong Unlikely to refer to coal, either literally or by its colour. It may refer to *cole*, now called oilseed rape. This was grown in the Stratford area from the mid 16th century; the oil was used for lamps. The compiler of the terrier may have been unfamiliar with this, so used the homophone 'coal' instead.

Colly Croft Furlong Probably again refers to cole. *Croft* more usually refers to an enclosed area. This furlong was enclosed by the brook on one side and possibly a hedge on another.

Cotway Furlong The name of two furlongs on either side of the former road to Quinton. It may be a shortened version of Quinton-way – the road was also known as Cotway – or refer to the surname Cotterell. The area was known as Cotterell's Bush Ground in the 1820s.

Crabtree Furlong Occurs twice in Preston Field. It refers to crabapple trees.

The Croft; Little Croft A croft was a small, usually enclosed piece of land. The Little Croft belonged to Thomas Smith and comprised four lands planted as an orchard. The road from the new bridge was laid across it. The Croft was the nearest furlong to the village, and is now an orchard. It was enclosed on three sides.

Cross Furlong Found three times in Preston Field. The lands lie or *shoot* perpendicular to the surrounding furlongs.

Down, Long and Short The term *down* is subject to speculation, but may link to the dialect word *doe*, meaning 'to fatten cattle'. The two furlongs were long and short respectively.

Drawthorn Hedge Furlong Next to Drawthorn Hedge, which once divided Moor Meadow Quarter and Brook Quarter.

Farm Twelves Twelve acres in size. Part of the demesne land or farm-piece: land owned by the lord of the manor. The term *farm* as we define it today originated after the enclosures.

Farm Piece See Farm Twelves.

Gorse Furlong Area where gorse grew. Gorse would have been rooted out in the furlong itself, but may have grown in the adjacent grazing area called Cotway Leas.

Gravelly Furlong; Gravelly Butts Land with gravelly soil.

Greenhill; Long Greenhill; Greenhill Butts; Greenhill Hedge Furlong Green land. Either a grazing area, as was Greenhill in Beast Leasow Quarter, or a particularly wet area where the soil turned green with algae. This may apply to Long Greenhill in Church Quarter, which incidentally isn't on a hill. This soil is Lias clay, particularly prone to waterlogging.

Greenway Furlong; Furlong Below the Greenway Next to the Wimpstone Road, once known as the Greenway.

Hanging Furlong Adjacent to Admington Gate Furlong. *Hanging* may be a corruption of *Admington* – the road was known as Hangway – or it may refer to a spot for hanging criminals or allotted to a hangman. No evidence survives to support this latter theory.

Hard Furlong Relates to the texture of the soil. The soil here is white marl, which dries especially hard in summer.

Hen and Chickens Another name for bird's-foot trefoil, a small, yellow-flowered wild plant which can form a dense blanket over harvested stubble. It may have favoured this spot.

Hill Furlong On top of a hill.

Homeward Brook Furlong; Upper Brook Furlong; Small Brook Furlong The first two refer to the Humber Brook. The Small Brook was a tributary.

Horsegrass Meadow Where horses were grazed. The name may date from the 17th century when heavy horses began to replace oxen.

Humber Furlong Next to the Humber Brook. This furlong cuts across the current Wimpstone road: the road is more recent than the field layout.

Lake Meadow *Lake* derives from the Old English *lacu*, meaning 'watercourse'. The river Stour flanks this field on two sides.

The Lenches Derives from the Old English *hlinc*, meaning a terrace of sloping ground, or a ledge of land on a hillside. This area drops sharply towards the Stour and was used for grazing. It is known today as Linch Bank.

Six Acres, Long and Short Six acres in size; long and short areas respectively.

March Meadow Also called Marsh Meadow. Adjacent to the Marchfont Brook. Before the brook was straightened in the 19th century, the area was notably boggy. *March* also refers to a border land; the brook is the boundary between Preston and Radbrook manors. This may be the area called The Marshe in 1597, to which Frances Hunckes ordered a gate erected at the manor court.

March Furlong See March Meadow

Middle Furlong In the midst of the other furlongs.

Moor Meadow This is fertile soil near the river, so unlikely to refer to moor-like or poor quality ground. Its meaning is obscure.

Oathill, Upper and Lower Land where oats were grown. Oats were grown in relatively small quantities in Preston, mainly as a fodder supplement or for horse-feed. These furlongs were probably devoted to that crop.

Patch Corner; Patch Pool Butts Next to the pond called Patch Pool.

Penny Meer Meadow; Lower, Middle and Upper Penny Meer Furlong *Meer* refers to land on a boundary. Penny Meer Meadow lies on the boundary between Preston and Radbrook Fields. The others may be transferred names. *Penny* may be a derogatory term to imply little worth, or may refer to an early rent value. There are examples of a Penny Field elsewhere in Gloucestershire originating in the 13th century.

Redlands, Upper and Lower The soil type here is red marl.

Ridgeway Furlong Along a ridge. This section of the Admington road was known as Ridgeway.

Roundabouts Refers to land entirely surrounded by streams, trees or roads. Quinton Ditch lies on the south; the Admington Road on the east; and hedge to the north and west.

Shakersway Furlong, Upper and Lower Adjoining the road called Shakersway.

Sir Roger's Furlong No record of a Sir Roger is known in Preston. One explanation is that the original furlong name, having become meaningless and obsolete, was adapted into this similar-sounding but meaningful term. See Rambling Meadow in Alscot Field.

Styeway Access track in Church Quarter. Its meaning is obscure.

The Thoroters Also spelt Throughters or Thoroughts. Land whose boundaries project across neighbouring areas.

Watching Hill Also spelt Watchen Hill. Probably relates to its location on a hill, with a good view over a wide area. It may once have been the site of a signal beacon.

Watery Butts Appears twice in Preston Field. Butts are short or odd pieces of land. These two were probably prone to becoming waterlogged.

Whitelands Way An access track across Beast Leasow Quarter. The soil type here is white marl.

Worrall Slade Furlong Two adjacent furlongs in Moor Meadow Quarter and Brook Quarter. See Blackpit Slade Furlong. Worrall was the surname of a farming family in Preston in the 16th and 17th centuries: the land may have connections to them.

Farming in the Open Field

The fertile soils of the Midlands were well-suited to both arable and pastoral [livestock] farming. Every farmer in Preston grew corn and most kept cattle or sheep. After harvest, livestock were grazed on the stubble. They would help with weed control and manure the fields. Cattle were housed during winter, fed on the harvested grain and littered on the straw. After they were turned out in spring, the winter's manure would be spread on the fields to fertilise the new crop.

Preston Field was divided into four areas: Church Quarter, Beast Leasow Quarter, Moor Meadow Quarter and Brook Quarter, divided the Radbrook and Quinton roads and a hedge near the Wimpstone road.

Each quarter was devoted to one crop in rotation: wheat; barley; peas and beans; then a fallow year. This helped control the life cycles of weeds and pests and allowed the land to rest.

Wheat was grown for bread. Barley and pulses were mainly fed to cattle – the high protein content of pulses boosts milk yield – and barley was also malted for brewing. Oats were grown in smaller quantities: the grain was fed to horses, or the entire plant was mown and dried for cattle fodder.

The fallow year was replaced in the 18th century with leguminous crops such as sainfoin, clover or vetches. These were a valuable feed supplement and nourished the soil. Vetches, a type of wild pea, were most favoured in Preston but were later supplanted by clover. Sainfoin, not native to Britain, was unsuited to heavy Midlands soil and didn't become popular. A field in Alscot Field was named Sainfoin Ground by 1818; the only suggestion of its cultivation in Preston.

Greatly improved yields followed these crops, but it was two centuries before the reason was discovered. Legumes are 'nitrogen-fixing' plants. Bacteria-filled nodules in the roots convert atmospheric nitrogen into solid nitrogen compounds, vital for plant health.

John Timbrell (1566-1622) the first recorded freeholder of his family, was a typical mixed farmer. His agricultural assets on his death comprised :

Eight score [160] sheep	£30
Ten horses and mares	£20
16 great beasts [oxen] and 4 calves	£30
Pigs and poultry	£4
Crop of corn and grain on 4 yardlands	£90
Carts, ploughs, harrows and other trumpery of husbandry	£6
Hay, wood and coals	£8
One year's wool	£4

Thomas Blakeman rented a sizeable farm, possibly Church House, until his death in March 1755. He had about 100 acres under cultivation. His agricultural assets included:

79 lands of wheat	£42
70 lands of peas and beans	£34 10s
82 lands for sowing barley	£36 18s
Wheat rick and 28 bags of wheat in the barn	£18 4s
10 quarters [2.5 tons] of barley	£7 5s
13 tons of hay	£21
Beans and peas	£1 17s 6d
Oats in straw	£1 6s
6 horses	£32
8 cows	£26
2 hogs	£4 4s
3 store pigs	£1 7s
3 hog troughs	4s
One bacon rack	10s
38 sheep	£9 10s
The fowl	10s 6d

Thomas' inventory was taken in late March: he hadn't yet planted his spring barley. His lands in each quarter were devoted to wheat, pulses and barley, while the fourth lay fallow or would be planted with vetches. His oats had been dried for fodder for his cows. Like all farmers he kept a few pigs to fatten. Their destiny is clear from the next entry: a bacon rack.

Beasts of Burden

Oxen, the first beast of burden, had many advantages over horses. They were less prone to disease and foot problems and could thrive on poor hay and straw that a horse wouldn't touch. Until the 17th century, horses were predominantly used for warfare, hunting and transport by those who could afford them. Henry Taylor, a wealthy Preston yeoman who died in 1561, owned 24 oxen and twelve horses. John Maunsell alias Alexander, another wealthy man, owned six horses in 1601. It's unlikely these did farmwork.

The Medieval destriers or warhorses, capable of carrying a fully-armoured knight into battle, evolved into heavy horses such as the Clydesdale and the Shire Horse. These replaced oxen from the 17th century. Horses were more nimble, especially when turning the plough, so were better suited to cultivation work. And farmers were becoming more prosperous so could afford their upkeep.

John Timbrell owned sixteen 'great beasts' and ten horses in 1622. By the end of the 17th century, oxen seem to have disappeared from Preston. Robert Phipps had seven horses and no oxen in 1695, and no evidence survives of their presence after this date. Every farm had at least one stable for horses in 1721.

The heavy horse retained its role on the farms until replaced by a new rival, the steam engine. And later still, the tractor.

Sowing root crops in Wimpstone c.1930. Henry Ashby of Home Farm is leading the horse; farmworker Charlie Mayo guides the drill. Courtesy of Richard Parnham.

The Wool Trade

The wool trade had been thriving since the 13th century and many fortunes had been made. British wool, the jewel of the realm, was in high demand in Europe and was the backbone of the British economy. Sheep comprised the majority Britain's livestock until the 18th century.

Henry Taylor had a huge flock of over 500 sheep in 1561. Preston had pasture for 905 sheep, so Henry's comprised over half the village's flock. The wool trade was no doubt the source of his wealth. Other farmers kept more modest flocks. John Maunsell alias Alexander owned 90 sheep on his death in 1601. Thomas Timbrell owned 160 sheep in 1622.

The wool trade was probably the reason behind the early enclosure of Alscot Field, completed long before Preston Field. When William de Willicotes held Alscot manor in 1411, the land was mainly arable with six acres of meadow. Several people were living at Alscot, essential for the labour-intensive cultivation work. The land comprised the usual open field layout.

Sheep shearing at Wimpstone c.1930. Handheld shears had been used for millennia; mechanical clippers were an innovation embraced by the younger generation. Courtesy of Richard Parnham.

A century later, around half had been converted to pasture. This probably coincided with the fact that only one house was now occupied in Alscot. The settlement had decayed and been abandoned, and the arable land was turned into sheep pasture which needed a fraction of the labour force. By 1571, Alscot comprised 400 acres of grassland, 160 acres of wood and furze, and no arable. Much of the woodland was also soon converted to pasture.

The depopulation may have a more sinister cause. Many villages were forcibly depopulated and their ploughlands converted to more valuable sheep walks. Acts of Parliament attempted to curtail the clearances – the displaced labourers were believed to become vagabonds and criminals – but it was half-hearted. Wool was too important.

During the 17th century, cotton imports from the New World put the wool trade in jeopardy. The vast sheep-walks began to disappear, and the fortunes made were now lost. By the 1650s, Thomas and Cuthbert Taylor, descendants of Henry Taylor, rented a house and modest amount of land. The prestigious farm of their forebears was gone. The family disappeared from Preston within a generation. An Act of Parliament in 1678, a desperate measure to boost trade, decreed that all corpses were to be buried in a shroud of wool – Preston's burial registers contain a record of this – with a £5 fine otherwise. It did little to help.

Alscot's fields seem to have been brought back under the plough around this time and divided between three individual farms. Whitehill Farm and Beecham Farm were built in the 1660s. Cotterell's Farm, home of William Cotterell from at least the 1690s, may have been built at a similar time. By 1723 the latter was gone – perhaps burnt down – but the fields called Cotterell's House Ground and Cotterell's Great Orchard betray its existence. Alscot Farm, now called Rough Farm, was built on the site *c.*1730.

There were no more large sheep flocks in Preston. Instead, dairy cows began to graze its pastures.

To Stratford

N

Alscot Farm

Whitehill Farm

Beecham Farm

River Stour

(Further Lane Furland)
(Further Holt)
The Holts
Elm Ground
Sand Pit Gr.
Marl Pit Gr. (Homeward Holt)
(Homeward Lane Furland)
(Elm Holt)
Forty Lands (Cotterell's House Gr.)
Barn Gr.
Holt Meadow
(Little Meadow)
ALSCOT PARK
Whitehill Meadow
Shooters Hedge
(Long Meadow)
(Lower Ramb Close)
(Middle Ramb Close)
(Upper Ramb Close)
Pike Gr. (Picked Gr.)
Little Back Hill
Whitehill (Homeward Whitehill)
Red Field
To Preston
Tithings Meadow
Great Ground (Broom Field)
(Poulters Close)
Broom Field
Upper House Gr.
Lower House
Clover Gr.
Brook Furlong
Brick Gr.
Yard
WHITEHILL FARM
Rambling Meadow (Ramb Lamb Meadow)
Broom Hill
Round Ground (Broom Hill)
To Shipston
Little Ground (Broom Hill Meadow)

Dairy Farming

Many households kept one or two cows, but the first record of any sizeable dairy herd in Preston – thirteen cows and a bull – belonged to Matthew Phipps of Whitehill Farm in 1690. The date coincides with the declining wool trade. His brother Robert, who succeeded to the farm, owned eight cows in 1705. John Smith of Lower Farm owned a huge herd of 22 cows and a bull on his death in 1729. Thanks to the time-consuming process of hand-milking, dairy herds would rarely surpass this for another two centuries.

John was a progressive dairy farmer, and his assets on his death illustrate the care with which he managed his herd. They included:

| 40 quarters [10 tons] of wheat | £50 |
| 75 quarters of barley | £100 |

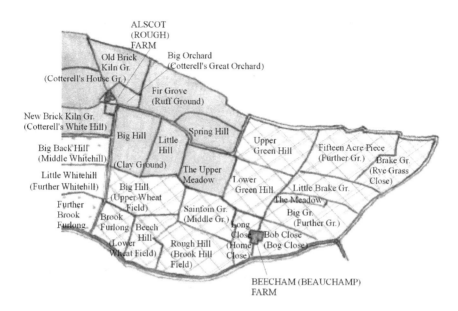

ALSCOT
(ROUGH)
FARM

Old Brick
Kiln Gr.

Big Orchard
(Cotterell's Great Orchard)

(Cotterell's House Gr.)

Fir Grove
(Ruff Ground)

New Brick Kiln Gr.
(Cotterell's White Hill)

Spring Hill

Big Hill

Little
Hill

Upper
Green Hill

Fifteen Acre Piece
(Further Gr.)

Big Back Hill
(Middle Whitehill)

Brake Gr.
(Rye Grass
Close)

(Clay Ground)

The Upper
Meadow

Little Whitehill
(Further Whitehill)

Lower
Green Hill

Little Brake Gr.

Big Hill
(Upper Wheat
Field)

The Meadow

Further
Brook
Furlong

Sainfoin Gr.
(Middle Gr.)

Big Gr.
(Further Gr.)

Brook
Furlong

Beech
Hill

Long
Close

Bob Close

(Lower
Wheat Field)

Rough Hill
(Brook Hill
Field)

(Home
Close)

(Bog Close)

BEECHAM (BEAUCHAMP)
FARM

Alscot fields in 1818. Names in brackets indicate names in 1723 if changed. Dashed lines indicate boundaries removed by 1818. Field names are discussed later.

53 quarters of peas	£53
5 quarters of vetches	£1
A bay of black oats	£13
8 ricks of hay	£48
One ton and a half of cheeses	£30
2 cheese presses and vats	£1
8 horses and 3 colts	£67
22 cows and 1 bull	£57 10s
47 sheep and lambs	£18 10s
5 pigs	£10
2 dung carts and a roll	£3 10s
1 great harrow and 2 small ones	£1 5s
3 wagons	£13
6 ploughs with irons	£1 10s
2 wheat staddles	10s
Hurdles, sacks, ropes and other utensils of husbandry	10s

John's cows were in fine condition, valued at just under £3/head. Robert and Matthew Phipps' were worth only £2/head.

Like all farmers in Preston Field, John grew wheat, barley and peas in equal quantities. Vetches had now replaced the fallow year. Being a wild plant, they yielded a fraction of the domestic cereals. The inventory was taken in September: John's harvest was complete and the grain was threshed and bagged. The low quantity of wheat may indicate a poor harvest or it had perhaps been sold.

Matthew Phipps also grew wheat, barley and peas. As his fields were enclosed and independent of other farmers, he could cultivate them as he wished. In 1690 he'd grown twice as much wheat – the more profitable crop – than barley and peas. He also had the freedom to experiment with other crops. He'd just harvested a rick of rye, a nutritious cereal crop recently discovered to boost milk yields. Robert Phipps eventually abandoned rye for vetches, proved the superior feedstuff.

John had an entire bay of black oats, a leafier variety of the common oat, in his barn. No other farmer in Preston is known to have grown them. They are still valued today: dairy cows fed on them retain high milk yields for a longer period. John certainly wasn't one to rely on hay to feed his herd.

The result of his hard work is evident. His cheese room contained an incredible 1½ tons of cheeses, valued at £30. Matthew Phipps' cheese was worth only £6.

Before refrigeration and railways, there was little market for liquid milk. It wouldn't keep fresh over the long journey into urban areas, and people in rural areas kept their own cows. So the majority was used to make cheese. This would store for several months, was transported with minimal detriment and made a good profit. All dairy farmers in Preston made cheese in some quantity.

A cheese typically weighed 56lbs or ½ cwt; John had sixty of these. It was September and the herd had been milking at their peak on the fresh summer grass for several months. A pound of cheese requires about eight pints of milk: 450 pints to a cheese. Each cow may have yielded 20 pints a day, so John could easily make a cheese each day.

The process has barely changed. The milk was mixed with a bacterial starter culture in the cheese vat. Rennet was added to coagulate the milk protein. A solid mass of curd was formed along with liquid whey, which was drained off. The whey was fed to pigs, as was the buttermilk left over from butter-making.

The curd was pressed and left to mature in a cave, a cellar or a specialised cheese-room. The latter was usually on an upper storey and had a stone floor. This kept the cheese cool and damp but allowed air circulation. A cheese-room was added to Locke's Farm in the 18th century.

Every farm and district had their own methods, which led to the vast array of regional farmhouse cheeses still available today.

The Parliamentary Enclosures

By the late 17th century, industry was growing, global frontiers were expanding, and Britain was fast entering the modern era. In many areas including the Midlands, an agricultural system barely altered for millennia was facing a revolution. New crops and technologies gained in popularity. Agricultural literature was widely read. Uncultivated land was pressed into production. Improvement became a national concern involving all farmers. Yields of grain, meat and milk soared. The agricultural revolution gained pace and pushed Britain into the Industrial Age.

The ancient open field system, outdated and hopelessly inefficient, was now a major hindrance. Parliament decreed that all remaining open fields should be enclosed. The arable-growing areas of the Midlands were hit hardest. The poorer lands of south-west, for example, unsuited to arable, had been predominantly enclosed for several centuries.

The peak of the enclosures (or inclosures) was between 1760 and 1780. Nearly 7m acres in 3000 parishes, around 20% of British farmland, was forcibly enclosed. Field boundaries, roads and footpaths were all redefined as the entire rural map was rewritten. The commoners' rights which had often stalled private enclosures were ignored, and a centuries-old way of life was swept away.

The system improved the prospects of wealthier farmers, but the poorer people were forced to give up their few animals upon which they depended. An increase in rural poverty followed. The smaller landowners were also forced or coerced into selling their land.

Preston Field was owned by nine people when the commissioners arrived in 1757.

James West, lord of the manor, held 13 yardlands: 12 yardlands in his possession and 1 yardland held by **Mrs Day** for her life.

Robert Burton: 2 yardlands.

John Smith: 1½ yardlands, expectant of his mother›s death who is 70 years of age.

John Souch: 1½ yardlands.

William Timbrell: $1^2/_3$ yardlands.

Thomas Locke: 1½ yardlands.

William Salmon: $1^2/_3$ yardlands.

John Mansell: 2½ yardlands.

James West

Richard Marriett, lord of the manor in 1721, had died in 1738. The estate passed to his son Richard, who died a bachelor in 1743. The estate then passed to his brother-in-law John Lowe, who sold it to antiquarian James West. James now owned the same 13 yardlands as Richard Marriett in 1721.

Mrs Mary Day

Mary was the widow of William Ryland, who had died in 1739. The copyhold in Preston was transferred to Mary for her life. In 1743, Mary remarried. Her new husband was yeoman Edward Day from Cherington. Mary moved to Cherington and leased her land to Thomas Locke.

In September 1759, shortly before the enclosures were finished, Mary signed an agreement surrendering the messuage and land to James West, in return for a lifelong annuity of £16. The farmstead, in what is now the Lower Park, was on the site of James' proposed park extension. It was demolished soon afterwards.

Robert Burton

Robert Burton owned two yardlands which had belonged to Thomas and John Yeats in 1721.

Robert was the son and heir of Thomas Lingen of Radbrook Manor (d.1742). Robert's mother was Ann Burton of Longner Hall in Shropshire. Robert inherited this seat in 1748, on condition that he change his name from Robert Lingen to Robert Lingen Burton.

A Thomas Yeats, maybe the farmer, was buried in January 1728. His house, probably Church House, and his half yardland passed to William Yeats, maybe his nephew, and were purchased by Thomas Lingen or Robert Burton. By 1749, William was leasing the house from Burton. His death in 1758 is the last record of the family in Preston.

John Yeats had died in 1734. It seems his house and land had already been sold. His will, written three days before his death, bequeathed a single shilling to each of his four siblings. His land was owned by Robert Burton by 1749; the fate of his farmhouse is unclear.

John Smith

John was the eldest son of John Smith of Lower Farm, who had died in 1729. His 39-year-old widow Muriel took possession of the farm thanks to her marriage settlement, although John was the legal heir and owner. He leased a farm at Willicote from his marriage in 1741.

John Souch

John Souch, now 69 and in failing health, was still living at Milcote. He died shortly before the allocations were finalised in 1759. His memorial on the east wall of Preston church states that he was '*pious and devout before his God, of much probity in his worldly dealings, and according to his abilities ready to succour his distressed neighbours.*'

His son Goodwin, a wealthy tanner living in Shottery, inherited The Old Vicarage and the land at Preston.

William Timbrell

William was the third son of Thomas Timbrell, who had become very wealthy and never returned to Preston.

John Jones, who leased the farm in Preston, died in 1732 and William returned to The Cottage with his wife Sarah. Sarah died later that year and William married twice more, but remained childless.

Thomas Locke

Thomas was Thomas Locke's only son. Thomas senior had lived an elaborate lifestyle at Milcote and ran very much into debt. He died in 1735; his memorial stone is in the nave of Preston church.

There was scant inheritance for his children so his wife Sarah, who had possession of the farm thanks to her marriage settlement, transferred it to her son, providing she keep the parlour, parlour chamber and garret, and had use of the brewhouse. She also wanted two beds with their blankets, coverslips, bolsters, pillows, sheets, valances and curtains; six cane chairs; two looking glasses; a chest of drawers and the table in the parlour chamber. She retained all this until her death in 1745.

William Salmon

William's fortunes had changed dramatically. Still a carpenter by trade, he owned a substantial amount of property including The Old Manor, formerly owned by his father-in-law Thomas Smith. This was a far cry to his tiny rented holding of 1721.

Thomas Smith had died in 1738. His farmland was bequeathed to his son John, and the house was shared between John and his sons-in-law, William Salmon and Richard Wilkes. A month after Thomas' death, the land was divided between the three heirs. The reason is unclear. Perhaps John was in poor health; a poor businessman; or followed another trade. John sold his share to John Mansell, who sold it to William Salmon. William probably bought Wilkes' share as well.

John Mansell

John was the eldest son of Thomas Mansell, who died in 1748 aged 84. Thomas owned land in Preston and Armscote: John inherited the former and his brother Robert the latter.

John, now classed a gentleman, was a shrewd businessman. He bought and leased properties and land in the local area and leant capital to other men. He remained a bachelor for his life.

The Fate of the Other Farmers

Giles Smith, who rented Lingings Farm in 1721, left Preston later that year. He leased Admington Manor and thirty enclosed fields, and died in 1727 with assets of £3001 (£258,000 today). Three of Giles' sons farmed in Admington and became wealthy and respected gentlemen. They all kept their ancestral village in their hearts: they baptised their children there and were buried in its churchyard. Giles' grandson Thomas would later return to Preston.

John Albright owned ¼ yardland in 1721, and relied on common of pasture to keep his few cows and sheep. He may have been forced to sell before the enclosures as his tiny holding would quickly become untenable. There is no further record of his family in the village.

John Simkins was still renting his farm from Richard Marriett in 1735. By 1748, now aged 60, he was renting a cottage from Thomas Mansell. This is the last record of him in the parish.

The Beginning of the Enclosures

The enclosure process began in 1757. Mr Richard Peters, the appointed commissioner, confirmed that the lands were 'dispersed in the fields and inconvenient and for the discouragement of industry,' and the bill was passed to the landowners for their agreement.

Mr West appeared and consented to the bill. Mrs Day signed the bill, as did Robert Burton. Peters then ran into difficulties.

Mrs Smith did not object to the inclosure, Peters reported, but she had never put her hand to anything and would not begin then. Her son John, whom the bill stated owned the land 'expectant of his mother's death', did sign. One wonders whether Muriel's death was desired sooner rather than later.

William Timbrell was willing to have the inclosure, and was not against signing, but desired first to have an answer from a person in London.

John Souch said he was infirm and was unable to look after an inclosure, but he would sign if the rest would.

William Salmon consented to the inclosure, and wondered why it had not been signed before. He believed they would all sign, but as he was a tradesman he did not choose to sign first.

John Mansell said he would sign if the rest would, but was unwilling to sign first.

Thomas Locke was very desirous that the field be enclosed, and he would sign if Mr West would take a farm on the further side of the field.

Peters eventually gathered all the necessary permissions. The enclosure could proceed. It took a further two years to complete. A land surveyor valued each furlong, meadow and piece of lott ground. The Field was divided into allotments so each landowner would receive land equivalent in value, if not in acreage, to what they'd previously held.

The requests of the gentry – James West and Robert Burton – were heeded. Burton would receive an enclosure near his manor house at Radbrook. West would receive the land below Shakersway which he wanted for his park. The requests of the smaller freeholders – especially that of Thomas Locke – were ignored.

Even so, the commissioners' decisions were not always met favourably. James West wrote:

> *To the commissioners for inclosing Preston Field*
> *London, 20ᵗʰ November 1759*
> *Gentlemen,*
> *I have always been unwilling to give you the least trouble but left everything of my property to your free and impartial determination, but I*

understand that a mistake has happened in your survey's allotment. I do hope that no part of the pasture allotted to me shall be taken from me and I hope the proportion of the 10 acres over allowed to Mr Burton shall be laid contiguous to my pasture farm. I hope you will all bear in mind that there has been less (excluding what the parliament has directed) contiguous land to my home estate allotted me than to any other freeholder in Preston and that everyman's land but mine is laid together.

> *I am gentlemen your faithful humble servant*
> *J West*

The reply from one Lewis Bradley stated that:

We have taken all the care we could that justice be done to you in every particular, but no yardland is of equal value to another. If the whole is examined, I believe you'll find yours improves more than any estate in Preston. I have given Mr Peters all the assistance I could in setting your estates as much to your advantage as possible.

The expenses provoked further bad feeling. Richard Peters' bill and the commissioners expenses – including carriages, dinners, wine and breakfasts over a nine month period – fell to the landholders. The total came to £39 19s 6d. A further letter from James West complained:

I think it highly unreasonable that these expenses which amount to near £40 should be allowed. You receive enclosed the file listing the proportions to be paid by each freeholder which amount to a considerable sum, but not near so much as our neighbouring inclosures.

> *I can see no reason to give up a farthing that I have to people who have no sense of honour or gratitude. You'll be pleased to remember that this day is fixed for the signing the award, payment of expenses and finishing this whole affair.*

The Allotments in Preston Field

		Size			Value		
		Acres	**Rods**	**Perches**	**£**	**s**	**d**
James West	Church Farm [now Park Farm]	192	3	27	145	17	5
	Part of Moor Meadow	6	0	2	6	9	8½
	Preston Pastures Farm	255	3	28	139	0	9¼
	Sweet Knowle Farm	210	3	17	100	17	1¾
William Timbrell	In Church Quarter	55	2	38	42	2	4
Thomas Locke	In Church Quarter	38	3	39	31	11	½
	Part of March Meadow	8	2	5	6	7	11½
Robert Burton	In Beast Leasow Quarter	58	3	7	49	15	4½
William Salmon	Most-ly Moor Meadow Quarter	60	3	15	42	5	7½
	The Croft [now an orchard]	2	0	5	1	19	10
Muriel Smith	In Moor Meadow Quarter	44	1	15	36	7	4

John Mansell	Most-ly Moor Meadow Quarter	87	3	17	62	8	3½
	The Croft [now an orchard]	1	1	6	1	5	9
Good-win Zouch	Most-ly Beast Leasow Quarter	49	0	14	37	19	5½
TOTAL		**1073**	**0**	**35**	**705**	**8**	**½**
	Add the measure of the roads:	26	2	2	20	15	9
TOTAL		**1099**	**2**	**37**	**725**	**3**	**9½**

The New Fields in Preston

Each farmer had to plant perimeter hedges and divide the fields as he saw fit. Many furlong names were reused in the new fields, although sometimes in different places. Long Greenhill, Horse Grass, Penny Meer and Watching Hill are examples. Some were named after the quality, location or function of the ground, such as Far Ground or Coppice Ground. Some were generic: Thomas Locke's arable fields were named Third, Fourth and Fifth Ground. Some names have been altered several times; others have remained constant for several hundred years.

Allotment Field Two fields in the 1830s: Great Greenhill and Two Furlong Ground. Part was used for allotments from the 19th century.

Atherstone Hill On the new road to Atherstone on Stour. Previously Big Hill.

Back Hill; Back Field Fields at the back of the farm.

Barn Hill; Barn Field Adjacent to post-enclosure field barns.

Beast Leasow A pre-enclosure name.

Bridge Ground Of uncertain meaning. It contains no bridge or reason for a bridge.

Bungalow Field A modern name. Once Penny Meer Meadow.

Burnt Ground Brash or stubble was sometimes burnt off. It may have become overgrown with scrub during depression years.

Bushy Leathard, Hither and Further *Leathard* refers to hard, stubborn soil. The land had probably reverted to scrub during depression years. Now known as Leasow and Windmill Field.

Church Ground; Little Church Ground; Ploughed Church Ground Near to the church. Transferred from Church Furlong.

Coles Transferred from Coal Furlong.

Coppice Ground With an area of coppiced trees. Appears twice in Preston Field.

Cotway Pre-enclosure name. Known as Cotway Butts in 1788; Cotterell's Bush Ground in the 1820s.

Crabtrees, Upper and Lower With crabapple trees. Transferred from Crabtree Furlong.

Cross Ground The lands cross the field on an angle.

The Croft Transferred from an adjacent furlong. Includes the Little Croft.

Dairy Ground Used to pasture dairy cows. There is a long tradition of dairy farming at Preston Pastures.

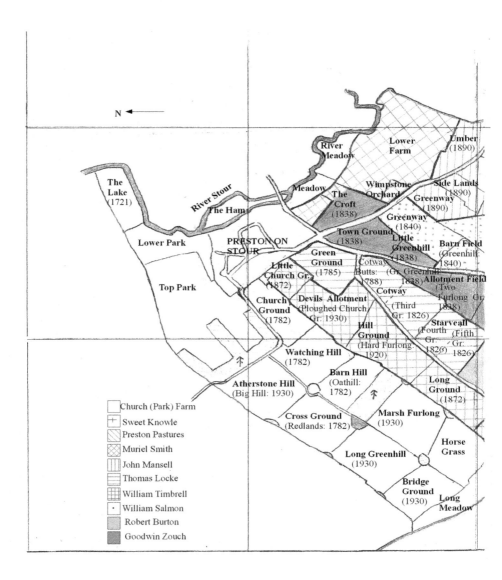

N ←

The Lake (1721)

River Stour

The Ham

Lower Park

Top Park

PRESTON ON STOUR

River Meadow

Meadow

Lower Farm

Umber (1890)

The Croft (1838)

Wimpstone Orchard

Side Lands (1890)

Greenway (1890)

Greenway (1840)

Town Ground (1838)

Little Greenhill (1838)

Barn Field (Greenhill 1840)

Green Ground (1785)

Little Church Gr. (1872)

Cotway Butts: (Gr. Greenhill (788) 1838)

Allotment Field (Two Furlong Gr. 1838)

Church Ground (1782)

Devils Allotment (Ploughed Church Gr: 1930)

Cotway (Third Gr: 1826)

Starveall (Fourth (Fifth Gr: Gr: 1826) 1826)

Hill Ground (Hard Furlong 1920)

Watching Hill (1782)

Barn Hill (Oathill: 1782)

Long Ground (1872)

Atherstone Hill (Big Hill: 1930)

Cross Ground (Redlands: 1782)

Marsh Furlong (1930)

Horse Grass

Long Greenhill (1930)

Bridge Ground (1930)

Long Meadow

Church (Park) Farm

Sweet Knowle

Preston Pastures

Muriel Smith

John Mansell

Thomas Locke

William Timbrell

William Salmon

Robert Burton

Goodwin Zouch

146

To Wimpstone

Humber Brook

To Ilmington

Long Meadow

Lower
Crab Trees

Short
Meadow

Upper
Crab Trees
(1920)

Meadow

Long
Ground
(1890)

Gad Field
(Garfield
Piece: 1920)

Rickyard
Ground
(1920)

House
Ground: 1920)

Coppice
Ground
(1890)

Mushroom
Field
(Long Ground
1920)

House
Ground

The Hill
(1890)

Coles
(1890)

Lower
Hailes
(1920)

(Burnt
Ground:
1920)

Flat
Ground
(1920)

Fair Field
(Fir Field: 1920)

Nine
Acres
(1840)

Drawthorn
(1840)

Top
Drawthorn
(1840)

Hailes
Burnt
Ground
(1920)

Lower
Long

Short Downs
(1721)

Back Hill

Lower
Piece
(1920)

Top Stumps
(Upper Far Gr.:
1838)

Ridgeway
Ground (1920)

Upper
Long

Gravel
Pit Ground
(1920)

Tanzy
Piece

Gate Piece
(1920)

Bottom Stumps
(Lower Far
Gr.: 1838)

Leasow
(Further:
1880)

(Wheat Ground:
c.1880)

House
Ground
(c.1880)

Middle
Hill
(c.1880)

Far Hill
(Beast
Leasow:
c.1880)

Preston Bushes
(Roundabouts:
1880)

Bushy
Leathard
(Whites Ground:
1780-1842;
Penny Meers: 1920)

Windmill
Field
(Hither
Bushy
Leathard:
1920)

Dairy Ground
(Pool Piece:
1920)

Flat Ground
(c.1880)

Second
Flat
Ground

Old Cover:
1880)

Fox Cover
(1920)

To Quinton

Pig Field

Upper Penny
Meer: 1780-1842

Withy
Tree Gr.:
1920

Long
Field

Bungalow
Field

First
Meadow
(Rail Meadow: c.1880)

Radbrook
Meadow

(Coppice
Gr.: 1920)

(Pasture Ground: 1842;
Penny Meer Meadow: 1780)

Quinton
Ditch

Second
Meadow

Second
Quinton
Ditch

Further Quintons
(Quinton Pasture:
c.1880)

(March
Meadow:
1785)

Radbrook

(Lower
Quintons:
1920)

Quinton
Ditch
Cover

Marchfont Brook

Enclosed fields in Preston. Current names are in bold; dates indicate first known record.
Older names are in brackets. Dashed lines indicate removed boundaries. Post-enclosure
allotments are marked.

Devil's Allotment First recorded in the mid 20th century. Maybe derogatory.

Drawthorn, Top Drawthorn Pre-enclosure name.

Fair Field A corruption of Furfield. On a 1920 map it was called Fir Field. Perhaps it was a particularly good field.

Far Ground, Upper and Lower The furthest fields of Goodwin Zouch's allotment. Later renamed Top and Bottom Stumps.

Far Hill The furthest field of Preston Pastures. Formerly Beast Leasow.

Flat Ground Found twice. The ridges were plausibly levelled at an early date.

Fox Cover An area left as scrub for foxes to lie up. Foxhunting was a key aspect of estate ownership.

Gadfield Garfield Piece in the 1920s. Maybe relates to a man of that name. Unlikely to refer to the carpenters: this family died out in the 1770s.

Gate Piece Reminiscent of Admington Gate Furlong.

Gravel Pit Ground Where gravel was dug. Adjacent to the old enclosure called Gravelly Furlong.

Greenground Known as The Green in 1785; Greenground by 1826. It was converted to pasture soon after the enclosures and has remained so ever since.

Greenhill; Great Greenhill; Little Greenhill; Long Greenhill Pre-enclosure names.

Greenway; Upper Greenway; Lower Greenway Pre-enclosure names.

Hailes Burnt Ground; Lower Hailes Adjacent to the ancient Hailes Barn Hedge. Hailes may derive from the Medieval term *haye*, meaning hedge.

Hard Furlong Pre-enclosure name.

Hill Ground Field on a hill.

Horsegrass Pre-enclosure name.

House Ground Next to both Preston Pastures and Sweet Knowle farmhouses.

Lake Pre-enclosure name.

Leasow Grassed land. Formerly Further Bushy Leathard; Wheat Ground earlier still.

Long Meadow; Long Ground Appears several times. A field longer than the surrounding ones.

Marsh Furlong Pre-enclosure name.

Middle Hill Adjacent to Far Hill.

Moor Meadow Pre-enclosure name.

Mushroom Field Where mushrooms grew. Long Ground in the 1920s.

Old Cover See Fox Cover. This was common ground used as fox cover by the 18th century.

Park, Upper and Lower Became part of James West's park in the 18th century. Now returned to farmland.

Penny Meer Meadow; Upper Penny Meer; Penny Meers Pre-enclosure names.

Pig Field Adjacent to a pigsty. This was three fields until the mid 20th century.

Pool Piece Contains a reservoir to supply water to Preston Pastures.

Preston Bushes This land probably reverted to scrub during the depression years of the 1870s. It was woodland by 1920. Formerly Old Cover and Roundabouts.

Quinton Ditch; Lower Quintons; Further Quintons By the Quinton Ditch.

Radbrook Meadow Meadow nearest Radbrook. Formerly Marsh Meadow.

Rail Meadow May have been the haunt of water rails, a bird which favours marshy ground. Now divided into First and Second Meadow.

Rickyard Ground Adjacent to a rickyard.

Ridgeway Ground Pre-enclosure name.

Roundabouts Pre-enclosure name. Now part of Preston Bushes.

Short Downs Pre-enclosure name.

Sidelands The lands shoot perpendicular to those in the adjacent field.

Starveall Derogatory name for poor land.

Stumps, Top and Bottom May have grown with scrub and trees following depression years.

Tanzy Piece Suggests it grew with tansy, a yellow-flowered wild plant.

Town Ground Field in Goodwin Zouch's allotment closest to Preston.

Two Furlong Ground Comprised part of two old furlongs: Middle Furlong and Bratch Piece Furlong. Now part of Allotment Field.

Umber Pre-enclosure name.

Watching Hill Pre-enclosure name. Also spelt Watchen Hill.

Wheat Ground Used for growing wheat. A very large field later divided into three.

Whites Ground First recorded in 1780. Now incorporated into the Pig Field. The soil type is white marl. Whitelands Way ran nearby.

Windmill Field Contained a windmill which pumped water from a well into a reservoir to supply Preston Pastures. See Pool Piece.

Withy Tree Ground Growing with withies – willow trees in Midlands dialect.

The Enclosed Fields in Alscot

Barn Ground Field with a barn in or near it. This would have belonged to Alscot Farm.

Beech Hill Where beech trees grew. Probably leant its name to Beecham Farm.

Bob Close Bog Close in 1723. This is in a valley near the brook and was probably often waterlogged.

Brake Ground; Little Brake Ground *Brake* is waste ground covered in brush wood. The most distant point in the field, it was probably the last area to be cleared for cultivation.

Brick Kiln Ground, New and Old Near a kiln, probably dating to the farms' construction. The kilns were mentioned on a 1723 map.

Brook Furlong; Further Brook Furlong Adjacent to the brook – a former county boundary – separating Alscot and Alderminster.

Broom Hill; Broom Field Land abundant with broom, a shrub once used for broom-making.

Clay Ground With clay-rich soil. See Marlpit Ground.

Clover Ground Where clover was grown. Clover was widely planted from the 18th century. See also Sainfoin Ground.

Cotterell's House Ground; Cotterell's Great Orchard; Cotterell's Whitehill Adjacent to William Cotterell's Farm. By 1723 the house was gone but was later rebuilt as Rough Farm.

Forty Lands With forty lands.

Further Lane Furland; Homeward Lane Furland Next to the turnpike road. The furthest land of Rough Farm, the former especially so.

Gravelpit Ground Containing a gravel pit.

Great Ground Now the Big Ground. This was two fields in 1723, later combined.

Greenhill, Upper and Lower A grassed field on a hill.

The Holts; Elm Holt; Further Holt; Homeward Holt A holt is a small wood or thicket.

House Ground, Upper and Lower; Home Close Next to Whitehill Farm and Beecham Farm respectively.

Marlpit Ground Where marl was dug. Marl was used for brick-making – brick kilns were sited nearby – and also to neutralise acidic soils. The field was renamed from Homeward Holt by 1818.

Pike Ground Picked Ground in 1723. From the Old English *pic*: a pointed piece of ground. The field is triangular in shape. 'Pike' is a term still used for the odd corners of a field.

Poulters Close Connected to a keeper of poultry.

Ramb Lamb Close, Upper, Middle and Lower; Ramb Lamb Meadow Where ram lambs were kept. They were separated from the females to prevent unwanted pregnancies. While the silent 'b' has been dropped from *ram*, it remains in *lamb*. The first three were incorporated into the Deer Park *c.*1760.

Rambling Meadow An interesting confusion resulting from the archaic spelling of *ramb*. Ramb Lamb Meadow was altered to Rambling Meadow by 1818, an example of how a 'Chinese Whispers' effect can give a similar name with very different meaning.

Red Field The soil is red marl.

Rough (Ruff) Ground; Rough Hill Probably some of the last land to be cleared for cultivation, still abounding with scrub and stones. Rough Farm was named after this area.

Round Ground With a curved boundary.

Ryegrass Close Ryegrass was a particularly nutritious fodder crop for cattle.

Sainfoin Ground Renamed from Middle Ground by 1818. Sainfoin is an artificial grass introduced in the 18th century, perhaps trialled here. It was unsuited to the local soil; this is the only reference to it in Preston.

Sandpit Ground Where sand was dug.

Shooters Hedge Land used for shooting.

Spring Hill A spring still runs here.

Tithings Meadow Land allocated for the tithes. A tithe was a tenth of all profit from agriculture, due to the church. Formerly paid in kind – grain, meat or wool – it later became a monetary payment and land was devoted to its fulfilment.

Whitehill; Little Whitehill; Homeward Whitehill; Middle Whitehill; Whitehill Meadow The soil type is white marl. It also gave the farm its name.

Six: A Rewritten Landscape: The New Dawn of Agriculture

After the Enclosures: Boom and Bust

Unimpeded by the ancient open field system, farmers could now cultivate and improve their own block of land as they wished. They treated poor-yielding soil with marl; installed drainage systems; dug ditches; straightened watercourses and experimented with new crops. An understanding of genetics led to the development of myriad breeds of sheep and cattle – meatier, milkier, woollier – each carefully suited to their particular environment. Cereal crops underwent similar development. The corn-threshing engine was developed in 1786, and within fifty years the most labour-intensive task of the farming year had disappeared.

Crop rotations were planned years in advance. William Timbrell, now in his seventies, leased his land to William Dudley in 1780. The agreement shows the foresight and skill now required of the successful farmer.

One field was pasture. Dudley was not to mow or crop it, but graze it with cattle. An arable field was to be planted with clover and rye grass. Yields were probably falling and this would allow it time to recover. Another pasture field was to be ploughed in two years time, planted with turnips, then three crops of corn, then laid with grass again. Turnips had been recently introduced. They were a 'cleaning' crop: planted in wide rows and easily hoed. Handheld or horse-drawn hoes were the only method of weed control until the advent of chemical weedkillers.

Productivity rose and as demand surged – the UK population doubled between 1821 and 1881 – agriculture went from strength to strength. Even the poorest land was cultivated. Science and technology could now conquer anything. Vast amounts of money were invested, rents rose, and fixed-term leases meant those farmers who struggled could be removed.

The Napoleonic Wars began in 1792. Trade with Europe ceased and prices soared in consequence.

The more prudent land agents cautioned against unnecessary expenditure, with considerable foresight. The fickle British weather proved unconquered. Poor ground yielded far less than the investment ploughed into it. With vast debts, a single bad harvest could mean ruin. When the Napoleonic Wars ended in 1815, the European trade routes reopened, coinciding with a series of crop failures across Europe. Years of agricultural depression followed.

Edward Humphries leased Preston Pastures in 1824. In 1831 he couldn't pay his poor rates of £4 5s, and before the end of the year he had abandoned the farm. He was just one of many.

Robert Smith, the younger son of John Smith of Lower Farm, was a modern farmer: enterprising, foresighted, seduced by the capabilities of science. He lived with his wife and eight children in Locke's Farm, then owned by Thomas Cox. He also farmed his father's land and rented Park Farm and Sweet Knowle. This totalled nearly 400 acres, considerable even by 20th century standards. Robert spared no expense in stocking and equipping this land – he even had his own four-horsepower threshing engine.

In December 1823 he had to give up Sweet Knowle. In July 1824, he was forced to sell up Park Farm. Farm sales are usually held in September: it seems Robert was desperate for money. His ricks of wheat and hay, the growing crops of wheat, oats, beans, clover and vetches, almost ready for harvest, 170 sheep and 22 cattle were all sold by auction, along with his wagons, carts, ploughs and his prized threshing engine. Within three years he left Preston. His subsequent fate is unclear.

Parliament proposed a ban on corn imports as long as the market price was under 80s/quarter [eight bushels, approx. ¼ton.] This would keep prices high and aid farmers. The proposal was opposed by urban groups who cited the starving poor, but as the rural gentry controlled parliament the Corn Laws were passed. They were finally repealed in 1849. This had little impact for two decades: as poor harvests in Britain were usually mirrored across Europe, there was little scope for cheaper imports.

In the 1870s, railways and steam shipping revolutionised global transport. Refrigeration techniques allowed imports of meat from the vast herds of New Zealand, Australia and Argentina. Cheap grain began to pour across the Atlantic from the Canadian and US prairies, coinciding with a succession of bad harvests in Europe.

Import tariffs were raised in all European countries except Britain, and British corn prices plummeted. Fields reverted to scrub as farmers hadn't the capital to plant them. The labour cost of hoeing and tending the fields was unaffordable. Weed-ridden crops yielded poorly, and so the downward spiral continued.

The depression forced many out of business. Frederick Silvester sold The Cottage and his farmland to James Roberts-West in 1872. John Smith, who farmed over 300 acres at Meon Hall and had recently inherited Lower Farm, sold the latter to James Roberts-West in 1875. Five years later he gave up Meon Hall and moved to Warwick where he became a brewer. He was still wealthy enough to employ three servants to look after himself, his wife and his thirteen children.

Joseph Taylor gave up his tenancy of Sweet Knowle in 1880 and moved to a much smaller farm in Blackwell. George Salmon, who took over Atherstone Hill Farm on his uncle's death in 1848, also abandoned farming in the 1870s. He moved to Stratford where he became a shopkeeper. John James took over Whitchurch Farm in the 1880s. Its previous tenant, Henry Gilbert, had badly neglected the farm. After his first harvest, John bagged up all the weed seeds and sent them on to Henry.

Thomas Salmon Smith of Park Farm recalled in 1921 that it was only thanks to Alscot Estate that his father and many others had managed to pull through – the Estate had dropped the farm rents by 50%. Henry Ashby of Preston Pastures also recalled these times. His father Robert was one of the few farmers who had managed to thrive, and Henry applauded the ethos of the estate and lamented the breakup of similar large estates.

The Two World Wars

By 1914, 80% of wheat and 40% of meat was imported. As war ravaged Europe, German submarines began to attack British supply ships. Home production was pronounced vital, but farmers met great impediment. Their horses were commandeered for the war effort. Their labourers were conscripted. Feed costs were high and fixed prices meant the farmers lost money on every beast they sold.

The Corn Production Acts of 1917 and 1920 guaranteed minimum market prices to stimulate grain output. All abandoned land had to become productive to deal with the aftermath of the war.

In 1921, the Act was repealed without notice. Prices plummeted. Another depression followed what became known as the Great Betrayal.

And then a new war loomed. In 1936, the War Agricultural Executive Committee (War Ag) was set up to tackle the woeful deficiencies of British agriculture. 70% of British food was now imported, and all unproductive farmland had to be cleared and cultivated.

This was the responsibility of the landowners. If unable or unwilling to do the work, it was taken over by the War Ag. Horses were incapable of drastic clearance work or hauling a plough through heavy, stony ground, so the War Ag would arrange machines to do the work. This was considered one of the outstanding features of wartime agriculture.

A 'bush-pusher' was a huge crawler which bent the stems of trees, cut through them, then scooped out the roots. They were pushed into heaps and burned. Nardey Bush near Whitchurch and Crimscote Downs were reclaimed in 1943. Ridge-and-furrow grassland was broken up using a 'ridge-breaker' which simply split the ridges in two and tipped the soil into the furrows.

Farmers were forced into the mechanical era as tractors and combine harvesters replaced the heavy horses. Agriculture would never look back.

From an advertisement by the Ministry of Agriculture in the Stratford Herald, 1943.

Preston's New Farms

There were ten individual farms in Preston following the enclosures: seven small units belonging to the freeholders and three large farms created from James West's allotments. The latter were held by a succession of tenant farmers. Six of the freehold units were purchased by the West family in the 19th century.

The land was still worked in strips. This didn't change until the reversible plough was invented in the 19th century, which allowed ploughing to proceed steadily across the field rather than circling a central strip. The ridges then began to be levelled.

Ponds were dug in most new fields to water livestock and horses. Typically quite small, many have silted up or been infilled. Pre-enclosure ponds were bigger and often planted with willow trees. Patch Pool, behind Numbers 1&2, is one of these ancient ponds. The name is at least 300 years old and of uncertain origin, but could have Anglo-Saxon origins.

Coppices were also planted. Locally-harvested wood was the source of furniture, hurdles, gates, fences, baskets and countless other products. The straight stems of young trees were cut through, either at ground level or at six feet: coppicing and pollarding respectively. This encouraged the tree to send out many new stems which in time would be harvested themselves. Pollarding prevented animals browsing the new stems.

Woodland crafts largely died out in the latter 20th century as plastic and metal replaced wooden products. The coppiced trees now grow freely, untouched for fifty or a hundred years. The multiple thick trunks shooting from a single butt betray a tree's use in once-managed woodland.

Patch Pool (left); a once-coppiced tree (right).

Preston Pastures

Work to build new farmsteads amidst James West's two furthest allotments began shortly after the enclosures. The most important consideration was water supply. Commissioner Lewis Bradley wrote to James West in January 1760:

> *I think the sooner you give orders for sinking wells for water where you propose building, the better, as they will be some time about, and you cannot carry any materials for building until you have found water. As there are two farm houses to be built, I think there is no time to be lost.*

At Preston Pastures, a windmill was devised to pump water from a well into a reservoir in the Dairy Ground, from which it was piped to the house and fields.

These large, modern farms – Preston Pastures was 255 acres and Sweet Knowle 210 acres – were intended to rake in the profits afforded by science and technology, but both farms proved rather unsuccessful. The expenditure to hedge, drain and improve a farm of this size was immense. Many farmers didn't have the capital to do this effectively, and were reluctant to spend much on land they may only be farming for a few years.

The land was also poor quality. Preston Pastures was valued at 10s 9d/acre after the enclosures in 1759; Sweet Knowle at 9s 6d/acre. The other allotments averaged 15s/acre. Being the furthest land from the village, it had perhaps received less manure and attention than the nearer furlongs.

The first farmer at Preston Pastures was James Jackson, followed by his son George who left c.1775. At least ten more farmers followed, some lasting as little as six years.

Robert Ashby from Tysoe took the farm in 1860. Robert seems to have been the first to achieve success. He was perhaps more shrewd, and benefited from the improvements already undertaken. Within ten years he was also leasing 85 acres of Sweet Knowle. His son Henry then grandson Fred continued the tenancy.

The Ashbys had a large and successful dairy herd. The reason for their success is probably due to converting the poor-yielding fields back into pasture for which it was better suited. The farm was soon notable for the soundness of its pasture land and the excellent stock it produced.

The family were tenants until Fred Ashby purchased the farm in the 1920s. He sold up in 1936. It was briefly owned by a few more farmers until purchased by Vera Perry c.1950, who owned it for over fifty years. These farmers also all kept quality dairy herds.

Sweet Knowle

The first tenant of Sweet Knowle was David Malins, who took a 21-year lease in 1760. His daughter Elizabeth married Robert Fletcher from Alveston in January 1770, and their first son Edward was born at Sweet Knowle four months later. It is interesting to note that while Elizabeth could sign her name in the marriage register, Robert could not.

Robert took over the farm in 1781 and his sons Edward, Nicholas and Robert later worked with him. His daughter Elizabeth married John Mansell from The Gables. Robert died in 1820 and the family left the farm.

It had at least eight tenants before it was taken by Richard Jaques from Newbold on Stour in the 1880s, followed by his sons Arthur and Richard. The brothers rented the farm until 1921 when it was sold to William Stanley of Mickleton.

It was later sold to Major Spenser Flower, whose family owned Flower's Brewery in Stratford, then passed to his daughter Heather and her husband John Taylor. In the 1960s it was purchased by Hedley Harding whose son Rex farms there today.

Church Farm (Park Farm)

This was the third of James West's new farms and was allotted a farmhouse in the village. It was called Church Farm as its land was in Church Quarter, later renamed after the deer park. It is the only working farm in the village today. The 192-acre allotment was reduced to 145 acres after the park was expanded.

Joseph Prentice was probably its first tenant, followed in the 1780s by Thomas Bumpass of Admington. Its occupancy after this is unclear until Charles Ward, who farmed at nearby Wincot, took the tenancy in the 1820s. A decade later his son John took over and Charles returned to Wincot. John remained until *c.*1860.

It was then taken by John's nephew Giles Smith, the great-grandson of Giles Smith who'd rented Lingings Farm in 1721. Giles had been living at Church House with his parents and had recently married Sarah Silvester of The Cottage.

On his death in 1900, it was taken over by his son, Thomas Salmon Smith. On Thomas' death in 1927, it was taken by his niece Elsie (Nancy) and her husband Alwyn William Mansell Spencer, followed by their son Bob. Bob's son Will farms there today.

Locke's Farm

Thomas Locke never married. The church register records the burial of: *Thomas Locke, an ancient yeoman, a bachelor,* on January 5th 1781. He was buried in an elaborate brick tomb inscribed:

> *In the memory of Thomas Locke, son of Thomas and Sarah Locke, who according to his particular desire is interred beneath this tomb. He departed this life on the 1st day of January 1781 aged 71. He was esteemed when living and lamented when dead.*

The farm passed to his sister Elizabeth Timbrell. In 1785, the farmstead and land were sold to Edward Townsend Kenwrick, Rector of Atherstone on Stour.

When Kenwrick died the farm passed to his nephew, Revd Thomas Cox, who sold it to James Roberts-West in 1827. The house was divided into four dwellings and the land leased with other holdings.

Thomas Locke's grave.

The Old Vicarage

Goodwin Zouch remained in Shottery and the farm was managed by a steward. The Preston burial register records that: *Thomas Ward, a middle-aged man, manager of Mr Zouch's farm*, was buried in February 1780.

Goodwin died in 1788. He was buried in the family vault in Preston where his father, brother, wife and four of his children already lay. The farm was inherited by Goodwin's son John who lived at Milcote. John married widow Mabel Hill in 1784 but had no children. He died in 1804.

Mabel soon remarried, first a gentleman named Thomas Sparkes and later a fourth husband, and died in 1831. The farm was sold to James Roberts-West in 1838. It remained a working farm until the 1850s. The house was then leased to a succession of retired farmers, apart from a brief spell as a vicarage, and the land incorporated with other holdings.

Robert Burton's Farm

Robert Burton died in 1803. The estate at Radbrook passed to his son Robert, and then Robert's son Robert, both of whom lived at Longner Hall in Shropshire. In 1842, Radbrook manor and farm, including the 58 acres in Preston Field, were sold to James Roberts-West. No property in Preston was included in the sale, but Church House was the property of Alscot Estate by the mid 19th century. One half remained a working farmhouse until the 1850s.

Radbrook Farm was sold into private hands in the 1920s. It still includes Robert Burton's allotment today.

The Old Manor

William Salmon died a wealthy man in 1761. He left The Old Manor and the farmland to his eldest son Thomas, and other properties in Preston to his younger sons Richard and Joseph. Thomas leased Atherstone Hill Farm and 170 acres of pasture from Sarah West. Thomas' son William, who inherited The Manor and farmland in his turn, continued the lease. The Old Manor was divided into three in the 1830s. In 1840, William sold the house and land to James Roberts-West. He never married and lived at Atherstone Hill with his nephew George until his death in 1848.

The Cottage

William Timbrell became one of the wealthiest farmers in Preston. When he died in 1790, aged 87, he left legacies of around £1000 to various family members. Among his other bequests were silver tablespoons, a gold piece of James 1st and a silver dollar.

He took diligent care with his funeral arrangements. He dictated that he was to be buried in a vault and tomb in the manner of his brother-in-law, the late Mr Locke – he left £30 to his executors to cover this – and his three tenants and his servant were to carry his coffin to his grave. They were each to have a new brown coat worth two guineas for the occasion. William worried over this last clause, and a year after signing his will added a memorandum revising this to a coat, waistcoat and breeches.

William's vault has not withstood the test of time, but that of Thomas Locke, after which it was designed, still stands.

The farm passed to William's great-nephew John Timbrell, the vicar of Beckford and later Archdeacon of Gloucestershire. John had no interest in farming and sold it to Richard Salmon, the grandson of William Salmon of The Old Manor.

Richard married late and had no children, and on his death in 1836 the farm passed to his nephew Samuel Richard Silvester. Samuel changed his name to Richard Salmon Silvester in recognition of his considerable inheritance. He moved to The Cottage with his wife Charlotte and their six children. In 1843 he suffered a fatal epileptic seizure and Charlotte ran the farm until their eldest son Richard, then eleven, would succeed.

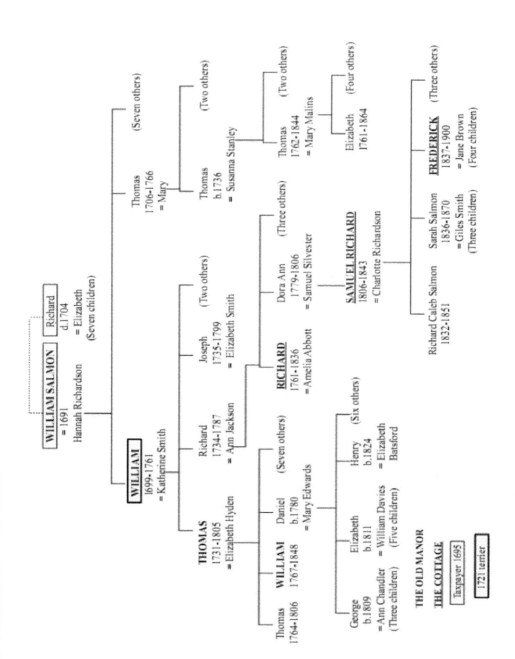

THE OLD MANOR

THE COTTAGE

Taxpayer 1695

1721 terrier

161

But Richard contracted tuberculosis and died in 1851, aged 19. His younger brother Frederick went on to inherit. Frederick became a victim of the agricultural depression of the 1870s and sold the house and land to James Roberts-West in 1872. The Cottage ceased to be a working farm.

The Gables

John Mansell was the first of his family to attain the rank of gentleman. He never married, and on his death in 1777 the house and lands passed to his nephew Thomas.

Thomas' sons John and Thomas farmed in Preston. William built much of Mansell Street in Stratford. John inherited the family farm, followed by his son, also called John. John's own son, another John, was set to inherit in his turn.

In 1873, tragedy struck. John was struck down by jaundice. He ailed for a fortnight, then the illness moved into his brain. Within 48 hours he was dead. He was 39. His father, widowed and frail, moved in with his younger son Robert who farmed in Stratford. Robert returned to The Gables following his father's death three years later.

Robert had no children, and when he died in 1905 the family name died with him. His widow Sarah remained at The Gables until her death and the farm passed to his sister Ann's children.

Ann's grandson, Cecil Lees, built Mansell Farm on the family's farmland in 1939. Descendants of the family still live there today.

Lower Farm

Muriel Smith died in 1761 after 32 years a widow. Her son John remained at Willicote for his life and leased out Lower Farm.

John and his wife Elizabeth had fourteen children, several of whom died in childhood, including with particular tragedy their sons William, buried at Preston on 1st June 1763, and Thomas on 7th June. They are adjacent entries in the burial book.

Elizabeth died in July 1764, shortly after the birth of her last child Robert, who himself died at seven months. John died in 1772 and Lower Farm passed to his only son to survive childhood, John, now aged 18.

John lived at Lower Farm for his life. His eldest son, also called John, took a farm at Meon Hill in Quinton, and his younger son Robert farmed the land in Preston with a vast amount of rented land.

On their father's death in 1826, John took over Lower Farm. He remained until his death in 1843. His widow Jane had a life interest in the farm and their son, another John, moved to Meon where his thirteen children were born.

Jane retired in the 1850s and the farm was leased out. When she died in 1873 it passed to John, who sold it to James Roberts-West two years later. A series of tenant farmers followed. In 1922 Harvey Smith of The Old Vicarage, no known relation to the earlier family, exchanged with Harry Gould who was retiring. Harvey retired in 1955 and was followed by his son Harry, who remained until his death in 2003. It then ceased to be a working farm.

Life on the New Farms

A good farmer in the 19th century could live well, educate his children, employ a few servants and maintain his position as a respected and diligent member of the community. Preston Church Council and the School Board were almost exclusively made up from farming families.

Giles Smith of Park Farm (1831-1900) despite his retiring disposition was known for his zealous work in the local community. He was churchwarden for several years, a Guardian of the Poor and was also on the Highways Board. He was a farmer of great enterprise, a liberal employer, and his character obtained the esteem of the whole neighbourhood. Robert Mansell of The Gables (1838-1905) was of a similar character. His conduct in all matters of life was marked with thoroughness and strict integrity, and these qualities won the respect of everyone.

Agriculture still provided employment for the majority of men, women and boys in Preston. Those who didn't work directly on the farms were employed as carpenters, wheelwrights and blacksmiths for whom the farms provided a great deal of work.

Of four hundred inhabitants in Preston in 1841, 77 were farm labourers. The eldest of these was 84-year-old William Russell, who had five non-working dependants. The youngest was eight-year-old William Horseman, whose father Richard was also a labourer.

Preston School was built in 1848, but children weren't legally obliged to attend school until 1880. Children from poorer families, with a new baby all too often arriving each year, had to start work at a young age to supplement the family's meagre income. Boys would begin their working life as plough boys or bird scarers before moving on to harder manual work.

The rising population led to a fall in wages and employment during the 19th century. Servants in husbandry became less common, as it was now more economical to employ labourers on a daily basis without the expense of food and lodging. The loss of commoners' rights following the enclosures and the decline of cottage industries such as spinning which had provided women with an income meant life became very bleak for the farm labourer. The staple food for many families was barley bread and a good meal was unheard of.

Thomas Walton (1852-1936) a labourer's son, lived most of his life in No.40. He recalled shortly before his death that he began work aged four, scaring crows off the newly-planted corn. He would earn 2d a day and wouldn't see a soul except when his dad brought his dinner. When he took his dinner with him, he ate it on the way there and had to make do with a swede instead. When he was seven he began working as a plough-boy which earned him 7d a day. He continued with farm work until he started his own carrier's business in the 1890s.

Labourers on Alscot Estate c.1882. Second right, Giles Horseman? From WI collection.

Joseph Arch, a farm labourer from Barford, spoke out against rural poverty and campaigned for labourers' rights. He complained that the labourers were dismissed as unskilled, when in fact they had to be adept at all areas of arable and livestock management: sheep shearing; milking; horse-work; hedgelaying; ditching; thatching and scything to name a few.

Joseph drew people from across the country to his cause, and in 1872 he started the National Agricultural Workers' Union. Its main aim was a fair labourers' living wage. Those who joined the Union often lost their jobs and homes but in some places they achieved success.

In January 1874, the midst of the depression, employers were attempting to reduce wages again. Farmers could now ill afford labour costs. In Preston and other places, labourers had been on strike for five weeks. Who they worked for is unclear.

It seems Preston's farmers had divided opinions on the matter. Giles Smith of Park Farm was a Guardian of the Poor, a liberal employer, and his relationship with his hands was of the happiest character. Henry Ashby of Preston Pastures and Robert Mansell seem to have been of similar disposition. When Henry's youngest son Fred married in 1914, he organised a supper with music and dancing for all his twenty employees. It may be significant that Henry Ashby and Robert Mansell were Baptists, more inclined to equality than the Church of England.

John Smith, who inherited Lower Farm in 1873, may have had a different attitude. In February 1874, around the time of the strikes, a suspicious fire broke out in his barn. Although the fire brigade was summoned, it destroyed several buildings. Normally when a fire broke out, everybody rushed to help. In this case, it was reported in *The Leamington Courier*, the villagers 'showed a disposition anything but creditable, refusing to work unless drink – the bane of society – was supplied to them.' John Smith was obviously very unpopular in Preston. He may have lowered wages or sacked employees for Union membership. The arsonist was never identified.

The Political System

Only landowners were eligible to vote until the early 19th century, with requirements varying between boroughs. In 1811 there were three voters in Preston: Thomas Mansell of the Gables, Richard Salmon of The Cottage and William Salmon of The Old Manor and Atherstone Hill Farm.

In 1832 the requirements were standardised to freeholders and those occupying land of a certain value – not necessarily in the voter's district of residence. In 1853 the electorate comprised:

Name	Abode	Nature of Qualification	Location of Property
Robert Fletcher	Preston	Freehold house and garden	The village [Beer House]
Richard Hughes	Preston	House and land as occupier	Near the village [Zouch's Farm]

James Jaques	Preston	House and land as occupier	Sweet Knowle
John Mansell	Preston	Freehold house and land	Near the village [Mansell's Farm]
Joseph Tipping	Whitehill	House and land as occupier	Whitehill Farm
Henry Walton	Preston	Land as occupier	Preston Pastures
Charles Ward	Wincot	House and land as occupier	Near the village [Park Farm]
James Roberts-West	Alscot	Freehold house and land	Alscot

In 1884 the vote was extended to any man who owned or rented property worth £10/annum and had lived in it for a year. This now included many labourers.

Parliamentary radicals – 'radical' referring to anyone seeking any form of change – formed the Liberal party in the mid 19th century. They campaigned for social change and political reform and gained rapid support, especially among the working classes.

The Liberals or Radicals had a strong presence in Preston, no doubt linked to the striking labourers of the 1870s. A Liberal meeting was held in Preston in November 1885 with 'curious interruptions by a local farmer', as reported in the *Stratford Herald*. What they were and who he was are unfortunately lost to time.

James Roberts-West was keen to stamp out this Radical presence. Labourer Joseph Rouse (b.1835) of Alderminster paid his rent on time, kept his garden tidy and nobody had any complaint about him. His only fault was to join the Liberal committee to choose an election candidate in 1885. Shortly afterwards he was evicted from his home, where he'd lived for 18 years. He and his sons also lost their jobs. Mr West told him he 'couldn't have these goings on in the village', and also spoke of 'the abominable union'. Joseph had once been a member of the Labourers' Union but was no longer.

As nobody dared quarrel with Mr West, Joseph and his family had to leave. By 1891 he was living in Offenham, Worcestershire and had found work as a gardener. His 12-year-old son Walter was also a gardener. His sons George and Charles had found work on the railways.

Labourer William Timms (b.1846) had lived and worked in Preston without fault for his entire life, and was also vocal in his support of the Liberal party. He supported Lord Compton, the Liberal MP for Stratford, in the 1885 election and was served with an eviction notice for his house. This was withdrawn, but William continued to cause trouble. In July 1889 he was voted into the chair for a well-attended Liberal meeting in Preston, with the speakers standing in a farm wagon. He entertained the speakers to tea at another meeting in July 1892. The Tory candidate, Colonel Thomas Chester-Master, was described at this meeting as 'a fossilised old Tory who ought to have lived in the time of King Charles'.

The next day land-agent James Stokes gave William notice to quit his allotment. He was told that another would follow for his house. The whole village was indignant, but Stokes claimed it wasn't for election purposes. The case was strangely reported in the *Dundee Courier,* which regularly published anti-establishment articles.

William was forced out and in 1901 he was working as a bricklayer's labourer in Stratford; in 1911 he was a caretaker in a water works in Snitterfield.

The Twentieth Century

The dawn of the 20th century heralded a new era for the farm labourer. Only two working farms now remained in the village itself. Fewer people were needed on the land thanks to the increasing use of machinery, and compulsory education meant more career paths were open to the lower classes. Those who chose to remain farmworkers were no longer the lower end of the social scale.

Joe Newland (1901-1993) started work on Radbrook Farm aged 13. Ploughing, drilling, hay-making, harrowing – all with horses – and many other tasks filled his working days. It was bleak work in wet weather; he would tie potato sacks around his legs and shoulders in an effort to keep out the rain.

Joe found himself to be a natural horseman. He learnt to gain their trust and would always make sure they had a good pile of clover to eat while the wagons were unloaded. The horses had to be ready for the working day which began at 7am. After work, they had to be fed, watered, groomed, and stabled or turned out to grass. The tack had to be cleaned and the scurf and sweat cleaned off the collars, all before the men could tend their own needs.

Eric Dale (1920-1975) worked at Atherstone Hill Farm and then Park Farm until tragically killed in a farm accident. He could also turn his hand to any task.

Both men were champion hedgelayers. Creating a thick, stock-proof hedge was a skilled job. The hawthorn stems had to be severed almost at ground level, laid flat and woven around the other stems. They would shoot and form many new stems which would fill the gaps. Woven hazel laths supported the structure. A perfectly neat job was a matter of pride.

Rick-building was another skilled job. They had to be built tightly and securely: one error and several tonnes of sheaves would avalanche to the ground. When finished, a waterproof covering of thatch was added. Eric Dale's son Fred (b.1942) spent days at a time thatching ricks, a job he loved and got very good at. Joe Newland was also an expert thatcher.

Mowing was another deceptively difficult task. Horse-drawn reapers replaced hand mowing from the 19th century, but smaller areas were still scythed by hand.

Farm workers gained a deep and quiet understanding of the countryside. Ethel Davies, nee Newland (b.1944) followed her dad up and down the fields as a child, carrying their sandwiches and bottles of cold tea as he pointed out all the birds, insects and flowers to her.

Daniel Hopkins of No.2 (1862-1955) held for some time the title of Preston's oldest resident. He was a real countryman of the old school. He started work for Henry Ashby at Preston Pastures in his teens, and worked for Henry's son Fred and grandson Henry before retiring in his eighties. He also did brick-making, draining and well-sinking for Alscot Estate.

Bill Reason (1877-1969) was born in Birmingham where his father Henry worked in a gas works. The family moved to the Stratford area where Henry began farmwork, and Bill began work as a groom at Park Farm c.1910. When most of the horses were commandeered for the war effort he worked as a cowman and general farmworker. In later years, as he told the *Sunday Mercury* in 1956, now aged 79, 'I only do a bit of gardening now.' He finally retired in 1963, aged 85.

Thomas Salmon Smith (1861-1927) a former draper, took over Park Farm on his father's death in 1900. His only child Thomas was much-liked, healthy and enthusiastic about farming. In August 1907, aged 17, he jumped on his bike at first light to go and feed his fowls. He fell and cut his knee. A few days later, he complained of stiffness in his back and jaws. He couldn't eat his dinner properly. Tetanus [lockjaw] was diagnosed. An infection caused by soil-borne bacteria contaminating a deep wound, tetanus triggers uncontrollable spasms in all muscles, which lock rigid. In the 1900s it was untreatable. Within four days, Thomas was dead.

Bill Reason, 79, and Will Spencer, 2, outside Park Farm in 1956.

In 1927, Park Farm was taken over by Alwyn (Will) Spencer (1882-1936). Will was a keen huntsman and always had a pile of dogs around him. He walked puppies for the Warwickshire Hunt and won several prizes at the annual Puppy Show. He was also a keen bee-keeper. A labourer called Hathaway, woodsman Jack Day and gamekeeper William Noyce often worked on the farm. Will would say in the mornings, 'Noyce Day, Hathaway!'

Harvey Smith (1884-1956) moved to Lower Farm in 1922. He was renowned as a good farmer and had a real affection for the land he tilled. His obituary in the *Stratford Herald* described him as a strong and forceful character. Ivy Ashby, nee Noyce, remembered he was known as 'bugger 'em' for his constant swearing.

The children were quite frightened of him as he would shout at them – quite rightly – for playing on the bridge wall, but he actually had a soft spot for children. James Stredder, who lived at The Dell, remembers that Harvey had a dog called Carlo. One day he wasn't in his kennel.

'Where's Carlo, Mr Smith?' he and his brother Robert asked.

'Well, last night, a big helicopter came down from the sky, and its blades were spinning round and round, and it picked old Carlo up and it took him off to heaven.'

Carlo had in fact been put down.

Harvey Smith, courtesy of John Smith. Alwyn William Mansell Spencer, courtesy of William Spencer.

Farmers needed a critical eye for horses, and most kept hunters as well as working horses, the latter the responsibility of the carters and waggoners. Harvey Smith was an excellent judge of Shire horses, of which he was especially fond. The Alderminster and District Shire Horse Society was set up in 1920, largely through the efforts of Thomas Salmon Smith, also a keen horseman who won several prizes at the Warwickshire Hunt Show. The Society advised on breeding programmes, arranged sales and held one of the best shows in the Midlands with over 200 entries.

Alwyn (Will) Spencer was also a keen horseman and kept several prize-winning hunters, all of which had to be sold after his death in 1936. He fell from a wagon of hay in the Lake Meadow and was knocked unconscious.

Margaret Leese of Field Barn Cottage was helping with the hay-making and her five-year-old son John witnessed the accident. They only had a bottle of tea to revive him – it was John's job to hold it – and they sent for brandy from Alscot Park. Will was taken to hospital where he was found to have four broken ribs and a punctured lung. He died a few days later.

George Beauchamp came to Preston in 1945 to work for Alfred Bishop at Rough Farm, then later worked for the council. His son Ray (1944-1993) worked for Harry Smith. Ray helped out a lot of people in the village, particularly the elderly, and was a familiar sight delivering logs with his old tractor. He was quite a character, and would come out with comments such as; 'I might be green, but I ain't a cabbage,' and 'It's better to be daft and knows it than daft and not knows it.'

Joe Spencer's wife Bett from Whitehill was always in a hurry. She was driving down the Cow Lane when Ray flagged her down.

'Are you in a hurry, Mrs Spencer?'

'Yes, I am rather, Ray.'

'You'd best carry on, then.'

When she came back she stopped. 'Was it anything important, Ray?'

'Not really. I just wanted to tell you, you'd left your umbrella on the roof of your car.'

Women on the Farms

Women worked on the farms at haymaking and harvest when no pair of hands could be spared, and dairy work was traditionally a woman's job. It was believed that cows had fewer teat problems and udder infections when milked by women, as they were gentler. Butter had to be churned slowly; men had a tendency to rush it.

Many widows or married women from poorer households worked full-time as farm labourers. There were eleven female labourers in 1841. The eldest was 83-year-old long-time widow Elizabeth Allen. Her widowed daughter Mary, a laundress, and four grandchildren lived with her.

Mary Manners, 40, lived in a dilapidated cottage on the main village street with her five children. Three years earlier, her husband William, a labourer, had contracted bronchitis, a term applied to any infection or inflammation of the airways. It was August, and exacerbated by the heat and dust – William had probably been working at the harvest before he fell ill – his condition rapidly deteriorated. With no antibiotics yet developed, his airways choked with mucus until he lost his fight for oxygen. He was 38.

Mary, her youngest child just a few weeks old, had to labour in the fields herself. Her 14-year-old son John was also a labourer, and her 12-year-old daughter Eliza probably minded the younger children.

Mary struggled alone for fifteen years. She was in receipt of Poor Relief for a good deal of this time, but life would still have been insufferably hard. In 1855, now aged 53, she remarried. Her new husband was Sampson Robbins, a labourer and bachelor who'd lived in Preston all his life. Her daughter Phoebe had married a few months earlier: the entries are adjacent in the church register. The couple moved to Temple Grafton, ten miles away, and Mary died a year later.

The number of female labourers declined as the 19th century progressed. Only six – known as field women – were recorded in 1871, including Sarah Timms, 52, and Elizabeth Gibbins, 51, both labourer's wives. Elizabeth had two young children at home. Sarah's four children were no longer at home.

The decline in female labour was celebrated by the social reformer Joseph Ashby, a distant cousin of the Ashbys of Preston Pastures. He believed it would be an advantage to society if it were made a crime for women to work in the fields.

'If a woman were out at work all day,' he questioned, 'what muddle must the house be left in, with no comfort for the labourer or his wife when they returned home? Children would play truant and older girls, who need careful training for service and home-making duties, would instead be learning the worst vices.'

Women were forced into the fields well into the 20th century. In the 1930s, out-of-work farm labourer Albert Leese, who had been employed at Beecham Farm, moved into Field Barn Cottage with his wife and five children. In 1935 he suffered a fatal heart attack. His widow Margaret, her youngest child aged 3½, had to work on the farm herself, as well as doing the laundry at Park Farm. Even so, her son John (b.1931) remembers, the children were all too often hungry – they would sometimes eat raw rhubarb and linseed-based cattle cake – and life was very hard.

Margaret remarried in 1936 and the family moved to Stratford where life was much better. But Preston retains a magnetic hold over John, who still visits his childhood home seventy years on.

Pea picking and potato picking were usually jobs for women and children. Potatoes – grown to quotas during the Second World War – were spun from the ground with a machine then picked up by hand. If the work wasn't finished by the end of the summer holidays, the children involved were allowed extra time off.

The Second World War brought thousands of women into agriculture when the Women's Land Army (WLA) or Land Girls made up the labour shortfall. Many had no agricultural experience. Some were as young as seventeen and away from home for the first time. They lived on farms or stayed in hostels and travelled to farms as needed. A hostel was built at Long Marston, and the WAAF site on the Atherstone on Stour aerodrome, adjacent to Whitehill Farm, also provided accommodation. Local women helped at the hostels – cleaning, preparing meals and providing sympathy and care to the young girls. Rose Horseman of No.8 often had Land Girls round for tea.

Land Girls remained at Whitehill for several years. In December 1947, Florence Hamilton was persuaded by another Land Girl to steal a hen from Bett Spencer's hen house to take home for Christmas. When Mrs Spencer visited the hut to make inquiries, Florence gave her a false name. She appeared in court and was dismissed, but ordered to pay £1 costs.

Mary Watts, nee Spencer (b.1923) of Park Farm was working as an apprentice hairdresser when war broke out. She faced the choice of the women's forces or farm work, and returned to work on the family farm.

Mary's first job each morning was feeding the calves. This involved lighting a fire under a copper in the old wash house, heating water, making gruel and carrying it out in buckets. She grew adept at both tractor and horse-work. The bulk of the hard labour was done by the men; Mary would drive the tractor at harvest time while her brother Bob worked the binder. If there was no farm work to be done, she would work in the garden or in the house.

When Mary married farmer Bertie Watts in 1946 and they moved to their own farm, her new skills proved very useful; the work force comprised only Bertie and herself.

Harvest at Lower Farm, 1942.
Renee, Doreen, Brenda, Peggy and Ruth Smith, with John and Harry Smith.
Courtesy of John Smith.

Farm Buildings

The farmhouse and buildings were arranged around a central yard. Locke's Farm and The Old Vicarage are obvious examples on the 1760 map. Park Farm still retains this layout. Houses were built separately to their buildings from the mid 18th century.

In 1721 each farm had at least one barn, stable and yard. Open yards were later supplemented with covered shelter-sheds. The barn was usually to the north or against the prevailing winds to shelter livestock. The stables, cowsheds and shelter-sheds were on the west, maximising exposure to the winter sun. The house and other buildings were arranged on the remaining sides.

Farmers often erected buildings in the midst of newly-enclosed fields. Harvested sheaves could be quickly stored; cattle could be housed near their pasture ground; and the manure could be easily carted to the fields. The buildings now belonging to Park Farm a mile from the village comprise a barn, built *c.*1760, and other 19th century buildings. The buildings along the Admington Road were built on William Salmon's allotment after it was sold to James Roberts-West in 1840.

The porch of the barn at Park Farm facing the yard, complete with small side door, is unusual. The upper door on the northern side of the Admington Road buildings was for unloading feed from wagons. Dashed lines indicate feed troughs.

The Barns

The barn was the most important building, used to store sheaves until threshing commenced. A barn usually had three 16ft bays. Sheaves and threshed straw were stored in the outer two, while the central bay was used for unloading and threshing. The ears of corn were beaten with flails until the grain was separated from the straw and chaff. The huge doors allowed laden carts to pass through and the breeze aided winnowing.

Timber-framed barns were built in a similar manner to the houses, except the wattled panels were left undaubed. This kept birds and vermin out but gave ventilation. Barns were built with brick after the 18th century. The diamond pattern of gaps in the brickwork was for ventilation.

Two timber-framed barns survive in Preston. The oldest – early 17th century – is at The Gables. The panels have now been plastered. That at Park Farm has brick panels which replaced the earlier wattles.

Fires in the tinder-dry sheaves were common. The barn at Park Farm was once badly damaged by fire, evidenced by charred timbers at the northern end. It was originally four bays, but was rebuilt half a bay shorter.

The Rickyards

As farms grew in size, the barns were soon filled at harvest. From the 18th century, ricks of hay and corn were built outdoors in rickyards. The rick was built on a staddle: a wooden framework supported on staddle stones. These mushroom-shaped stones, now used as garden ornaments, were designed to prevent rats climbing into the ricks.

Two farms in Preston had rickyards in 1721. They soon became commonplace and the old barns fell into disrepair, although open-sided Dutch barns were commonly built from the late 19th century.

The Granaries

Grain was stored in sacks in a granary. This was on an upper floor, often over a cartshed. The dry air circulating beneath aided storage. If kept above a cowshed, the warm, damp air spoiled the grain. The granary had outside steps which stopped below the door to hinder gnawing rats.

A granary opposite Park Farm was built in the 18th century. There were probably once steps to the upper door, removed when the building was restructured. The hole in the door was to allow cats in for vermin control.

The Cartsheds

Only Giles Smith's farm had a cartshed in 1721, but within fifty years they were commonplace. Farmers now had valuable equipment and could afford a building to store it. Those in Preston were typically three to six bays. Cartsheds always opened away from the fold-yard so livestock didn't damage the equipment.

The Stables

The valuable horses were usually stabled. Every farm had at least one stable in 1721. They often had a loft to store feed. Oxen were also housed. They needed stalling of four feet apiece, and were worked and stalled in pairs. This is why a bay in timber-framed buildings was 16ft: to house two pairs of oxen.

The Cowsheds

Shelter-sheds – roofed buildings, open on one side – replaced open yards from the 18th century. They aided feeding, especially in inclement weather, and kept drier. Individual pens for cows and calves were often added. Stalled cowsheds were common, especially for dairy cows.

The building at Park Farm angled at 100 degrees to the barn in 1760 was probably a cowshed. It was a low, timber-framed building – the joints are still visible in the barn – and may have been destroyed by the same fire that ravaged the barn. A brick cowshed was built on the spot in the 19th century.

The Pigsties
The Enclosures Act revoked the right to keep pigs on the common ground so alternative housing was needed. Pigsties were almost ubiquitous on farms and in cottage gardens until the mid 20th century.

Livestock

Sheep were now big and meaty, although there was a healthy trade in wool and sheepskins, the latter taken to the Stratford tannery where they fetched a few shillings apiece.

Enclosed fields allowed careful breeding strategies. The South Down, a hardy and quick-growing sheep with quality meat, was developed in the 1800s and was commonly kept in Preston. It became the genetic parent of many modern breeds. James Roberts-West started a pedigree flock in 1836, and Alscot rams were winning championship prizes seventy years later. The entire flock had to be sold due to financial problems in 1918.

In 1880, Joseph Taylor of Sweet Knowle owned a flock of Grey Face Cotswold sheep. The Cotswold sheep had once carried the wool trade, but now had limited popularity.

South Downs at Alscot Park c.1882. Note the handmade hurdles. From WI collection.

Cattle ranged from a motley group with doubtful parentage to carefully-bred pedigree herds. Herefords were the most common beef cattle in the area. James Roberts-West was one of the earlier breeders, and had a herd of pure-bred Herefords by 1824.Charles Crawford, a Stratford farmer who emigrated to Canada *c.*1840, also kept Herefords which may have been imported from Alscot. He named his new holding 'Alscot Farm'.

The Stratford spring cattle show in March 1941 saw a good number of Preston cattle among the 500 entries. Elsie Spencer from Park Farm entered 42 cross-bred Herefords, which took first and second prizes in their class. The trustees of Alscot Estate also took a first prize with their Herefords.

The Aberdeen Angus was a newer breed, arguably producing the best beef, and in 1902 land-agent Robert Burra attended a high-class sale of these, probably with a view to supplementing Alscot's herd.

Most farms kept their own bull. Harvey Smith kept his in The Ham where it would frighten the children. John Leese of Field Barn Cottage remembers, aged three, his father sitting him on a bull. His mother once looked out of the window and exclaimed, 'The bull's out!' John was so panicked he wedged a chair against the door so it couldn't get inside.

Prize Hereford bull at Alscot Park c.1882. From WI collection.

Local butchers visited the farms to choose animals for their shops. In December 1851, William Gibbs, a Stratford pork butcher, had a display of meat of such quality that 'if any of the peculiar race [Jews] came within sight of the forbidden meat, it would certainly shake their fortitude.' This included three delicate and excellent porkers bred by Frederick Silvester of The Cottage.

Delivering the animals to the slaughterhouses in Stratford was a boy's job. In 1868, Robert Fletcher from the Beer House was knocked down by a cow being led to a slaughterhouse in Bridge Street. He suffered a cut hand and a broken thumb, but after medical attention was able to walk the four miles home.

Meat was now routinely inspected for quality. In 1868, a carcass for sale in Stratford Market, owned by butcher George Sims of Alderminster, was examined by the Inspector of Nuisances. It was soft, flabby and greenish. The inspector believed the animal had some sort of disease and seized the carcass.

Sims claimed the cow had come from Frederick Silvester, who was summonsed to the Petty Sessions along with William Gibbins who tended his livestock.

Frederick said he sold the cow to Sims a fortnight earlier, and a boy had fetched her a week later. He'd bought her with a calf in the spring, but she was now barren. He claimed she was perfectly healthy when he sold her. William Gibbins confirmed that he'd been feeding the cow on oil-cake and hay for two months, and there was nothing at all the matter with her – she was healthy as any cow in England.

It was suspected that the carcass for sale was not the same beast, and Sims was sentenced to 21 days' imprisonment.

Pig-keeping was encouraged during the Second World War. Many houses had pigsties; others were kept in yards and gardens. Preston and District Pig Club was formed *c.*1940, and by 1946 had 110 members.

Members would rear a pig and have a supply of meat when the animal was slaughtered, in return for forgoing their meat coupons and giving some meat to the government. An annual membership fee of four shillings included an allocation of meal and insurance should a pig die. Members pooled their expertise in pig-keeping.

Schoolmaster Harry Lord was secretary until his death in 1942, replaced by accountant Bob Stredder. Percy Beavington was the treasurer; the sacks of meal were kept in the outbuildings by the bakery. William Fletcher, the great-grandson of Beer House keeper Robert Fletcher, was the pig-killer or 'pig-sticking man'.

In 1948, Mrs West was the president; former mayor Robert Mansell Smith and Cecil Lees from Mansell Farm were vice presidents; farm worker Eric Dale was secretary; and army veteran Peter Jones was treasurer. Domestic pig-keeping was now declining; this is the club's last recorded year.

Dairy Farming

Most farms kept a few dairy cows. Until the 1940s most herds were fewer than twenty cows, but Preston Pastures, with a long-established dairy herd, had stalling for 38 cows in 1920, and Eric Carte kept 62 cows there in 1943.

Dairy herds traditionally comprised Herefords, where a breed was identifiable. The Dairy Shorthorn became common in the early 20th century, and Friesians were introduced to the area in the 1920s by cattle dealer Frank Francis, who worked for Alan 'Mac' James at Whitchurch Farm. These were good milkers, the Friesian especially so, but only more progressive farmers kept the costly Friesian. Mac James was one. Eric Carte kept both Friesians and Shorthorns.

JC Gamble moved his entire farm from Preston Pastures to Audlem in Cheshire by train in 1950. Twenty wagons were loaded with feeding stuffs and equipment. The cows were milked while the young stock were brought in by lorry, then the cows and dairy utensils were moved. These filled a further six wagons. The train pulled out at eleven and Mr Gamble sped off by car. He reached Cheshire in time to supervise the unloading, and by 3.15pm the herd were grazing in their new fields.

The cows at Park Farm were pastured in the Churchground or Little

Churchground and walked down to the farm twice a day for milking. Chris Daniell (b.1946) remembers going with her grandfather Bill Reason to call them down. The cows at Lower Farm were pastured in The Croft. The road they were walked along is still known as the Cow Lane.

Friesians walking along the Cow Lane from Lower Farm to pasture c.1965.
From WI collection.

The vacuum milking machine, which became commonplace during the Second World War, revolutionised dairy farming. A set of milking clusters fitted onto the cow's teats and sucked the milk into a bucket. This was poured into a milk churn and the machine was moved to the next cow. A good hand milker could manage twelve cows. With a machine this could reach thirty, so herd sizes rapidly increased.

At Park Farm, the cows were milked by hand until the early 1950s. Mary Watts, nee Spencer remembers one old cow would stand in the yard and allow them to milk her into a jug if they were running short in the house.

Hygiene was now of considerable importance. The churns were wheeled to the outside dairy where the milk was filtered and passed through a cooling system before being returned to the churns. John Horseman, who collected the milk for Preston school, enjoyed watching this in progress.

The next innovation was the milking parlour. Harry Smith of Lower Farm had a purpose-built parlour installed in the early 1950s. This was more hygienic, and as the cows stood on a platform, it was much easier for the milker.

Harry's parlour had space for four cows, milked simultaneously. This was far quicker than the bucket-milker system which milked one at a time. A place for a fifth cow was soon added. Harry milked forty cows, which took two hours twice daily; 5-7am and 5-7pm. He did this for fifteen years without a break, and people would always come to see him at milking time as they knew where he would be.

The Dairy Work

Thanks to the expanding railway network, milk could now be transported to urban areas before it soured. Most milk was now sold in liquid form. The churns were left for the milk lorry to collect each day and empty churns were left in their place. The empties made an almighty racket; it was always obvious when the lorry was approaching. Cliff Jones of No.36 drove a milk lorry in the 1960s. When he set off for work at 5am he caused more than a few rude awakenings.

Milk was also sold locally. It was often a children's job to collect it. Dennis Vickers (b.1939) remembers Mrs Spencer ladling it out into billy cans. Nellie Smith, nee Brookes (1896-1966) from Atherstone Hill Farm got home from school then walked back into the village with milk for Robert Burra's baby. Valerie Bliss, nee Jaques, would collect the milk on the way home from school. The children would swing the cans round as they walked. When the milk ended up in the road, Valerie would be sent back for more.

From 1921, $^1/_3$ pint of milk was supplied to schoolchildren to combat malnutrition. Preston School was supplied by Park Farm. In the 1940s, milk monitors were sent to collect it. Fred Dale (b.1942) remembers each child fetching their own bottle and carrying it back very carefully – woe betide anyone who dropped it. Elizabeth Lyne, nee Beavington hated it, especially in winter when it was frozen and it had to be thawed in front of the school fire.

Fetching the milk from Park Farm. Phyllis Wood; Elizabeth Beavington; Jenny Gibbins; Christine Keeley; John Spencer; Kenny Paxford c.1954. From WI collection.

Dairy schools were set up in the late 19th century to teach women about science and hygiene, a far cry from the traditional methods their families had used for centuries. Farms now had purpose-built dairies. They faced north and were on a lower level for coolness. Flagstone floors and a stone setlass – a raised platform for settling milk and cream – were ubiquitous.

Nellie Brookes worked in the Atherstone Hill dairy after leaving school. Carrier Thomas 'Tat' Walton took their butter into Stratford for sale. Henry Ashby's three unmarried daughters, Ellen, Rosa and Lily, were all working in the dairy at Preston Pastures in 1911.

Cows were milked at Atherstone Hill in the 1940s. The cream was left to settle in wide bowls for butter-making, and Valerie Bliss would often get into trouble for leaving finger marks in it. Bigger farms now used mechanical cream separators. These had an elaborate system of gears which quickly spun the cream from the milk. One at Park Farm remained until the 1960s.

Valerie and her sister Barbara often had to churn butter, and argued bitterly about who had done the most turns. A thud in the barrel indicated when the butter had finally 'come'.

Farmhouse dairy work declined after the mid 20th century, as factory-made cheese and butter became commonplace. Cows were milked at Park Farm until 1958; at Lower Farm until 1973. There are no dairy herds in the village today.

The Age of Technology

As surging yields fed the Industrial Revolution, machinery and technology filtered back into agriculture. Steam engines threshed grain; they ploughed heavy, stony ground beyond the capabilities of horses; they chopped straw and turnips, and ground beans and oats for animal feed. Feed engines were found on farms of all sizes by the late 19th century. At Park Farm, an engine to clean and chop mangolds was used until the 1960s.

Threshing, which had comprised most of the workload in winter, now needed a fraction of the manpower, and engines were vandalised by out-of-work labourers. Many believed that machinery would never match good labourers, and Joseph Arch claimed that yields on mechanised farms were far lower than those using man-labour.

Threshing engines were affordable only on the largest farms, but by the 1830s portable engines were touring farms at threshing time. Threshing was now arduous work for eight men. Two pitched the sheaves down from the ricks to the engine. One cut the strings. One fed the sheaves into the machine, taking care he didn't slip down himself. One dealt with the outpouring grain, directing it into sacks, tying and replacing them. One cleared the ever-mounting piles of chaff and straw. Two men built the straw into ricks. It could be dangerous work. George Day, 41, a labourer from No.44, fell from a rick in November 1870. He was badly injured and died five days later in the Union workhouse.

The engine required a copious supply of water so it didn't 'run out of steam'. The first task boys were entrusted with was carrying buckets of water to the engine. Joe Newland remembered it would splash and freeze into his clothes on an especially cold day. Horses could be used to draw water, but were often frightened of the engine.

Harry George from Quinton worked the threshing engine in the 1930s. The day's threshing began at 7am, so Harry had to set out for the farm on his bicycle well before 5am to get steam up.

Harry was a heavy smoker, and Harvey Smith said he didn't want to see him smoking with all the loose straw about.

'Well clear off across the farm, then you won't see.'

The engine itself produced a constant stream of sparks, only obvious when it was working at night.

For centuries, harvest had involved scything the corn and binding it into sheaves which were stood in pairs or 'shocked' to dry. The pairs were known as stooks or shocks (pronounced shook). They were then pitched into wagons and stored in ricks or barns. Twelve men could harvest five acres a day in this way.

The horse-drawn reaper-binder was invented in the 1870s. It cut and bound the corn in one action and left the sheaves at intervals across the field. This allowed four men – a driver, a man on the binder, and two men shocking – to harvest an acre an hour. The implications were tremendous.

Binders worked in a circular motion around the perimeter of the field, reducing it to a progressively smaller area in the centre. The corn was full of rabbits which were pushed into this piece. When the field was almost finished, the villagers gathered with sticks, and when the rabbits were forced to bolt everyone would try to nail a few for the pot. Bob Spencer remembered 107 rabbits were once caught in Radbrook Meadow.

When tractor-drawn binders appeared, less rabbits were caught, as the noise bolted them too early. When myxomatosis devastated the rabbit population in the 1950s, the rabbit-catching tradition came to an abrupt end.

Tractors

The reaper-binders and threshing engines were consigned to the history books in the 20th century as a new development, the internal-combustion engine, found its way into agriculture.

The first tractor appeared in the UK in 1915, when a lack of men and horses and a desperate need to increase productivity necessitated their use. They grew in popularity and by 1939 the number of working farm horses had fallen by half. There were now 55,000 tractors in Britain. By 1945 it was 170,000, as the Second World War pushed farmers forcibly into the mechanised era. The Fordson factory at Dagenham in Essex manufactured over a hundred a day. The orange-painted tractors were an easy target for the Luftwaffe, who would bomb stockpiled machines and strafe those in the fields, so they were painted green for camouflage.

It was the younger generation of farmers who embraced the new technology. Harvey Smith was very fond of Shire horses and for him much of the joy of farming went with their passing. His son Harry (1922-2003) was much the opposite. He was keen on technology and anything which saved time or improved efficiency. He owned a Landrover from the 1960s – a jeep to the village boys – but when his eyesight deteriorated in the 1990s he became a familiar sight pedalling around the village on his bicycle, with his little dog on a string running alongside.

Park Farm owned a tractor from the early 1930s. John Leese remembers the

Spencers getting it stuck in the mud outside its shed, and watching with interest the efforts to get it out.

Alfred Bishop of Rough Farm also had trouble with his new tractor. On his first bout up the field, he reached the top and shouted 'Whoa!' The tractor didn't listen. It bored through the hedge and into the next field. Alfred turned it round, drove back through the hole and carried on down the field.

By the mid 20th century, men were employed solely as tractor drivers. Dennis Maton of No.12 was a tractor driver at Park Farm. He was meticulous about his work and could plough a perfectly straight furrow. Tommy Walton, an enthusiastic and well-liked lad, also worked as a tractor driver at Park Farm until he was killed in a motorbike accident in 1954, aged 23.

David Smith of Lower Farm using the most modern tractor, the Fordson Super Major, and a buck-rake to fill the silage clamp c.1965. From WI collection.

Horses and tractors co-existed for many years. Horses carted fodder to livestock and pulled harvest and hay wagons; tractors did cultivation work where the greatest time could be saved.

Many farmworkers lamented the loss of connection with the land which came with the machinery, and the fact that the working pace was now so much faster. The impersonality of the machines was another issue: a horse could be a friend. Others just stoically accepted it as the way things now were.

The Modern Harvest

The combine harvester, which reaped and threshed grain in a single action, reached the UK in 1936. A hundred were in use in 1940, rising to 3500 by the end of the war. The first models needed a driver and someone to manage the sacks into which the grain flowed. The most labour-intensive process of the farming year was now a two-man job.

When the sacks were full, they were tied and dropped down a slide. A string released a door and the sack dropped onto the stubble. In winter, when the machine was standing idle in the shed, the slide and door doubled as an excellent playground for small boys.

With no cab, air-conditioning or breathing apparatus except a handkerchief over the mouth, it was a horrible, dusty job, as anyone watching the dust billowing from a combine harvester today will know.

The scattered sacks of grain were collected each evening. The sacks – 2 ¼ cwt or 114kg each – were stood on end, tipped over an iron bar and lifted by two men onto the trailer. A third man would stack them.

It was a boy's job to drive the tractor and trailer, and they began as soon as they were heavy enough to press on the clutch. Will Spencer remembers, aged six, he wasn't looking where he was going and ran into one of the sacks. The front of the tractor started to lift into the air. Luckily he managed to stand on the clutch and was rescued before any further mishap.

The 'bagger' combine soon became outmoded. Corn yields were rising, thanks to advances in agronomy. While two tonnes of wheat per acre was considered excellent in the 1970s, four tonnes is common today. So the 'tanker' combine was developed. This stored the grain in a tank which was emptied into a trailer, a great improvement on the 'bagger'. Harry Smith and Alfred Bishop clubbed together to buy their first tanker combine.

The combine-harvester left the threshed straw in rows in the field, and a new operation had to be added to the farming calendar: straw-baling. The straw was collected by a mechanical baler and packed into tight bales of around 20kgs each. Up to 20,000 bales were made each year on a large farm. Two men would throw the bales onto the waiting trailer, first by hand then using a pitchfork as the courses got higher, and a man on top would stack them. In the 1970s, the Perry Loader became available to load the trailers. The bales now had to be stacked, two wide and three deep, in the field, then picked up by the machine.

The Spencers, as a matter of stubborn pride, continued to pitch them by hand. Their employees didn't share their enthusiasm. When Eric Dale saw the loader standing idle in the field and the three Spencers all pitching by hand, he scathingly said, 'It's like having a dog, and barking yourself.'

Harry Smith next door, with no qualms about pride, did use a Perry Loader. It became a matter of honour to see who could clear a field the fastest.

Bales were stored in stacks of up to twenty courses in rickyards or Dutch barns. An elevator – once horse-driven, now engine-driven – ferried them up. Fred Dale once got the tines of his pitchfork stuck in the elevator. The fork tottered up towards the top of the stack.

'Hey, get my pitchfork!' he shouted to Mike Spencer on top. The fork reached the top of the elevator, swung round, then succumbed to gravity. Mike had a good clout across the head.

The farm workers would always go to the pub after the day's work. Those that weren't old enough would have to sit in the truck – with a ginger beer and packet of crisps if they were lucky – and wait.

Seven: Employment Outside Agriculture

The Soldiers

During the Middle Ages, manors were often held on military tenure; the holder had to provide a specified number of men, horses and weapons if required by their overlord. The first recorded freeholders in Preston – John Wylcotes and Thomas Franklin in 1419 – both held their land on tenure of military service.

All able-bodied men were liable for military service. This amateur army, originally called the *fyrd*, was started by Alfred the Great in the 9th century. All men had to keep and practice with a longbow on Sundays and holidays. A manor court in 1596 recorded that wealthy freeholder John Maunsell alias Alexander was exempt from this.

Muster Rolls were compiled of all able-bodied men aged between sixteen and sixty in each county. A general muster, or formal inspection, was held every three years. Each man had to bring arms according to his means, ranging from a longbow and helmet to horses and full armour. The eligible men in Preston in 1608 included husbandmen John Timbrell and Giles Smith, whose families became wealthy yeomen for several generations, and labourer Thomas Garfield, probably the ancestor of the renowned carpenter family.

The permanent British army has its roots in Parliament's New Model Army of the Civil War period, and became officially established in the 1660s. Officers and lower ranks were denoted according to social class.

As the British Empire expanded, several young men from Preston joined up in search of excitement and opportunity. They served as far afield as North America, South Africa and India. In 1914, many volunteered for Kitchener's new army. Two years later, conscription took many more. Not all would come home. Four names were inscribed on Preston's war memorial.

William Paxton, 34, a carpenter with a wife and young son, volunteered in March 1915. He was posted to the Royal Engineers in France shortly before his daughter was born. On 1st July 1916, two artillery shells fell among William's company. He was one of fifteen fatalities. He was buried in Bienvillers Military Cemetery.

Thomas Kingston, 35, was the son of former coachman Henry Kingston of Alscot Lodge. He was married with two daughters and was working as a gardener when he volunteered in 1915. He was posted to the Machine Gun Corps in Greece. He was wounded towards the end of the war and died on 28th November 1918, a fortnight after the armistice was signed. He was buried in the Mikra British Cemetery in Kalamaria.

Francis William (Will) Porter was the son of Aubrey and Margaret Porter of No.8. He had emigrated to Canada in 1912 and was married with a young son. In March 1916, Will volunteered for the Canadian Overseas Expeditionary Force and served in France. On 11th October 1918, he was killed in an attack on enemy lines. He was buried in the Niagara Cemetery in France. He was posthumously awarded the Military Medal.

Richard John Green from Peckham moved to Preston in 1915 to become the farm pupil of Thomas Salmon Smith at Park Farm. He was called up in April 1916, just after his eighteenth birthday, and posted to the Royal Sussex Regiment. On 2nd November 1918, he was killed by an exploding shell. He was buried in the Harlebecke New Military Cemetery in Belgium.

In 1939, new battlefields opened up across the globe. Three more names were added to Preston's war memorial.

Major William Reginald James (Reggie) Alston-Roberts-West had served in the Grenadier Guards before inheriting Alscot Estate. He rejoined his unit at the outbreak of war and arrived in France three weeks later. He was killed in a counter-attack on German lines near Flanders in May 1940 and is commemorated in the Dunkirk Memorial Cemetery.

Private Reginald Henry (Reg) Maton, the son of Ernest and Emily Maton, was enlisted into the Royal Berkshire Regiment and served in Burma. He was killed in action on 4th January 1945, aged 24. He was buried in the Taukkyan War Cemetery in Myanmar.

Lieutenant Colonel Wilfred George Newey, whose family had lived at Whitehill Farm, was a territorial soldier in the Royal Artillery. He was evacuated from Dunkirk and served in the Middle East. On 1st February 1945, he was on board an aircraft carrying personnel involved in the Yalta conference which crashed into the sea. Wilfred one of many fatalities. He was 37 years old. He was buried in the Imtarfa Military Cemetery in Malta.

The Carpenters

Carpenters and sawyers were the second-most common trade in Preston until the 20th century. They were indispensable for constructing carts, wheels, tools, furniture, and until the 18th century, timber-framed buildings. Robert Moore was recorded as a carpenter on the 1608 Muster Roll. He was in his forties or fifties, and may have helped build the oldest surviving houses such as The Old Manor and Locke's Farm.

The next recorded carpenters are the Salmon and Garfield families. The Garfields had lived in Preston since at least the 1600s. Thomas Garfield, an aged labourer 'of the merest stature' was recorded in 1608. John Garfield (b.1681) was a carpenter, as was his father, also called John. John senior paid 6d tax in 1695 (see Chapter 3), indicating he was a fairly well-off tradesman.

The hey-day of timber-framed houses was now over, but moulded beams, decorative woodwork and oak panelling provided much work. In 1708 John Garfield – whether the father or the son is unclear – submitted designs for an elaborate concave ceiling to no less a client than the Earl of Coventry.

John senior died in 1709, and a year later his son married. He had at least five children, the eldest, John, born in 1711. By 1721 the family were renting a house with an orchard and garden on the site of No.20. The kink in the boundary between No.20 and the village hall follows the edge of this house, as a comparison of the 1760 and 2015 maps shows.

The house was a three-roomed building typical of 17th century timber-framed houses: a hall, kitchen and workshop with a room above each. One of John's forebears had probably built it. In common with most villagers, John kept a couple of cows and a pig on the common, and more unusually, a mare, which indicates he was a man of some means.

In 1729, John fell ill. He quickly wrote his will and was buried six days later. He was 48 years old. He bequeathed all his possessions, including his tools, lumber, animals and books, to his son John, now married and working in the family trade, and £100 to John's young son.

John junior was to be the last of his line. His only son and his wife Elinor died three months apart in 1750. John himself died in 1779, and the last record of the family in the village is his burial: *John Garfield, an ingenious mechanic, aged nearly 70.*

William and Richard Salmon, carpenters and probably brothers, moved to Preston in the 1680s and raised families. Both paid 6d tax in 1695, indicating they were respectable tradesmen. When Richard died in 1704, his possessions were valued at £47 including lumber and planks, three cows, a pig, some poultry, corn and books.

William's sons William and Thomas followed into the family trade, as did Thomas' son Thomas. William proved a shrewd businessman. He leased a small piece of farmland and married wealthy farmer's daughter Katherine Smith, a move which proved fortuitous. William inherited a good deal of his father-in-law's property and went on to purchase more. Several of his sons went on to glowing agricultural futures.

Carpenter William Dodd moved to Preston from Atherstone on Stour in the 1830s. He moved into part of The Dell in the 1850s. His three sons also worked as carpenters. Thomas left Preston in the 1850s. William married labourer's daughter Mary Horseman in 1842. She died from consumption a year later, just after her 20th birthday, and William also left Preston. John married and remained in Preston for his life.

William senior died in 1861. His widow Rebecca remained at The Dell until her death in 1868 then John moved into The Dell. In later years he employed three men. He died in 1891.

William Paxton, a sawyer's son, began working as a carpenter in the 1850s. In 1861 he was living next door to John Dodd – he may have been apprenticed to the family. He later moved into No.18 where he remained for the rest of his life. His only son William also became a carpenter and was killed in France in 1916.

The Blacksmiths

For two thousand years, from the Iron Age to the Industrial Revolution, the blacksmith had an unchallenged and vital status. As well as shoeing farm, coach and stable horses, the blacksmith would make and repair all manner of ironwork: gates, railings, plough shares, iron tyres, farm tools and more. Nails, a deceptively difficult task, were the first job of an apprentice blacksmith. Only when he had mastered this would he be allowed more complex work.

The first recorded blacksmith in Preston was Thomas Yeats, who married around 1540 and died in 1583. He didn't work at the present forge: the house dates to the late 16th century and the forge itself to the 17th century, although they could be rebuilds of earlier buildings.

Thomas had eleven children. Frances married well-off farmer Henry Smith, and Elizabeth married Thomas Timbrell. Thomas bequeathed Frances' children £3 and three sheep; Elizabeth two stacks of bees and two swarms; his son Jerome's children three sheep; and the remainder of his goods to Jerome himself.

John Robbins was the next recorded blacksmith, working for at least twenty years in the mid 17th century. He would certainly have used the current forge. His house was owned by Thomas Yeats, the grandson of the earlier smith. This strengthens the case that the current forge replaced an earlier one. The property was inherited by Thomas Yeats' eldest son Thomas, and then to his brother John. Its subsequent ownership is unclear.

John Robbins' son John was born in 1635. He wasn't a tax-payer in 1695 although he was still living in Preston, which suggests he wasn't a smith at this time. The Robbins family, all now labourers, remained in Preston until the 1850s.

In June 1782, the church register recorded the burial of: *John Elvins senior, blacksmith of ye village.* John was 68 and had two sons, John and William. William didn't long survive his father; John was also a blacksmith.

John owned The Dell, now divided into two and leased to labouring families. The forge and house were now owned by the West family, from whom John held a lease. He was still working in 1798, and died in 1814 aged 80. He had one son, Thomas, who inherited The Dell. Thomas lived in Stratford and seems not to have been a smith.

Thomas Gardiner, a blacksmith from Alveston, married Alice Hornsby from Preston in 1813 and took over the forge. The couple had four children. Thomas died in March 1820, aged 31, and a year later his young widow married another blacksmith, Henry Bryan. They had a further seven children. Henry remained at The Forge until his death in 1869, then his son James, now 36 and with a family of his own, took over.

James moved to Mickleton during the 1870s and a new blacksmith, Amos Winter from Loxley, took over. Amos had recently married Preston girl Sarah Allibone. By 1891 their eldest son Thomas James (Jimmy) was working in the forge, and when Amos died in 1910, Jimmy took over. Jimmy married late and had no children. He remained at the forge until his death in 1937.

William (Bill) Gilks from Quinton was now the only blacksmith in the area. He cycled to the forges in Preston, Wimpstone and Crimscote every week. As well as shoeing horses – fourteen carthorses in a day on one occasion – Bill made plough shares and all other ironware. George West of Alscot Park remembers taking his pony to Bill to be shod, as does Mary Watts from Park Farm. Dennis

Vickers enjoyed watching him at work, and liked the burning smell as the red-hot shoe was applied to the hoof.

The death knell had sounded for the village blacksmith. Factory-made goods and motor vehicles decimated their workload, although in many places they adapted to a new role – the car mechanic. This wasn't to happen in Preston, and in 1948 Bill retired and the forge closed for good.

The Millers

Milling has been an central aspect of life for millennia. Wheat was milled for flour; oilseed rape for lamp oil; oats and barley for animal feed; cutlings – coarsely ground oats or barley – for pig feed. This was probably the function of Cutlin Mill, an ancient mill whose house survived until recently in Atherstone on Stour.

To control water supply to the mill, a second branch to the river, known as the 'back brook', was often dug. A weir on the back brook – in Preston that furthest from the village – channelled water into the 'front brook' and took away any excess. A mill race ran either side of a second weir on the front brook. The drop in elevation gave a fast flow-rate to turn the mill-wheel.

The land between the two streams is called The Ham. 'Ham' is an old name for a riverside meadow, deriving from the Old English *hamm*. It often applies to a meadow by a mill. The field is shaped like a joint of ham, but this is coincidence. The upper part was once the mill orchard.

The road into Preston once crossed the Stour near the mill at the bottom of The Ham, first via a ford and then a bridge. When the current road and bridge were built in the 1760s, the back brook was lengthened and The Ham extended. The piece above the bridge is called Blackcurrant Island for unknown reasons.

The first record of a mill in Preston is in 1327: John Miller, a *molendinarius* [miller] paid 6d tax. This is an interesting example of surname evolution. John, the miller, had become John Miller.

In 1496 there were two watermills in Preston, leased to William Humphrey and John Salbrugge of Alverscotte [Alscot]. 'Mill' refers to a set of millstones; more than one mill could be under the same roof.

In 1662, two water corn mills were leased for £50/annum to William Lowe, who also leased The Ham. The mills were next leased by William Farr, who moved to Preston with his wife and two children *c.*1686. He was appointed churchwarden a year later and had four more children. In 1695 a third mill was included in the agreement. The annual rent was now £30 – almost half what William Lowe had paid. Perhaps the mill was falling into disrepair.

William Farr died in 1702. His sons William and Thomas remained in the village and raised families. By 1721 the three mills were managed by Thomas. He paid £47 rent for the house and mills in 1735, with 7s 6d for the water. This is the last record of the family in Preston.

In 1746, two mills were recorded in Preston, the miller's name unknown. This is the last record of their existence. When James West built a new weir at Atherstone to turn the river into a picturesque water-feature, there was no longer enough flow to keep the millwheel turning. The millers went out of business. No mill is marked on the 1760 map and none has stood in Preston since.

The Weavers

Wool was almost exclusively exported to Europe during the Medieval period, but by the 15th century weaving had become a British cottage industry. Cloth was woven from yarn (spun wool) or linen (spun from flax or hemp.) Revd Harvey Bloom wrote in 1896 that Preston once had a large weaving shed near the river.

Widow Hannah Alcock (d.1693) had spinning wheels for both wool and linen. Jane Kite, wife of cordwainer William Kite, also spun wool and linen, as probably did most local women until the Industrial Revolution. Jane had a good stock of 'fleece wool', 18lbs of shapen yarn and 14lbs of spun hemp on William's death in 1729.

Hemp preparation was known as 'retting'. The plants were soaked in the river for several days to break down the fibrous stems. The rotting plant material was smelly, polluted the water and choked the streams, and the issue was often presented to the manor courts. In October 1594, every householder except John Maunsell alias Alexander was prosecuted for washing hemp in the Stour. It didn't deter anyone. They had no other option.

Dye was manufactured from the woad plant. A field in Atherstone on Stour next to the Preston boundary was known as Wad Leasow in the 18th century. 'Wad' is a corruption of 'woad'. The field is called The Lezzer today.

William Hartwell is the first recorded weaver in Preston. He owned his own cottage with a shop [workshop] in 1721. He was in late middle-age and had lived in Preston for at least thirty years. He paid 4d tax in 1695, indicating he was a less well-off tradesman.

In September 1721, his only daughter Mary died aged 31. Four weeks later, his wife, also called Mary, died as well. William then divided his house into two. On his death in 1736 he bequeathed one half to John Smith, a Stratford schoolmaster, and the other half to young labourer Thomas Gasey and his wife Anne, 'for taking care of me during my sickness.'

The next recorded weaver is William Pardoe or Pardy. William was born in 1733 and died in 1771. The burial register stated he was a weaver of middle age. John Pardoe, probably William's son, married in the 1780s and raised a family. He worked as a weaver until at least 1800. A George Pardoe, who lived in Preston at a similar time, was also a weaver.

By 1813 John Pardoe, now in his fifties, was working as a labourer. John's wares probably couldn't compete with the cheap textiles flooding from the towns. His two sons had died in childhood and when he died in 1853, aged 90, the family name died with him.

Over a century later, Betty Dale, daughter of farm worker Robert Dale, began work at Clifford Mill, now a weaving business run by master weaver Tibor Reich. The Mill was chosen by the Wool Board to weave a furnishing fabric for Princess Elizabeth (the present Queen) on her marriage in 1947. The fabric was designed by Tibor, and 23-year-old Betty wove most of the fabric herself. It was delivered personally to Buckingham Palace.

The Cordwainers

A cordwainer made shoes, distinct from a cobbler who repaired them. The term comes from a high quality leather called cordwain.

The first recorded cordwainer in Preston was William Kite (also spelt Kyte or Keyte) who rented one of John Souch's cottages in 1721. This was fairly basic: a single dwelling room, a workshop and a room over each, but it had its own close, yard and garden. William had several children, the eldest born in 1714. He took an apprentice, 13-year-old Charles Stanley from Mickleton, in 1721.

William was fairly well-off. He kept three cows, seventeen sheep and a pig – a considerable number for a commoner – and also owned a mare and colt. He even built an additional room to his dwelling.

He died in 1729. His youngest child was three years old. His possessions were valued at a respectable £252, including his animals, an allotment of hay in the common field, bags of wheat and oats, shoes, leather, implements of his trade and 'little things of the mercery trade'.

He was a general shopkeeper as well as a cordwainer. He owned £25-worth of 'sugar plumbs', a fashionable and expensive plum-shaped sweet. He also had two barrels of tobacco, two barrels of pitch and a good quantity of cheese, no doubt homemade. He probably brewed beer for sale – he had a good stock of hops and three barrels for drink in his shop.

William's wife Jane died two years after him and the family name disappeared from the village. The fate of their children is unclear.

William's apprentice Charles Stanley remained in Preston. In 1731, his wife Jane gave birth to twins, Elizabeth and John. They had two more children, Charles and Ann. In May 1770, the church register recorded the burial of: *Charles Stanley senior of Preston, shoemaker.*

John married and raised a family in the village. Charles junior married Elizabeth Townsend from Beecham Farm. Their first son William was born in 1772. Both men worked as shoemakers.

William also went on to become a shoemaker of good repute. In 1813 he was respected enough to earn the epithet 'Mr', rare for a tradesman at the time. His subsequent fate is unclear, but no Stanleys were living in Preston by 1841.

William Salmon from Quinton, of no known connection to the Preston family with the same name, married Martha Pardoe, daughter of weaver John Pardoe, in 1823. William worked intermittently as a cordwainer but mainly as a farm labourer. By this point the Industrial Revolution had moved many crafts to the factories.

Cordwainer John Hone from Brailes moved to Preston in the 1840s. His eldest son James was working in the trade by age twelve. John died in 1865 and James left Preston in 1887 after a brief spell as a baker.

The Tailors

The first recorded tailor is Nicholas Shepherd in 1608. The next is Thomas Bromley, who rented one of John Souch's cottages in 1721. Thomas was married with one daughter, Mary. In 1717 he took an apprentice, Robert Edkins, a husbandman's son from Welford on Avon. Robert was 22, unusually old to start an apprenticeship. He seems not to have remained in Preston for long.

When Thomas died in 1735, he was renting a bigger dwelling owned by Thomas Smith of The Old Manor, its whereabouts unknown. This comprised a workshop, kitchen, parlour and buttery [pantry] with three upstairs chambers. His household possessions were valued at £6 4s.

He was very particular about their fate. In his will he gave his wife his bed with its blankets; a cupboard; a table; the least looking glass; three chairs; the three least pewter dishes; six spoons; the biggest kettle; a fire shovel and tongs; a pair of bellows; two pairs of new hemp sheets; two little tablecloths and two towels. Everything else went to his daughter Mary.

The next tailor on record is William Stanley, son of shoemaker John Stanley. William was a pauper, and at least five of his ten children died in childhood. The church register hints why. When he married Ann Malins in 1780, he was recorded as 'William Stanley, *gibbosus*': a hunchback. Severe disability had destroyed his prospects. He was still working as a tailor in 1813, and died in 1826 aged 71.

Tailor Giles Tidmarsh moved to Preston around 1820, and lived at No.28 from at least 1841. His son Charles followed into the trade, but when Giles died in 1864, Charles moved to Stratford.

John Gardiner, son of blacksmith Thomas Gardiner, was working as a tailor by 1841. He lived at The Forge until his marriage in the 1860s when he moved to The Dell. When he left the village a decade later, the craft disappeared from the village.

The Wheelwrights

The wheelwright's trade flourished in Preston throughout the 19th century. These craftsmen made, tyred and repaired wheels along with every other component of carts, wagons and carriages for farm and domestic use. The newly-improved turnpike road provided much passing trade.

The George family were wheelwrights for three generations. William George, a labourer from Whitchurch, moved to Preston after his marriage in 1828. He worked as a labourer until *c*.1840, when he began to work as a carpenter. By this point he was living in Silvester's Row.

By 1861 he was working as a wheelwright, a natural progression from carpentry. Their yard was adjacent to Silvester's Row in the present cemetery. His sons Richard and Frederick worked with him. Richard's speciality was the interiors of stagecoaches. Frederick put his carpentry skills to another line of work; he was also the village undertaker.

Frederick married dressmaker Clara Bromwich in 1865 and they moved into another of Silvester's Row where their five children were born. They became tenants of Robert Mansell at The Dell *c*.1872 and their yard was moved there.

Clara died in 1900 and Frederick remarried in 1908. His bride was Flora

Smith, a servant 31 years his junior. He remained at The Dell until his death in 1922, aged 80.

His son, also called Frederick, worked as a wheelwright from the 1890s then moved to Wimpstone and became a carpenter.

The Beer House Keeper

There is no record of any public house in Preston, but in the 19th century there was a Beer House. This was a building licensed to sell beer and cider which could not be consumed on the premises.

Robert Fletcher was the Beer House Keeper for the entirety of its history. He was born in Preston in 1806 and was a carpenter by trade. He lived in one of several now-demolished cottages which stood below the village green, then purchased the largest of the three cottages once belonging to the Souch family. The Beer House was a sideline for his carpentry work.

Robert brewed his wares himself. Farm labourer Daniel Hopkins (1861-1955) told Dorothy Unett that Robert would brew his beer in an old dough kiver – a wooden trough for proving bread dough – in his outhouse. His chickens were accustomed to roost on it, and the lid was always thick with their droppings.

Nevertheless, the Beer House proved popular. Robert had a steady trade at social events and people gathered outside his house in the evenings. In 1872 he applied for a licence to sell alcohol for consumption on the premises, but this was refused.

In 1881, Robert, now 75, was working solely as a carpenter. The Beer House was no more. Robert died in 1889 and the premises, comprising a sitting room, kitchen, brewhouse, two bedrooms, two sheds and a carpenter's shop, was sold by his son William. It was now dilapidated and needed considerable outlay. The sale value was £60. Robert's personal effects were valued at £64, including his machinery, stock in trade. a donkey, a pig, crops of wheat, beans and potatoes, and a portable engine worth £25.

The Beer House was soon demolished and replaced with the present No.44.

The Roadmen

William Hewins, a former farm labourer who lived in part of Locke's Farm, began working as a road labourer in the 1840s. He maintained the unpaved parish roads and filled potholes and ruts. He probably began the long job of laying stones.

In 1877 he put in a bid to the Highways Board for the work, quoting £52 for the village roads and £22 for the turnpike. His bid was accepted – perhaps because Preston farmer Giles Smith was on the Board – and this was sufficient for him to call himself on the 1881 census, now aged 71, a 'road contractor'.

Richard 'Jack' Robinson, a former carter now living at No.16, was the roadman until his retirement in the 1930s. Fred Hartwell, (1893-1971) a market gardener from Binton, moved to Preston in the 1920s and worked as a carter. He moved into No.4 and became the roadman c.1934.

The roads were now tarmaced and Fred went around the village with his spade, broom and wheelbarrow keeping everything tidy. He trimmed the verges, made sure the rain ran into the ditches and also scythed the village greens.

Fred Hartwell outside Locke's Farm c.1950. From WI collection.

The Post Office

As well as delivering parcels and letters, the Post Office was the provider of telegrams and the telephone. Few households had their own telephone until the mid 20th century. People would ring the Post Office and the postmistress would deliver the message to the appropriate house.

The Post Office also provided newspapers. Whitchurch schoolboy Ray Francis delivered the papers to his village on his way home from school in the

1930s – excepting Saturdays and school holidays when people could have the luxury of reading the paper with their breakfast.

Preston Post Office opened *c.*1894 in No.10. Sarah Davis, a recently widowed labourer's wife, became its first postmistress. Sarah died in 1898 and farm labourer Giles Horseman moved into No.10 and became sub postmaster. His wife Sarah, the sister of baker Richard Beavington, aided him.

Letters arrived from Stratford sorting office twice daily – at 7.20am and 3.45pm – and were delivered by Giles to the appropriate addresses in Preston, Whitchurch, Alderminster and the outlying farms, a round of 15 miles each day. Letters were dispatched from Preston at 12.30pm and 5.55pm, with a limited Sunday service.

Giles returned to farmwork during the First World War and his teenage daughter Lucy took over the work. One morning in February 1916, as the weather was particularly bad, Giles did the round for her. He didn't return. Come mid-afternoon, Lucy and her brother William went to look for him.

Thomas Hutchings from Churchill Farm in Alderminster said Giles had visited the farm by mid morning, and went to help search. Giles was found face-down in a ditch near the farm. He had been dead for several hours.

A post-mortem found his heart was enlarged and fatty. He'd complained of dizziness on occasions, and it was concluded that a heart condition made him faint as he was crossing the ditch. He fell face-down and drowned in three inches of water.

Sarah and Lucy took over the post duties. Lucy delivered the mail on her bicycle to the outlying villages and farms, come rain, snow or shine, until 1938. The expanding network of Post Offices reduced her workload considerably. Sarah would always have a cup of tea and piece of cake ready for the postman when he brought the mailbags, and she knitted something for every baby born in the village. She was sadly missed when she died in 1945, aged 87.

John Horseman, a distant cousin, remembers that RES (Bob) Wyatt, Captain of the English cricket team from 1930-37, lived at The Forge in Whitchurch. The Post Office often received telegrams for him. Lucy would write it out, put it in a sealed envelope and get John to rush it over on his bicycle.

Lucy dealt with the mail until the 1950s when she broke her hip. John, who lived at No.8, dealt with the post while she recovered. The post van arrived at 6.30am. John sorted it on Lucy's table then toured the village with the mailbags before going to his regular job. He continued this for five years.

Lucy, now over sixty, gave up the Post Office in 1958 and moved to No.30. She was presented with a television set by the village.

Muriel Carvell, the wife of plumber Stan Carvell, took over and she and her family moved into No.10. They left Preston in 1964 and the Post Office moved to No.28, where it was run by Jeanne James, wife of brewery worker Peter James. Jeanne also kept a small shop on the premises. The postbox was set into a pillar at the bottom of the steps.

In February 1970 it moved to No.44 where it was run by Jenny Wilkins, nee Gibbins. Molly Ashby from The Old Vicarage kept geese and Maran hens, and many former customers remember being chased by these unfriendly fowl. Jenny ran the shop and Post Office until September 1973. It moved to the former school in 1974, and remains there today.

Sarah Horseman; Lucy Horseman outside No.10. From WI collection.

The Carriers

The carrier was a link between rural villages and the wider community, transporting goods to market, fetching shopping and taking people on outings. The carrier's cart was a respectable if lumbering mode of transport with reasonable prices.

Farm labourer Thomas 'Tat' Walton (1852-1936) was Preston's first carrier. He was born in No.40, where his parents and grandparents had spent most of their lives, and he lived there himself after his parents' deaths.

He acquired a brougham, (pronounced 'broom') a four-wheeled carriage for up to six passengers, and started a carrier's business in the 1890s when the tramway began to decline in popularity. He had an innate understanding of horses – he'd been working with them since he was seven – and his venture was successful. He kept his three horses tethered on the village green. The best two were commandeered during the First World War, a severe blow.

Thomas collected butter and eggs from the local farms to deliver to Stratford market, and took shopping lists from the villagers. He collected goods such as shoes on 'appro' (approval) and if suitable he took the money the following week. His wife Hannah was just as confident with the horses and took ladies on outings. When Thomas' eyesight began to fail, his son John, now in his fifties and still living with his parents, drove the vehicle.

In the 1930s, the new bus service sapped his business. Nobody now wanted to ride on a lumbering cart, and John went to Stratford only twice a week to collect vegetables. Thomas died in 1936, and when John died in 1943, the carrier's business came to an end.

Thomas and Hannah Walton outside the bakery. From WI collection.

The Bakers

The first recorded bakers in Preston are in 1813; William Heritage and Thomas Adams. Whether one or both lived in No.50, to which a purpose-built bakehouse was added around this time, is unclear.

Daniel Salmon, the grandson of farmer and carpenter William Salmon of The Old Manor, worked as a baker from the 1830s (see family tree in Chapter 6). His daughter Elizabeth married Preston labourer William Davis in 1836. Four years later William began working as a baker. He and his family lived in No.50, along with Elizabeth's brother Henry Salmon, a baker and biscuit-maker. By 1851 the family were well-off enough to employ a resident servant.

William died in 1860 and Elizabeth continued to run the bakery with Henry and her son Daniel, a baker and flour-dealer in his early twenties. It seems Daniel wasn't a good businessman. In July 1863 he was declared bankrupt. The family left the bakery and it was taken over by Ann Hone, a widow in her forties.

Ann ran the bakery and a grocer's shop aided by her son James, who also worked as a cordwainer. In April 1873, James was in Stratford with George Harris, a baker who presumably worked for the family. James left Harris with their horses and carriage, and when he returned he found Harris drunk. Harris then attacked him.

James reported Harris for both offences – being drunk in charge of a carriage and horses was contrary to the Licensing Act of 1872 – and a hearing was held a fortnight later. Harris was fined 10s plus costs for the drunkenness, and another 5s plus costs for assault. It's unclear who Harris was, but it seems he didn't stay long in Preston.

Ann retired in 1876 and moved to No.51. James ran the bakery alone, with sidelines as a grocer, cordwainer, pig-dealer and fruit-dealer. He continued to be beset with problems.

In May 1885, his teenage employee William Samman of No.3 was fined 2s 6d with 9s 6d costs for selling bread without the correct weights and scales. Loaves had to be specific weights and bakers had to carry scales on their rounds. They were heavily fined if their loaves were underweight.

In July 1887, James himself was fined 1s with 13s 6d costs for allowing his horse to stray. This proved the final straw. Two weeks later he was declared bankrupt. He had debts of £1127 and assets of £96. The bankruptcy hearing disclosed his woeful business skills.

James had entered the pig-dealing business with no knowledge of the trade, and had sent a large number of pigs to a London dealer. He received commission nowhere near the cost of rearing them. His fruit-dealing was similarly disastrous.

He'd allowed a carter named Butler, who earned 14s/week, to run up a debt of £14, one of many bad debts. He'd borrowed £100 from his mother and £100 from Clifford miller Richard Smith, the latter unpaid for eleven years.

All James' effects – three orchards of fruit, the contents of his shop, his furniture, a quarter-acre of potatoes, five porker pigs, eight bacon pigs, a sow with eight piglets, several pig troughs, a chaff machine, fifty fowl, twenty ducks, a three-year filly, a nearly new cart and harness and the all-important weighing machines – were sold at auction.

His young employee, A.R. Timms, probably the son of William Timms of No.17, a 'respectable young man of good character' was advertising for a position as a baker and confectioner in Birmingham a month later. James moved to Balsall Heath where he returned to the shoemaking trade. The bakery was taken by Richard Beavington, a farmer's son from Ebrington.

Richard married Elizabeth Paxton of No.18 and proved much more successful. The bakery was iconic of Preston for nearly a century.

Richard Beavington; Dick Beavington at work in 1956. Courtesy of Elizabeth Lyne.

Richard spent his working life in the bakery. Former farm labourer George Burrows worked as his assistant from 1891-1911, and Richard's sons Ernest Richard (Dick) (1893-1991) and Percy William (1899-1984) followed into the business. The bakery had a loyal following, not only in Preston but also Clifford Chambers, Atherstone, Whitchurch and Admington. A pony and trap was used for deliveries until 1924 when a van was bought.

Richard was churchwarden for 25 years but was forced to give up in 1918 because of the stress of war work, not to mention both his sons serving abroad. He suffered a stroke in 1919 and didn't work again. He died in 1941.

Dick often stopped on his rounds to chat with district nurse Margaret Hayward, who nursed Richard during his illness. The couple were eventually married and their daughter Elizabeth was born in 1945.

It was a long working day for the bakers. The fire was lit at 6.30am and the accounts and bills were completed at 10pm. Sacks of flour were kept above the bakery and tipped through an outlet in the floor into the mixer. The dough was mixed and left to rise while the bakers stopped for breakfast.

The risen dough was weighed and moulded for the tins. If not done properly, the loaf would be full of holes from the air bubbles. Elizabeth Lyne, Dick's daughter, remembers the brothers could mould two pieces at a time, one with each hand. George West of Alscot Park (b.1937) loved watching the bakers at work, and being allowed to 'help' knead the dough in the troughs. Temperature was crucial, and the bakers often had to remind people to shut the door when they dropped in for a chat.

The oven temperature was gauged with a handful of flour. It would turn brown when thrown in. The time it took told the bakers precisely when the oven was ready.

The loaves were loaded into the oven with a wooden peel, carefully done so no space was wasted. At midday it was ready, and the aroma permeated the entire village. Oven gloves, made from old flour sacks, were used to remove the hot tins – Elizabeth usually made these. The oven was cleaned using a flour sack tied to a broom handle – it was important that customers didn't find ash and soot adhering to their loaves.

Simple dough cakes, a throwback to food rationing, were made in the still-hot oven, with people bringing their own lard or dripping to add to the mixture. Their slabs of lardy cake were unforgettable. Mary Watts, nee Spencer, and Vera Watson, nee Noyce, who both left Preston in 1946, still remember them seventy years on.

Demand for hot cross buns at Easter meant the bakers were up most of the night preparing the dough. It was thought lucky to save a bun each year, and a number of them were collected in the flour room. They remained until the bakery closed.

Charlie Horseman of No.8 collecting his goose from the bakery, Christmas morning c.1960. From WI collection.

Christmas was another busy time, as the oven was used to cook the villagers' turkeys, geese and cockerels.

The family ran a shop from the premises, managed by Richard's wife Elizabeth, then their daughter Millie, then Dick's wife Margaret. The shop sold all manner of groceries – children would invariably spend their pocket money on sweets – and was the hub of local news. People had to wait until the first customers had finished their gossip.

In 1970 Percy and Dick, now in their seventies, retired and the bakery closed for good. Bread was delivered from a bakery in Stratford but, as former customers lamented, it never tasted as good.

The Gamekeepers

Alscot Park needed several gamekeepers. They nurtured game; killed foxes, crows and stoats; arranged shooting parties and shot game for their master's table. Breeding pheasants was the most important job. There had to be a sporting number of birds for a succession of winter shoots; if not, bad news for their future prospects.

The young chicks were vulnerable to stoats, foxes and birds of prey, who soon learnt where an easy meal was found. Vera Watson remembers her grandfather William Noyce patrolling the pheasant pens in the 1930s, with his gun to the sky, waiting for intruding hawks.

They had to vigilant for poachers: the temptation to snare a pheasant or rabbit for a meagre pot was great. The gamekeepers stretched strands of wire between the trees to catch unwary poachers, and man-traps were still in use.

Poaching was punished harshly. Landowners and gamekeepers could seize anyone poaching on their land. In the early 19th century, a convicted poacher would be transported for up to fourteen years. In 1857 this was commuted to a prison sentence. George Whiting, a Preston labourer who had recently moved to Stratford, was charged with killing a rabbit on James Roberts-West's land in February 1870 and fined £2 plus costs. A labourer's wage was around 12s/week.

John Leese (b.1931) remembers his father fixing a raisin onto a fish hook, which would catch in the pheasant's throat when it tried to swallow it. One day the gamekeeper called in at their cottage while one of the snared birds was cooking.

'That smells lovely, Mrs Leese! What is it?'

'A neck of lamb,' she quickly replied.

Henry Hibberd of Top Lodge c.1900. Henry with his eldest son Victor c.1893. Courtesy of Elizabeth Lyne.

The gamekeeper wasn't asked to stay for dinner.

Two new gamekeepers came to Preston from a rural district near Salisbury in the 1880s. Henry Hibberd and William Noyce were both young married men who would raise families in the village. Henry moved into Top Lodge and William into The Kennels. The 1891 census records Henry with his wife Selina and their children, Victor, 4, Reginald, 2, and Gertrude, 6 months.

Tragedy was soon to strike. Just three weeks later, Gertrude contracted measles. She then developed acute bronchitis. She died a few days later.

Two years later, a further tragedy. Victor, now a month short of his sixth birthday and showing a keen interest in gamekeeper's work, went out to inspect a trap which he and his father had set in the Park the previous evening. He didn't return. A search was mounted and baker Richard Beavington found his body in a pond in Alscot Park, now silted up. He had slipped and drowned.

Victor was buried with his sister in Preston graveyard. The epitaph on their gravestone reads: *Suffer ye little children, come unto me.*

IN AFFECTIONATE REMEMBRANCE OF DEAR LITTLE VICTOR HIBBERD.

In looking at the graves in Preston,
Two little ones my eyes did rest on;
On them were flowers, so rich and grand,
Just placed there by a loving mother's hand.
A boy lay there whom I had known in life,
God has taken from a world of sin and strife.
He in His love knows what is best,
So He kindly took him with Himself to rest.
I was a stranger to him, and yet I saw
That in his little mind there lay a store
Of knowledge which you seldom find,
In most things he was forward, in nothing far behind.
He was a bonny boy (at least, so I thought),
As he ran away to see what had been caught.
Once a large stoat was in the trap,
His merry laugh ran out, his hands did clap;
Then off he bounded, with Jim at his side,
His father watched him with a manly pride.
Who knows the hopes that in that father's heart
Lie buried, about that boy so soon to depart.
From him and the mother who loved him so well,
In a way so distressing the grief they can tell
It caused them, when ah! so sad to relate,
They found him in that pit in such a state.
All things were done, all means were tried,
Their hearts were nigh to break, and so they cried
In agony of soul, for soon they felt and saw
That darling boy was gone, and they should never more
Behold him, skipping over field and park;
That light was out, all seemed so dark.
But He who came the broken heart to heal,
Can pour in His love and make them feel
That in His wisdom, He has gathered home
The little lamb He would not leave to roam,
Among thorns and briars of this world so rough.
A little while He lent him, then said "It is enough,
Come to the Shepherd's arms, and in His bosom lie,
No longer stay below; come up with Me on high."
But Jim, the dog, is still alive and well.
How fond I am of him I cannot tell.
I link that boy and dog together in my mind,
And how to separate them a reason cannot find.
So these few lines with you I leave,
Forgive, if anything is here to grieve.   **W.H.H.**

William Noyce, who spent most of his married life at The Kennels, was of genial disposition, a staunch churchman, and his abilities as a gamekeeper were highly esteemed by his employers. He was popular and took a keen interest in all that went on in the village.

His son Frank also became a gamekeeper. He married Myra Emms, a shepherd's daughter, in 1902 and they moved into Top Lodge. Like his father, Frank was conscientious, respected and liked by all.

One evening in October 1913, William and Frank saw a man setting snares near Sheep Leys Cover by Clifford Chambers. William instructed Frank and his nephew William Shergold, also a gamekeeper, to try and catch him when he returned for his haul.

As dawn neared, the two men heard a rabbit squealing. It was caught in a snare. Almost immediately a man came up, took the rabbit and snapped its neck. They challenged him. He dropped the rabbit and ran.

Frank and Shergold chased after him. He cut across a field then clambered over a fence. They caught up with him and hauled him back by his coat. He fought hard, slipped out of his coat and punched Frank in the stomach. He was tall and powerfully built, but the gamekeepers managed to overpower him.

They started to walk back to The Kennels, but their prisoner became violent. He pulled a knife from his pocket. 'I'll rip your guts out if you don't let me go!'

They disarmed him, then he said he had a whistle in his pocket.

'If I blow it, I'll have four or five others here to help me,' he threatened.

Frank and Shergold glanced at each other and hurried their prisoner on. They reached The Kennels without further incident.

The man gave his name as Joe Smith from Stratford. William didn't believe him. He was loaded into a trap and taken to Campden police station. Superintendent Jones searched the man and found a two-bladed knife, some ferret lines and a policeman's whistle. The man now gave his name as George Smith from Northamptonshire.

Jones ascertained that the prisoner was one of a gang of gipsies encamped near Sheep Leys Cover. Over sixty snares were found in the Cover; fifteen had rabbits in them. Smith was charged with poaching and assault and sentenced to one month's imprisonment with hard labour.

The case was reported in the *Cheltenham Chronicle* with the headline *The Gipsy and the Rabbits: Gamekeepers' Exciting Time,* which reflects a fascination with all things criminal that doesn't seem to have changed.

William Noyce retired in 1931 aged 74, after 44 years as head-keeper. He died a few months later. Frank's son Bill married school teacher Ada Cale and moved into Top Lodge where he continued the family trade.

Frank had always suffered from poor health – he'd been rejected from the army in 1916 for medical reasons. In 1934 a mature tree on the village green blew down and blocked the road. He helped cut it up. A few days later, his daughter Ivy cycled home from church to find him collapsed at the foot of the stairs. He'd suffered a stroke. He died a few days later.

Bill continued as gamekeeper until another tragedy. Major Reggie West, the lord of the manor and a keen sportsman, was killed in action in France in 1940. The shooting tradition came to an abrupt end. Bill moved to Alderminster and found work in a corn mill in Stratford.

Gamekeepers were reinstated when Reggie's son James succeeded to the estate, and traditional pheasant shoots are still an integral part of the calendar today.

The Bailiffs and Land Agents

A bailiff was employed by James Roberts-West by the 1840s. The bailiff managed and improved the estate's farmland and dealt with rent collection, tenancies, building work and maintenance matters. They typically lived at Rough Farm.

By the 1890s the job was split into two: the land agent and the farm manager. The former dealt with estate matters; the latter agricultural matters. James Stokes from Huntingdon was the first land agent or estate agent. He lived at The Cottage and was involved with the eviction of at least two tenants in the 1890s.

In October 1892, labourer William Timms of No.17 was summonsed to the magistrates in Stratford. He was owing £3 8d rent. James Stokes and his clerk were witnesses. Timms was told to pay up, along with the witnesses' expenses of nearly £2.

The same month, carpenter William Fletcher of No.12 was summonsed by Stokes. Fletcher was owing one shilling rent for a pigsty, which he was ordered to pay along with expenses of 18s 6d.

If Stokes was rather unpopular, his replacement Robert Burra, who came to Preston c.1898 and also lived at The Cottage, seems to have been much the opposite. Robert organised and took part in village concerts and performances of the Alscot Estate Amateur Dramatics Society, which he informally set up. He also sat on the tribunal which considered service exemptions during the First World War. He inherited the Burra family estate in Sedbergh in Yorkshire, and the family left Preston in late 1918.

Employment at Alscot Park

Domestic Service

In 1871, around 4% of the national population, mostly women, were in service, working as housemaids, cooks, nursemaids and many other roles for wealthier families. This was the best prospect available for girls from poorer families, and charitable initiatives were set up to prepare girls for service.

Most farming families in Preston employed two or three servants, and the better-off tradesmen often had at least one. The youngest girl in service in 1841 was twelve-year-old Emma White, a general servant working for farmer John Mansell. Hannah Knight from Alderminster (b.1856) later the wife of carrier Thomas Walton, recalled to the *Herald* in 1936 that she went into service aged nine, and earned £1 (£43 today) for a year's work.

'I was a little drudge,' she said. 'But in those days, we girls were glad to go.'
Thomas added, 'There wasn't much grub to be had.'

The daily routine for a maid typically began at 6am and finished around 11pm. She would light the fires and empty the chamberpots, then begin laundry, cleaning, fetching water, beating carpets, polishing woodwork and any other task demanded of her. Those employed on farms would also make butter and cheese. Typically a maid would have a half-day on Sundays and a day off once a month.

These women often worked until their marriage, when they took on the full-time duties of a wife, and shortly afterwards, a mother. They were sought after by suitors; they could keep a house to a high standard.

Other women and men chose to spend their lives with the nation's wealthiest households. During the 19th century it became fashionable to employ as many servants as affordable. Newspaper advertisements show that good appearance was universally required of a high-class servant. Height, health and skills such as needlework were of lesser importance.

James Roberts-West, who lived at Alscot Park with his wife and daughter, had sixteen live-in staff in 1881, as well as many others who lived on the grounds or in the village. Few were born locally. A good servant could find employment in a large household anywhere in Britain. Those less career-orientated remained in their locality.

Those 'below stairs' had as strict a hierarchy as the gentry they served. The census return lists them in order of status. The butler and housekeeper were the most vaunted positions for men and women respectively.

Name	Age	Relation	Occupation	Place of Birth
James Roberts-West	69	Head	Landed Proprietor	Preston on Stour
Elizabeth West	58	Wife	-	Brinklow, Leic.
Elizabeth Ann West	33	Daughter	-	Preston on Stour
George Dicken	30	Servant	Butler	Earlsland, Herefords.
John Bowden	36	Servant	Gardener	Stokeinteignhead, Devon
William Woodhouse	38	Servant	Coachman	Richards Castle, Shrops.
Lewis Humphries	25	Servant	Under Butler	Kentisbeare, Devon
Alfred Garton	22	Servant	Footman	Lymm, Cheshire
Joseph Woodward	22	Servant	Under Coachman	Ilmington, Warks.
Daniel Creed	22	Servant	Stable Helper	Sculthorpe, Norfolk
Mary Stonehouse	27	Servant	Housekeeper	Tettenhall, Staffords.
Emily Beauchamp	31	Servant	Cook	Whiteparish, Wilts.
Helen Davis	30	Servant	Lady's Maid	Ombersley, Worc.
Betsy Facer	30	Servant	Housemaid	Coldashby, Northants.
Alice Wither	18	Servant	Housemaid	Alvechurch, Worc.
Elizabeth Rimell	28	Servant	Dairy Maid	Mickleton, Glouc.
Emma Evans	25	Servant	Kitchen Maid	Llangennith, Radnor
Charlotte Metcalf	43	Servant	Laundry Maid	Lincoln
Mary Ann Brain	18	Servant	Laundry Maid	Maidenhill, Warks.

The housekeeper was responsible for the general smooth running of the household. She held the keys, dealt with the accounts, paid the tradesmen's bills, supervised the maids and arranged food and linen.

The butler supervised the other male servants, hired and fired staff, served wine and attended the family in the dining room and drawing room. He dealt with important matters and paperwork beneath the attention of his master.

The footmen cleaned the silver, set the table, opened doors and assisted the butler. As they were often seen in public, they had to be good-looking, and most importantly, the same height. An unmatched pair would be insufferable.

The lady's maid attended all the needs of her mistress: dressing her, taking care of her clothes and hairdressing. As she was often seen in public with her mistress, it was important she was of tidy appearance and appropriately pretty.

The dairy maids processed milk into cream, butter and cheese, and often milked the cows.

The housemaids saw to all tasks necessary for smooth maintenance of the house – cleaning, dusting, laying fires, airing bed linen, arranging flowers – as directed by the housekeeper.

The kitchen maids helped the cook: peeling and scrubbing vegetables, basting meat and other less skilled tasks.

The laundry maids washed, dried, aired, ironed and folded the vast quantities of linen.

The scullery maid spent her working life cleaning dishes and pans, a full-time task in a large household with an inclination to banqueting.

The nursemaid cared for the mistress's young children and made sure they were out of sight and earshot of the adults.

The Coachman

The coachman was a lucrative position. He supervised the stables, oversaw the grooms and stable-boys, and drove the coach. He was superseded in the early 20th century by the chauffeur. John Reason of No.32 was a coachman from 1830 until the 1860s. William Woodhouse was coachman from c1874.

In November 1885, William suffered a tragic accident. He delivered a carriage to the coach-builders' yard in Stratford then began to ride back to Alscot Park. He met a coach belonging to surgeon Reginald Greene on the Shipston Road, and its lamps panicked his mount. The horse lunged, tripped and fell on him. Despite immediate attention from Greene, William died soon afterwards.

He wasn't local – the census states he was born in Shropshire – and nobody knew anything of his family, so he was buried in Preston, the first plot in the new cemetery. His gravestone bears the stark message; *In the midst of life, we are in death.*

The last recorded coachman was Henry Kingston of Alscot Lodge in 1901. By 1911 he was employed as a lodge-keeper.

The Chauffeur

Motor cars were kept at Alscot Park by the late 19th century, and by 1911 the coach and horses was consigned to the past. Two young chauffeurs, Ernest Viridge and George Dyde, lived at Alscot – a handsome car needed a handsome driver – and 18-year-old George Rough was employed wholly as a motor car cleaner. Appearance, of course, was everything.

Farm labourer William Job, later spelt Jobe, a quiet, unassuming and well-liked man, maintained agricultural machinery for Alscot Estate. His mechanical experience gained him a position as chauffeur *c.*1912, and he moved to a cottage on the grounds. He was enlisted as a driver during the First World War and returned to Alscot on his demobilisation.

In January 1933, he collected Miss Penelope Portman and her maid Dorothy Groom from Leamington Station in Captain West's Standard car. He collided with another car by Oxtalls Farm on the Warwick Road.

It was described as the most shocking crash in the district for many years. William was killed instantly and both passengers and the second driver suffered severe injuries. William was a careful driver and neither car was going at excessive speed, and it was concluded the sun had dazzled one driver. William left a widow and four children, the youngest seven years old. His widow Sarah moved to No.20 where she worked as the school caretaker.

Percy Armitt, who lived in Silvester's Row and then No.14, was a chauffeur in the 1950s. He was always well-dressed and well-spoken, and was on call day and night.

The Gardener

The head gardener was provided with a cottage at Alscot, and many other gardeners and garden labourers lived in the villages. Digging and maintaining the borders and beds, growing vegetables, mowing grass, tending hothouse plants and pruning trees provided work for over a dozen men. The lawns were mown with a horse-drawn mower, the horse wearing special overshoes so its hooves didn't mark the turf.

The gardens provided many a life-long career. James Knackston was head gardener for around thirty years until his death in 1879. In 1921, Samuel Garrett from No.37 had been working in the gardens for 46 years. Bernard Charles (Charlie) Horseman, (1903-1974) the youngest of Albert and Ellen Horseman's thirteen children, started work as a gardener in 1918 aged 14, and continued for over fifty years.

Jack Bloxham (1879-1952) moved from Atherstone to Preston with his wife Lucy and their children in the 1920s. He worked most of his life in the gardens and in 1933 he gained the position of head gardener. He moved to the gardener's cottage where he remained until his death.

Eric Reason (1915-2009) worked in the gardens after the Second World War and was awarded the Royal Horticultural Society's Long Service Medal. Fred Dale also worked in the gardens after leaving farm work.

The Dawn of the 20th Century

The first signs of a new era were creeping into Preston. In 1851, 75% of male villagers worked in agriculture. In 1911 it was 50%, and would fall rapidly over the coming decades. Only five lads under eighteen were in full-time employment, the youngest being 14-year-old Thomas Rimell who, like his father, worked on a farm.

Compulsory education meant children started full-time work later and could aspire to better employment terms than their forebears. The aftermath of the First World War triggered more social change. Farm labourer Giles Horseman became Sub Postmaster in 1898. Fred Dyde, a farm labourer in his thirties who was very good with figures, became an insurance agent in the 1900s.

Fred pedalled around the local farms on his bicycle, and met Emily Wright, a servant at Radbrook Farm. She soon became his wife, and he later took his young daughter Marjorie with him on the crossbar. The insurance deals were closed with a good helping of rough cider, and Emily would say it was his bicycle which brought him home at night.

People were looking further afield for employment. Many went to Birmingham; others as far as London and Sussex. Some were in service. Many found employment on the railways. Several were police officers. Aubrey John and Francis William Porter of No.8 sought their future in Canada.

In 1911, Kate Pitt, 26, and her younger sister Rebecca, daughters of farm labourer Thomas Pitt of No.14, were lodging in Edgbaston. Kate was a dressmaker and Rebecca a pinafore maker. Their brother Fred was a butler in London.

William Silvester, son of failed farmer Frederick Silvester of The Cottage, was working as a contractor in Bexhill, Sussex. George Dyde, son of labourer Jesse Dyde, was a police constable in Bristol. Betsy Smith, an labourer's daughter, was a cook for a wealthy widow in London. Edith Jobe, the sister of chauffeur William Jobe, was a housemaid in Berkshire.

This had a major influence on village structure. In 1861, 60% households comprised young couples or families. In 1911, this had fallen to 35%. People were also living to a greater age and could do so independently. Gentrification of villages, often thought a modern phenomenon, began over a century ago.

Those who stayed in Preston dreamed of glittering futures. Adverts for employment began to appear in the newspapers of nearby cities. In 1887, a young woman with initials 'T.N.' from No.12 advertised for a situation as a coffee-room waitress in the *Birmingham Daily Post*. Miss Fletcher, maybe the daughter of shepherd Frederick Fletcher, advertised for a situation as a domestic companion and help in Lichfield and Northamptonshire newspapers in 1925.

Walter Goodall, a 25-year-old gardener from No.15, advertised for a position as under-gardener in a big house in the *Leamington Courier* in 1909. He had seven years' experience and was well recommended, but he was still living in his father's household two years later. He eventually found a position in Kenilworth.

Some of those who gained employment found the streets weren't paved with gold after all. William Ernest Timms, the son of labourer William Timms of No.17, left Preston in his teens in the 1880s. He gained a position as a porter for a large draper's shop in Birmingham. Albert Ashby, the son of Henry Ashby of Preston Pastures, was apprenticed in the same shop. Both lads were living in the shop with several other apprentices and servants. Employees often slept beneath the shop counters; their wages didn't cover lodgings elsewhere.

At some point in the 1890s, William returned to the village of Alveston near Stratford. He worked as a bricklayer's labourer and raised a family. Albert, however, remained in Birmingham where he started his own draper's business.

Emily and Gertrude Horseman were two of the thirteen children of farm labourer Albert Horseman and his wife Ellen. Emily, aged twenty, was working as a housemaid in London in 1911. Gertrude, aged seventeen, was a servant for Preston schoolmaster George Clarke. She soon joined her sister and began working as a servant in Notting Hill.

In October 1915, Gertrude got married. Her husband was Russell Herd, 24, a Staff Sergeant in the Army Service Corps. The honeymoon was presumably quite short and Russell returned to his duties.

Two months later, Emily also married. Her husband was Ernest Maton, a sailor in the Royal Navy. The time he spent with his bride before returning to his ship was also presumably quite brief. Emily returned to Preston, but met her husband at least once over the ensuing four years. She had a daughter, Irene, born in August 1917.

Both men returned home safely and both couples eventually settled in Preston where they raised families.

Eight: Culture and Community

A strong sense of community and friendship epitomised village life. Nobody's door was locked and people would pop into each other's houses for tea and a chat. Fred Dale remembers that people would gather on the allotments on Sunday mornings, have a good chat and a few ciders while they dug the vegetables for dinner.

'Where've you been for the vegetables?' their wives would later ask.

The loss of this friendship is something many people lament. Everyone now lives behind closed doors, with TVs and computers for entertainment. They travel outside the village for a night out, and the sense of knowing everybody is gone.

Neighbours were prepared to do a good turn for one another, although some went to more effort than others. When Mary Smith's ponies escaped from their field, Monty Preston from next door got them back, helped by George Beauchamp. Mary gave them some home-made wine in thanks: both men were enthusiastic drinkers.

A week later, Monty met up with George. 'Let's let them ponies out again. Then we can catch them, and then we'll get some more of that wine!'

'No, we can't do that!'

'OK, we'll just say they were out, and we've already got them back in.'

So that was what they did.

Social events were held in the schoolroom in the 19th century. A dance was held until 2am in January 1900, a surprisingly modern touch. It concluded with the National Anthem.

An annual concert was also held. Land agent Robert Burra was a keen performer, and he also arranged amateur dramatics performances. These were hugely popular, not least because Mrs West played her gramophone during the intervals.

Fetes, held between hay and harvest, were an integral part of summer. An event in July 1923, comprising the usual stalls, refreshments, teas and sports, raised over £170 for the church restoration fund.

In 1958 it was suggested that the refreshments, which had been attracting poor sales, be passed into the hands of Preston's teenage girls. Freda Schofield, the Alscot Estate secretary, was appointed supervisor.

Despite the scathing and still-familiar opinion that youth had no inclination to give up time for others, Freda was overwhelmed by the enthusiasm of the girls, which included Pauline Reason, 15, and Elizabeth Beavington, 13. They made sandwiches, cakes and tarts, produced posters, and raked in a seven-fold increase in profit.

Gymkhanas were a regular attraction at Alscot Park. A gymkhana and pony show in September 1932 raised funds for Stratford Hospital. Alwyn Spencer of Park Farm oversaw the event, which included obstacle courses and mounted musical chairs. George Gibbins and Ernest Ashfield ran a 'guess the weight of a pig' competition and a coconut shy. Dick Beavington, Bill Reason and Fred Hartwell ran the bowling, the prize a pig. Eric Reason, Charlie Horseman and Bill Paxford ran the ladies' bowling. Their prize was a mere chicken.

A branch of the Mothers' Union was set up in the 1920s. Meetings were later held at Doreen Stredder's house, with an annual garden party at Whitchurch rectory. A Boy's Club and a branch of the Girls' Friendly Society were founded at a similar time. A youth club was held at Whitchurch rectory in the 1940s, and fireman Ted Coomber started one in Preston in the 1950s.

The Women's Institute started in August 1940 and ran until 2002. Elsie Spencer was appointed its first president and the inaugural meeting, with over thirty women, was held in the garden of Park Farm.

The Working Men's Club followed in the 1950s and met weekly in the Village Hall, playing table-tennis and drinking strictly soft drinks. Ray Beauchamp was a favourite target for the table-tennis balls, until he got annoyed and stamped on the ball.

The over-sixties club met on Monday afternoons. The group was run by Mary Preston, of rather different character to her husband Monty. Mary organised various bus trips for the group and also for the WI.

In the 1950s a fish and chip van visited every Thursday night, driven by a big man named Tiny who drove the grocer's van during the day. Tiny always had a good queue of customers, but John Horseman and Patrick Hall from Sweet Knowle had a trick up their sleeve. Patrick kept a pet white mouse in his pocket. He would join the queue then take out the mouse. This was especially effective if there were girls in the queue.

The WI's 40th birthday party at Alscot Park, 1980.
Val Maris; Connie Reason; Frankie Spencer; Lil Walton; ? Joan James; Isolde West [cutting the cake;] Doreen Dee; Marjorie Bishop; Queenie Coomber; Mrs Hunt; Mary James; ? Elsie Harding; Chris Daniell; Doreen Stredder. From WI collection.

The Village Hall

After the Second World War it was decided that a village hall was needed. The villagers acquired the wooden buildings of the now-defunct searchlight station at Alderminster and began to fashion them into the building they wanted. It was built through voluntary efforts with funds raised from from dances, whist drives, firewood-cutting and an hair-dressing service – 'a bob a bob'.

Enthusiasm for the project was at first commendable but gradually the volunteers drifted away. Only Francis 'Keggy' Gardner, a carpenter who lived at Field Barn Cottage, remained. He worked alone for several months until the work was finally finished.

Building the Coronation Hall c.1952. Farm worker Arthur Wurviell; Bob Spencer of Park Farm; third man unknown. Right: Keggy Gardner. From WI collection.

The opening ceremony coincided with the coronation celebrations of 1953 and the hall was named the Coronation Hall. It was the hub of Preston's social life, hosting bingo, whist drives, dances and parties, until it was demolished in 1998, replaced a year later by a brick building, again largely funded by village efforts, named the Millennium Hall.

The Parish Church of St Mary the Virgin

The first known reference to a church in Preston is in 1272. The advowson – the right to appoint a priest or incumbent to the parish – was bought and sold along with the manor, and the holder of that privilege could appoint whoever he pleased to the post.

The Church Structure

The church follows the simple layout of an east-facing chancel, a nave and a tower. The oldest parts – the tower and part of the nave – date to the 15th century. James West rebuilt the chancel and part of the nave in the 1750s, adopting a version of the Gothic style he'd favoured with Alscot Park. The church is noted as one of the earliest of the Gothic revival.

West commissioned mason Edward Woodward, who'd worked on Alscot Park. The chancel work began in 1753: the walls were rebuilt with ashlar (dressed stone); three elaborate windows were added; and a parapet with pinnacles was added to the roof.

The windows were intended to showcase James West's extensive collection of stained glass. The east window contains pieces of exceptional quality, much dating to the 16th and 17th centuries. The portraits of abbots in the north and south windows were taken from Evesham Abbey after the Dissolution, and eventually purchased by James West. The remaining portraits were commissioned to complement them.

The East Window. The inscription reads: James West took the trouble to create [this]. 1754.

In 1756 the north wall of the nave was rebuilt and two windows added to either side. The main entrance was moved to its current position in the tower, and a tower window was inserted. Edward Woodward's estimate for this came to £136 including:

	£	s	d
Taking down the north wall; digging the foundations; scaffolding	4	10	0
Ashlars	3	10	10
Thirty loads carriage of ashlars: 10s each	15	0	0
Two windows in the side wall as the great chancel window	22	0	0
Two hundred and a half of iron bars in ye two windows	4	13	4
Two windows for the south front	22	0	0
One stone dome case window at the west end of tower	2	0	0
230 strikes [460 bushels] of lime at 6d each	5	15	0
50 feet top coping stone: 12d per foot	2	10	0
20 loads carriage of sand from Alscot and digging	1	2	6
Propping up roof and finding props	2	15	0
Plastering inside the north wall, 122 yards at 6d a yard	3	1	0

Preston church. Frank Packer collection.

The churchyard was originally surrounded by wooden palings. Their maintenance was the responsibility of the various farmers, who each had a specific number of rails to look after.

There were two gates: one in the current position by the main doors, and one opposite on the south side, next to 'ye Widow Smith's house', by the present phone box. The latter was moved to its present position when the palings were replaced by a brick wall.

The church has remained essentially untouched since the 18th century, apart from a doorway added in the chancel in the early 20th century for the sole use of the West family, who sat in the choir stalls.

The Bells

Preston church has three bells, each with its own inscription:

Prosperity to this place. A.R. [Anna Regina, the Queen] 1713

Cum iuncundissima voce prosequor [I proceed with a most pleasing voice] *Henry Bagley 1635.*

Henry Baglee made mee 1633.

Bell-ringing has attracted a long succession of loyal followers. In the late 19th century, the bell-ringers, along with the village choir, were entertained to supper every Boxing Day in the servants' hall of Alscot Park. This was one of many events arranged by the West family, each diligently reported in the *Stratford Herald*. The party had a liberal supply of old English fare, comprising roast and boiled beef, roast mutton, plum pudding and mince pies. Like many other events, the supper was abandoned following the First World War.

Denis Maton from No.12, Tony Ashfield from No.9 and Tom Walton from No.38 were the regular ringers in the 1940s. A church meeting decided that Bob Stredder, a skilled bell-ringer who had recently moved to the village, would teach more young men to ring the bells. In 1949 John Horseman, Derrick Ashfield and George Nason – a regular ringer for nearly fifty years – began to 'learn the ropes'. John was only thirteen and had to stand on a box to reach.

It was a gruelling job. There were three Sunday services – 8am, 11am and 6.30pm – as well as weddings, christenings and funerals. Derrick was never good at getting up in the mornings, and John had to bang on his door to make sure he was ready.

They would sometimes ring at Ilmington or Alderminster church, which both had six bells. Bob Stredder's sons James and Robert would complete the team. They would then go to The Bell at Alderminster for a drink. Bob would sneak the teenage John through the back door and get him a bottle of Poacher beer. The flavour has stayed with him ever since.

The Sexton

Stephen Hall, a labourer who lived Silvester's Row, was appointed sexton in 1901. He did maintenance work around the church, chiefly digging graves and lighting the church lamps, for which he was paid £4 a year. He also tidied the churchyard and cleared the adjacent ditch. He retained the job until the 1920s. Now nearing seventy, it seems he didn't put too much care into his work. In 1925 Phoebe Smith of Park Farm complained to the Church Council about the untidy state of the churchyard. Stephen retired soon afterwards.

George Nason, who moved to Preston in 1945, took on the job for many years. His cottage, No.40, became known as the Sexton's Cottage.

Yew Trees

The yew trees flanking the church path are characteristic of many churchyards and probably date to the 18th century. More unusually, a pair of yew trees flank the entrance to many houses in Preston.

The yew, evergreen and with a potential lifespan of over a thousand years, has an ancient association with eternal life. The symbolism long pre-dates Christian times: yews were planted along roads and on burial mounds in the Celtic era.

The yew was believed to protect against attack by fairies, witches and such like, and was planted outside houses in more superstitious times. Many of the yews in the village can only date from the mid 19th century when the new cottages were built, and their builder, James Roberts-West, was probably not the superstitious type, so their purpose remains a mystery.

The Baptist Chapel

A Baptist chapel was built in Preston in 1885 on land owned by the Mansell family. It was funded by Ann Smith, nee Mansell, the wife of wealthy Stratford draper John Charles (J.C.) Smith. John, Ann and her brother Robert were all staunch Baptists.

The Baptist mission in Preston had been started *c.*1867 by Revd Morley of Payton Street Chapel in Stratford. Ann Mansell heard him preach and was impressed. Anxious about the spiritual life in the villages, she invited him to Preston. Morley preached under a tree on the green; held subsequent meetings; and a weekly service was soon conducted.

Services were held in the house of wheelwright Frederick George of Silvester's Row. When the property was sold to James Roberts-West in 1872, Frederick had to move out, but Robert Mansell allowed him to live in The Dell and the services continued. With up to eighty people at each meeting, it was very trying for both preacher and attendees, so an application for a chapel was made.

The chapel had accommodation for 150 worshippers. Even so, its first service on Good Friday 1885 was densely crowded. Three hundred people from many local villages attended tea in Robert Mansell's barn. An anniversary service was held for several years. That of 1890 was the largest ever attendance at the chapel, and the traditional tea had to be held in two sittings.

Henry and Hannah Ashby of Preston Pastures were a mainstay of the chapel, and their granddaughter Joan Spencer, nee Ashby (1914-2007) recalled being loaded into a pony and trap with her seven siblings to be taken to services each week.

When Henry's son Robert died of appendicitis in 1892, his funeral was held at the chapel, although the burial took place in the parish churchyard. The funeral of Frederick George's wife Clara was also held there in 1900, as was Robert Mansell's in 1905. Frederick's funeral in 1922 is the last one recorded.

The Baptist mission began under this tree c.1867. Frank Packer collection.

The popularity of the non-conformists – referring to any Protestant faith other than the Church of England – is revealing. Robert and Ann Mansell and Frederick George had all been baptised into the Church of England and converted later in life. J.C. Smith had converted in his youth while learning the draper's trade in London. The Ashbys were historically Quakers.

The Baptist movement, started in the 17th century, became very popular during the 19th century. It was an early advocate of spiritual equality and tolerance. The clergy and congregation of the Church of England, in contrast, were very hierarchical. Each family had its own pew: the nearer the front, the higher their status. The poorer families sat on makeshift benches or stood at the back, and had to take communion separately. Labourer Joseph Arch of Barford wrote bitterly about the hierarchical attitude of the Church towards the lower classes. This may have contributed to the growing popularity of non-conformist churches.

Few Preston families seem to have been overtly Baptist in the early days. Their landlord, employer and benefactor was Church of England, and so it was rather dangerous to break the mould. It is probably significant that Frederick George became a tenant of the Mansell family.

Much rivalry existed between church-goers and 'chapelites', even to the extent that church-goers didn't use 'chapel' tradesmen. This declined following the First World War. People no longer had time for church or chapel, and the vicar and his family, once an integral part of village life, became confined to an ill-attended Sunday service.

Ethel Davies, nee Newland, attended chapel during the 1950s. It was still well-supported, but was becoming very pentecostal which cost many attendees. The chapel was eventually closed and was converted into a private residence in 1979.

Sunday School

Sunday Schools first appeared in the 1760s to educate child factory workers on their day off. When compulsory education was enforced, Sunday Schools adopted their better-known format: providing moral education and the basics of scripture. Most children attended by the late 19th century.

By the 1890s there were two Sunday Schools in Preston: one attached to the church, and one to the chapel. There was some rivalry between the two.

Rewards were offered for attendance and both provided an annual treat for their pupils. The details were carefully reported in the *Stratford Herald*. In March 1897, the church Sunday School were provided with tea in the schoolroom, including bread and jam and bread and butter, rare treats for the poorer children. They played games and each child was given a packet of sweets, some crackers and an orange, all generously provided by Mrs West whom the children gave a hearty vote of thanks for her kindness.

In 1914 the 'right royal time' courtesy of Mr and Mrs West's generosity included the traditional tea and games, and each child had three lucky dips in a bran tub filled with toys. All went home laden with toys, sweets and oranges. The event was attended by children of all classes, although the better-bred children were strictly segregated.

Author Ursula Bloom, daughter of Wimpstone vicar Harvey Bloom, attended these events. She later wrote that at the close of proceedings, each child would file past Mrs West. The schoolmaster would announce the name of the child. Girls would curtsey; boys tug their forelocks. Mrs West gave the child 6d and a piece of cake and the next child would approach, the first moving on to curtsey to the vicar's wife and then the vicar's daughters, who would all gently approve of their actions.

In January 1901, the Baptist Sunday School were provided 'good things for enjoyment' courtesy of Ann Smith. Prizes were awarded and the children greatly enjoyed themselves. The children, no matter their breeding, were treated equally.

Joe Newland (1901-1993) recalled that Sunday School outings were the only ones they had. The carrier's carts would take them to Meon Hill or Beecham. If they were lucky they went as far as Bidford on Avon, ten miles away.

A single Sunday School was held following the First World War. By the 1930s, its superintendent was Ann Smith's daughter Kate, who lived at The Dell. Miss Smith was very good with the children, Vera Watson, nee Noyce (b1925) remembers, although she ran the Sunday School with a rod of iron. She allowed the children to play tennis on her court and arranged folk-dancing and other activities. The annual outing was now more adventurous: they would go to Weston-super-Mare or the Malvern Hills.

In 1933, Kate arranged for 67 pupils, teachers and parents to travel by bus to Stratford. They had tea and met Kate's brother, former mayor Robert Mansell Smith. Mrs West attended and took tea, perhaps to consolidate the new unity between church and chapel. The vicar, Revd Montagu Hunt, also accompanied the party. The group went on a steamer and Robert Mansell Smith took several out on his punt. Sports were held on the recreation ground, followed by a treasure hunt and ice creams. The outing was an experience the children would long remember.

Miss Mary Fortescue of The Cottage ran the Sunday School in the 1940s, followed by nurseryman Ernie Carter who lived on the Ilmington Road. It was now held in the chapel at 3pm every Sunday, and involved hymns and Bible stories.

The children would play outside the chapel until Mr Carter arrived in his Austin 8. John Horseman (b.1936) remembers Mr Carter was a quiet teacher who would allow the children to march about the chapel as they sang the hymn *Onward Christian Soldiers.* John only saw him lose his temper once. He was playing the fool and Mr Carter, who was holding a heavy, bound Bible, marched down the aisle and clouted him across the face with it. John was terrified his parents would find out – they'd have been furious he was naughty – but luckily they never did.

Sunday School pupils outside the chapel c.1950.
Front row: Jenny Telfer; Dorothy Telfer; Ann Harding; Roger Coomber; Kenny Paxford.
Middle Row: Gracie Beauchamp; Christine Reason; Pauline Reason; Christine Keeley;
Jenny Gibbins. Back: John Telfer

Millie Beavington from the bakery and Ann Clifford from The Old Thatch then took over, followed by Doreen Stredder in the 1960s. Mrs Stredder was much stricter than her predecessors and stood no messing about. She also ran the annual nativity play with a rod of iron.

The Sunday School was now held in the church at 11am. It involved the usual hymns and Bible stories, and talks on topical subjects. Most of the local children attended. They were given a stamp depicting a religious scene for each session, which they collected in an album.

Regular parties were arranged by Vera Perry at Preston Pastures, and the children went on a trip to the newly consecrated Coventry Cathedral in 1962, followed by an afternoon at Dudley Zoo. Mrs Stredder always gave Easter eggs to her pupils.

The Sunday School came to an end in the 1980s.

Sunday School pupils waiting to collect their Easter Eggs from Doreen Stredder c.1965. From WI collection.

A Year of Festivities

The Wake Feast

A wake was originally an all-night vigil preceding a holy day, which developed into a time of mere revelry. Preston Wake was held from Saturday to Monday after the first Sunday in May. The date may be linked to the consecration of the church. By the mid 19th century, the Wake was a relatively minor celebration on the Monday.

Elizabeth Beavington, nee Paxton (1862-1953) told Dorothy Unett that the Wake was held on the green with stalls, bowling and wrestling contests.

Dancing and merriment, fuelled by Robert Fletcher's Beer House, would follow. The festivities were carefully monitored: in 1872 it was made an offence to be drunk in a public place. In 1875, Sergeant Thomas Basson and PC Sollis, both based in Long Marston, were on duty in Preston.

Fifty people were dancing and drinking in the highway in front of the Beer House, liberally supplied with drink. Giles Samman, a sawyer from No.3, went to Robert's door. Both officers heard him ask Robert's son to fill him a pint of porter [stout]. Giles paid for it in coppers, then drank it on the highway close to Robert's door.

Robert was licensed to sell beer only for consumption off the premises. The highway outside his door was technically part of his premises. The rest of the evening passed uneventfully with the house closing at 10pm and everyone going home sober. So Sergeant Basson, a stickler for the law, in particular drinking laws, hauled Robert in front of the local magistrates.

The officers were cross-examined by Robert's counsel, who proved that no drinking had taken place actually inside his house, but the magistrate considered the case proven. Robert was fined £2 10s plus costs, with the offence endorsed on his licence. The Beer House was closed down soon afterwards.

The Wake celebration dwindled further. Harvey Bloom wrote in 1929 that it now comprised a stall selling sweets, then even this was abandoned.

May Day

May Day has an antiquity of over two thousand years. It was one of the eight major festivals of the Celtic calendar, marking the flourishing of life at the height of spring. The May Queen, who still leads the traditional procession, represented the ancient Mother Goddess in all her earthly glory.

Once a celebration for the entire community, it declined to a festival for children by the 1900s. Harvey Bloom wrote in 1906 that 'the May Pole has become a dressed-up broomstick and the May songs a nasal gabble sung entirely out-of-tune.'

Even so, May Day was still anticipated as much as Christmas today. The May Pole, with a crown-shaped garland decorated with tulips and daffodils, was carried by Charlie Roberts, Alscot's odd-job man. The May King, May Queen, Maid of Honour and the rest of the children processed behind him.

The King and Queen were chosen by the teachers. Nellie Brookes from Atherstone Hill Farm, Millie Beavington from the bakery and Jack Newland from Radbrook Cottages were all chosen. Ursula Bloom of Whitchurch Rectory was forbidden by her parents: it was beneath her position.

May Day parade c.1900 at Atherstone Hill Farm. Martha Nellie Brookes (centre) is May Queen. From WI collection.

The assembled procession went to Alscot Park where, Joe Newland (1901-1993) recalled, they were all given a penny and a glass of wine, and they sang songs they'd spent ages learning:

Happy May, blithesome May,
Winter's rain has passed away,
Hip hurrah, hip hurrah, let us all sing together,
Bright springtime is here.

The procession toured the bigger houses of the local villages, and by the time they reached Whitchurch Rectory the younger children were reduced to exhausted tears. The event ended with tea in the school and games in Alscot Park.

The First World War brought this all to an end. The last record of the May Day parade is 1915.

A smaller celebration was revived by the 1940s, where a May Queen was pushed round in a wheelbarrow and the children danced around the May Pole. The procession continued intermittently until the 1970s, and was revived as an annual event in 1989. It is still held today.

May Day parade c.1908. The miserable children standing in the rain rather deride the meaning of the song. Percy Beavington is 2nd left. Charlie Roberts is holding the May Pole. Millie Beavington is on his left in a large hat. Courtesy of Elizabeth Lyne.

The Flower and Produce Show

Preston Flower and Produce Show was set up by Preston Horticultural Society in 1960, following the success of a small WI-organised show two years earlier. The gardeners and allotment-holders in Preston and beyond all entered vegetables, fruit and flowers. Eric Dale and George Nason were key organisers, and Joan Spencer of Park Farm was its long-term secretary.

Showing was a tricky business. With no notion of what was growing under the soil, three specimens of equal size, shape and colouring had to be found. And one rampaging snail the night before could ruin a prize-winning dahlia.

The show regularly attracted over 700 entries, with a dozen cups awarded. Expert gardeners Eric and Fred Dale claimed many of the prizes, as did George Nason. By the 1980s Howard Walton of No.2 was giving them stiff competition.

Knitting and needlework classes were popular among the women. These included soft toys, lampshades and garments. Queenie Coomber was a regular winner. The cookery classes were also fiercely fought. The simplest, such as a boiled egg, were often the hardest. A black rim around the yolk where it was cooled too slowly was an automatic failure, but only evident after the judges cut it open.

The show ran until 2000, but the high point, with hindsight, was in 1985, when an up-and-coming RSC actress named Helen Mirren opened the show.

Harvest

Harvest is the culmination of the agricultural year and the high point of rural life. Every able-bodied man, woman and child helped with the harvest, the reason behind the six-week school summer holiday.

Gleaning – picking up dropped ears of corn – was a task for women and children, and could provide poor families with a good deal of their income. School attendance remained poor until late September when the children finished gleaning.

The completion of harvest has been celebrated with gusto since ancient times. Everyone rode on the last load home, bedecked in flowers and singing Harvest Home songs. Harvey Bloom recorded a local song in the 1900s:

Up! Up! Up! A merry harvest home!
We have sowed, we have mowed,
We have carried our last load!
I ripped my shirt and I teared my skin,
To get my master's harvest in!

A harvest supper of boiled beef and plum pudding was given by each farmer. John James of Whitchurch Farm still held a Harvest Home supper in 1911. A family tradition stated that Harvest Home couldn't be held after Michaelmas [30th September] so a late harvest meant no party.

The harvest supper in Preston survived into the late 19th century, but now arranged by the allotment-holders. Over seventy allotment-holders sat down in the school to hot meat, puddings and home-brewed beer in 1890. As always, the health of the Queen was drunk.

The harvest supper was restored by the Village Hall Committee in the 1960s and is still an annual event today.

The harvest festival is also a long-standing tradition. That in 1890 was little different to today. The church was decorated with fruit, flowers and vegetables, and various services were held with hearty singing 'expressive of the thankfulness which all should feel for a bounteous harvest and other blessings.'

Guy Fawkes' Night

Celebrating the deliverance of Parliament in 1605 from Guy Fawkes and the other conspirators – Robert Catesby being the son of William Catesby, former lord of Alscot – was met with enthusiasm since at least the 19th century. Bonfires were frowned upon for the danger to thatch and ricks. The flames could spook horses, so a statute directed fires must be a suitable distance from the highway.

In 1849, Giles Smith, 18, soon to become a respected local citizen, built a bonfire by the highway in Preston. A police constable noted the offence.

Giles was summoned to court, both for building the bonfire and because the officer claimed Giles had assaulted him. The assault charge was dropped on a technicality, but Giles received a one shilling fine for the bonfire.

In the 1880s, an annual bonfire was built on the green in front of the school. An anonymous former pupil recounted to the *Stratford Herald* in 1940 that schoolmaster Joseph Webb would get permission for the children to go into the fields to gather wood for their bonfire. A tar barrel on a pole and some fireworks completed the setting.

The event survived into the 1940s; John Horseman remembers the children collecting hedge trimmings from the local fields. The lighting was aided with plenty of old tractor oil from Park Farm. An annual bonfire was held on the green until the 1960s – the children would start building it in the summer holidays – and come rain or shine it was one of the highlights of the year.

Royal Celebrations

Around sixty reigning monarchs have come and gone since the first Anglo-Saxon settlement was formed in Preston. Many would have passed unnoticed. The seasons turned, fields were tilled and beasts were fattened regardless of who was on the throne.

People's frontiers began to expand in the 19th century. The world outside their parish became both relevant and accessible, and the royal family became a subject of national pride.

Long Live The Queen
The Diamond Jubilee of Queen Victoria in July 1897 caused nationwide celebration. She was now the longest reigning monarch in British history. In Preston, the celebrations were enthusiastic. The village was decorated with flags, the health of Her Majesty was toasted and the National Anthem played. A substantial dinner was held for the men and boys of the village, followed by a meat tea for the women and children. The leftovers were distributed among the widows and poor the following day. A programme of twenty different sports commenced and the remainder of the evening was spent with dancing. Jubilee Covert on the northern parish boundary was probably planted at this time.

Long Live The King
In January 1901, Queen Victoria died. She was 81 years old and had spent nearly 64 years on the throne. A mourning service was held in the Baptist chapel, attended

by farmers, labourers and tradesmen alike. Most were attired in mourning dress.

Her son, King Edward VII, was crowned a year later. A nationwide chain of beacons was built according to the wish of the new king, to be lit simultaneously at 10pm on 30th June. Preston's beacon was built on the top of Atherstone Hill by George Brookes of Atherstone Hill Farm. Most of the village gathered to watch many other beacons, those on Ilmington and Broadway Hills most conspicuous.

The celebrations continued for several weeks. Land agent Robert Burra planned an ambitious celebration in the Deer Park in August for around 700 local people. A band was engaged from Birmingham and an array of sports arranged. The children were entertained with a Punch and Judy Show and a comic singer.

A non-smiling competition was held for the ladies. Despite great efforts from the onlookers, the committee failed to induce no less than seven of these dames to produce a smile, so the prize had to be shared between them. One can imagine the personality of some of these dour Victorian ladies!

A sumptuous tea was held and Coronation medals were distributed to the children. The evening concluded with a firework display and the National Anthem.

The Silver Jubilee of King George V

In May 1935, Preston and Atherstone gathered to celebrate 25 years of George V's reign. Captain and Mrs West, in their customary generous manner, didn't spare themselves to ensure the success of the function, with not a dull moment for the 400 attendees.

The children assembled at the school at 1.30pm and proceeded to the park led by Stratford Town Band, where everyone joined in the National Anthem. The children were presented with Jubilee mugs by Mrs West then sat down to tea. A ventriloquist and a conjurer provided entertainment, and sports and dancing took place on the lawn followed by a firework display.

The Coronation of Queen Elizabeth II

King George VI died in February 1952 and his daughter, now Queen Elizabeth II, ascended to the throne. Her coronation was held the following year. Preston planned a suitable celebration.

The church bells rang at 6.30am, followed by an early morning church service. The opening of the new village hall, for which fundraising had begun ten years earlier, was a highlight of the festivities. It was named the Coronation Hall and officially opened by 17-year-old James West, the young squire. It was his first public speech and he wrote the draft of it while travelling up from London on the train.

A street party with huge joints of beef, provided by Alscot Park and cooked in Beavingtons' ovens, was the best feast the villagers had ever known. The children were given a Coronation mug and a tin of Cadbury's chocolate fingers, and took part in a fancy dress parade. A television set was installed in the school for the coronation itself, the first time many people had seen one.

A comic cricket match, where men in dresses played against women in suits, took place on the green and a dance was held in the new hall until midnight.

The Comic Cricket Match

Olive Clark; Brenda Smith; Beryl Coomber; Doreen Smith; Connie Paxford; Gladys Gibbins; Eric Reason; ?; Bob Stredder; Percy Armitt; ?
Derrick Ashfield; Rose Horseman; George Handy; Tom Harding; Rose Handy; Bob Spencer; ?

The fancy dress parade. Carol Spencer; Spencer Watts; John Cook; Mary Cook; Susan Paxford; Gillian Carvell; ?

The Diamond Jubilee of Queen Elizabeth II

On 5th June 2012, a street party was held to mark sixty years of the Queen's reign. Twelve people had attended the Coronation event sixty years earlier. The event included a sit-down three-course meal for around 300 people, entirely provided from the village's kitchens. The main course was single-handedly cooked by Jane Spencer of Park Farm.

The Diamond Jubilee 2012. Those who attended the coronation in 1953 were: Millie Turner, nee Dale; James Stredder; Chris Daniell, nee Reason; Phyllis Fox; Sue Reid, nee Ridguard; Jenny Waters, nee Telfer; John Telfer; Dot Harrigan, nee Telfer; John Spencer; Roger Coomber; Ann Hicks, nee Harding; Jenny Wilkins, nee Gibbins; Fred Dale.

A national chain of beacons was prepared; Preston's was again on top of Atherstone Hill, where a dozen other beacons could be seen.

It was a scene mirrored across Britain, and across time. Over a century earlier, a beacon was lit on this same hill to celebrate the reign of another monarch. And perhaps a thousand years or more earlier still, to signal messages across the realm. A two thousand year story, united with today.

Conclusion

Preston may only be a small village, but it is a part of the network of communities which together form Britain. It has played its part in national history, and has left its mark on its people. The village remains in the hearts of those it touches, and they are drawn back to their roots, fifty, sixty or even seventy years later.

From the beginning of this story to its end, there has been one constant factor. Human nature. We nurture our children; care for our parents; do our best for our neighbours and community. We look forward with trepidation; back with fondness and regret. We mourn the ever-turning wheel of time which will one day claim us all.

Muriel Smith of Lower Farm died in 1761 after thirty years a widow, and was buried in the same grave as her three-year-old grandson Giles, who had died a year earlier. We will finish with their epitaph, itself long since claimed by time.

Behold all ye that pass by me,
As you are so once was we.
And as we are so you must be,
Therefore prepare to follow me.

Centuries may pass. The world may change beyond all recognition. But its people remain ever the same.

Appendix

Units of Measurement

Distance

12 inches	One foot	[30cm]
3 feet	One yard	[91cm]
5.5 yards	One rod	[5m]
22 yards or 4 rods	One chain	[20.1m]
10 chains	One furlong	[201m]
8 furlongs	One mile	[1.61km]

Distances were measured with a yardstick. The length of this standard varied hugely across England until Henry I (1100-1135) fixed it as the distance from his outstretched fingertip to the end of his nose. This it remains.

Area

An acre is 4840 square yards; a chain x a furlong [22yds x 220yds]; 4 x 40 rods; or 0.41 hectares.

Originally the area of ground which a yoke of oxen could plough in a day, it was standardised by Edward I (1272-1307).

An acre is divided into four roods. A rood is divided into forty perches. A perch is one rod^2 (5.5yds x 5.5yds.)

Volume

4 gills	One pint	[568ml]
2 pints	One quart	[1.1 litres]
8 pints	One gallon	[4.54 litres]

Dry goods, in particular grain, were measured in volume as well as weight. Two gallons of grain was a *peck*; eight gallons a *bushel*. The bushelweight, i.e. the weight of a bushel, is still a measure of grain quality today.

Weight

16 ounces	One pound	[454g]
14 lbs	One stone	[6.4kg]
8 stone	One hundredweight [cwt]	[50.8kg]
20 cwt	One ton	[1.01 tonnes]

Money

A pound	20 shillings
A crown	5s
A half crown	2s 6d
A shilling	12d
A penny [1d]	4 farthings

Glossary

Advowson: The right to appoint a priest or incumbent to a parish. Usually sold alongside the manor.

Ag Lab: Agricultural labourer. Abbreviated to this in census returns.

Capital messuage: The main residence of a manor-lord, who commonly owned several properties and manors.

Close: An enclosed area of land in the open-field landscape. Now termed a field.

Cordwainer: A shoemaker.

Demesne: Farmland in the manor cultivated for the lord of the manor.

Enclosures: Also spelt inclosures. The division of the communal open field into individual hedged fields.

Field: In the open field system, the entirety of a manor's farmland. After the enclosures it took on its present meaning.

Hide: A Norman land measurement. Nominally the amount of land needed to support one household. In Preston around 92 acres.

Hundred: An administrative subunit of a county. Once 100 families or 100 hides of land.

Husbandman: A tenant farmer. A husbandman practised husbandry of livestock. A husband tends his wife in the same manner.

Land: A strip of ground in the open field. Each farmer could have hundreds of lands scattered about the field. Also called a selion.

Lord of the Manor: The owner of a manor. Not necessarily a peer.

Manor: From Norman times, an estate upon which dues were collected by its lord and services were rendered by its populace. Often synonymous with a modern parish.

Master (Mr): A lord of the manor or major landowner without a peerage. By the late 18th century it became a general term of respect.

Messuage: A property with its associated outbuildings, gardens and other attachments.

Mistress (Mrs): The female equivalent of Mr. A woman who owned property or business assets. From the 19th century it denoted a married woman.

Nogging: Brickwork in the panels of timber-framed buildings.

Parish: An ecclesiastical or civil administrative unit. The former is the land appointed to a particular church; the latter a governmental unit.

Pauper: Someone in receipt of Poor Relief, the equivalent of income support today.

Quarter: A subdivision of the open field. The quarters were cultivated with one of four crops in rotation.

Squire: A colloquial term for a lord of the manor. Not to be confused with *esquire*: a rank of the nobility.

Terrier: A land survey. From the Latin *terra,* meaning 'land' or 'ground'.

Yardland: The standard unit of land in pre-enclosure agriculture. Its value varied between districts and over time. Also known as a virgate, husbandland or ploughland.

Yeoman: A freehold farmer.

Sources

Oral, written and photographic information shared by many people was crucial for compiling this book. Also an array of local oral histories and photographs was collected in the 1950s-80s by schoolteacher Dorothy Unett and the Women's Institute.

Websites such as www.ancestry.co.uk and www.findmypast.co.uk contain a vast array of records including censuses, church registers, military records, electoral registers and apprenticeship records.

Census Records

The first census detailing every individual in the UK was taken in 1841, and every ten years since. They are publicly available up to 1911.

In 1841, the names, ages and occupations were recorded. From 1851, marital status, place of birth and relationship were taken. In 1911, married women were required to give the number of years they'd been married, the number of children they'd had, and how many were still living.

Birth, Marriage, Death, Baptism and Burial Records

From 1540, churches kept records of all baptisms, marriages and burials. The records of Preston are virtually complete excepting the mid 17th century.

It was normal for parents to name their children after themselves, often for several generations. And 85% of men in the 18th century shared six names: John, Joseph, Robert, William, Thomas and Henry. It can make for a very confusing family tree!

The incumbent would often add other details to the register: occupation, age or place of residence. Age was often left to the judgement of the incumbent. Thomas Locke, an ancient yeoman, was buried in Preston in 1781; William Pardoe, a middle-aged weaver, in 1771; William Sitch, an elderly labourer, in 1778; and Margaret Blundell, an ancient woman, in 1772.

A particularly sad entry is the burial of : *An Irish pauper, who died in childbirth, September 1ˢᵗ 1825.* Nobody even knew the name of this woman who had died so far from her home. How she came to be in Preston is a mystery.

Civil registration – the certification by law of all births, marriages and deaths – began in 1837. The indexes are available online at www.freebmd.org. uk. Certificates can be purchased from the General Registry Office.

Grave Stones

These became common in the 17ᵗʰ century. Preston churchyard contains gravestones from 1697-1905; the new cemetery from 1885. Frost and ivy have rendered many illegible but the inscriptions have been recorded. Only the wealthy could afford a gravestone. The raised mounds of soil mark the graves of those who could afford nothing.

Wills

A last will and testament was made by anyone who had something to bequeath. The National Archives (www.nationalarchives.gov.uk), local records offices and www.ancestry.co.uk hold many surviving wills proved before 1858. After this date, an application can be made to the Probate Registry.

Newspapers

Newspapers offer an invaluable contemporary account of daily life and national events. The *Stratford Herald*, first published in 1860, has reported on Preston's fetes, school reports, deaths, military service, reminiscences of the elderly and many more things besides. The Shakespeare's Birthplace Trust holds all back issues.

The British Newspaper Archive (www.britishnewspaperarchive.co.uk) is digitising all local and national British newspapers into a searchable database, and reveals other stories which reached the wider world.

Other Records

Local records offices are the depositories of vast amounts of personal and legal documentation. These can include court cases; property deeds and leases; agricultural records; settlement certificates and manor court records. A database of all archives is available at www.nationalarchives.gov.uk.

Heads of Preston Households

	1861 census			1871 census			1881 census		
	Name	Age	Occupation	Name	Age	Occupation	Name	Age	Occupation
1	Thomas Whiting	55	Ag lab	Giles Horseman	46	Ag lab	Giles Horseman	55	Ag lab
2	James Pratt	45	Carpenter	John Norledge	45	Ag lab	Charles Dyer	41	Ag lab
3	Peter Uriett	42	Bricklayer	Peter Uriett	54	Bricklayer	Giles Samman	39	Sawyer
4	John Neal	48	Sawyer	Hannah Neal	55	Former sawyer's wife	John Bishop	63	Ag lab
5	George Herbert	46	Ag lab	Mary Ann Herbert	48	Charwoman	Henry Job	29	Ag lab
6	John Flowers	45	Ag lab	John Neal	31	Sawyer	Daniel Greenway	42	Sawyer
7	George Neal	49	Ag lab	George Neal	59	Labourer	George Neal	69	Ag lab
8	Samuel Garrett	67	Ag lab	William Garrett	50	Gardener	Hannah Garrett	56	Charwoman
UN [Unnumbered]	William Garrett	41	Gardener's lab	(demolished)					
9	William Jeacocks	57	Ag lab	James Hone	22	Cordwainer	William Dyer	43	Ag lab
10	John Fletcher	60	Carpenter	George Holtom	29	Labourer	John Davis Phipps	52	Ag lab (J.R.West)
11	Samuel Wright	35	Plumber and glazier	Samuel Wright	44	Plumber, house painter	Samuel Wright	55	Plumber, glazier
12	William Day	54	Ag lab	William Day	64	Ag lab	Jesse Dyde	42	Ag lab
13	Caroline Parker	50	no occ	William Riley	50	Woodman	William Riley	59	Woodman
UN	William Parker	69	Parish Clerk	(demolished)					
14	Thomas Allibone	68	Ag lab	Ann Allibone	76	No Occupation	Thomas Pitt	46	Ag lab
15	Sarah Smith	78	former laundress	Sarah Smith	87	No Occupation	Job Sandalls	45	Carter
16	John Davis	59	Ag lab	Richard Horseman	49	Labourer	Richard Horseman	58	Ag lab
UN	John Davis	32	Ag lab	(demolished)					
17	James Paxford	41	Gardener	James Paxford	51	Labourer	William Timms	34	Ag lab
UN	John Neal	79	Former Ag Lab	(demolished)					
18	Thomas Dodd	34	Carpenter	William Paxton	36	Carpenter	William Paxton	46	Carpenter
19	Joseph Webb	27	National schoolmaster	Joseph Webb	36	Schoolmaster	Joseph Webb	46	Schoolmaster
20	Catherine Smith	55	No Occupation	James Paxton	71	Sawyer	James Paxford	61	Ag lab
21, Old Manor	William Tucker	45	Gamekeeper	William Harwood	62	Labourer	(uninhabited)		
22, Old Manor	Joseph Davis	55	Timber Dealer	Joseph Davis	65	Timber Dealer	Joseph Davis	75	Timber Dealer
23, Old Manor	Elias Weston	55	Timber Dealer	(combined)			(combined)		
The Gables	John Mansell	62	Farmer	John Mansell	72	Farmer	Robert Mansell	42	Farmer
The Dell (1)	John Hone	40	Cordwainer, shopkeeper	John Gardiner	51	Tailor	Frederick George	39	Carpenter
The Dell (2)	Rebecca Dodd	71	No Occupation	Mary Dodd	46	Carpenter's wife	John Dodd	52	Carpenter
Lower Farm	Richard Hughes	53	Farmer	Thomas Gibbs	34	Farmer	William Holtom	32	Farmer
Lower Farm Cottage	John Parker	62	Shepherd	John Parker	71	Shepherd	John Parker	27	Carter
Silvester's (23)	William Timms	57	Ag lab	William Timms	67	Ag lab	William Timms	77	Former Ag lab
Silvester's (24)	James Paxton	60	Sawyer	Daniel Greenway	35	Carpenter	John Dyde	42	Ag lab
Silvester's (25)	William Gibbins	46	Ag lab (F. Silvester)	William Gibbins	56	Ag lab	(uninhabited)		
Silvester's (UN)	Thomas Burrows	46	Ag lab	Thomas Burrows	55	Ag lab	(uninhabited)		
24	Thomas Paxford	44	Ag lab	James Gaydon	72	Ag lab	(demolished)		
25	William Salmon	69	Ag lab	William Salmon	82	Lab	(demolished)		
26	Samuel Dyde	65	Ag lab	Samuel Dyde	82	Ag lab	(demolished)		
27	(uninhabited)			David Hughes	60	Ag lab	(demolished)		
28, The Steps	Giles Tidmarsh	70	Tailor	Jesse Dyde	32	Ag lab	Esther Mumford	63	Grocer
29, The Steps	Elizabeth Rouse	74	No Occupation	George Rouse	59	Gardener	George Rouse	69	Gardener

	1861 census			1871 census			1881 census		
	Name	Age	Occupation	Name	Age	Occupation	Name	Age	Occupation
30	Richard Horseman	40	Ag lab	Sarah Tysoe	85	infirm	Thomas Paxford	66	Ag lab
31	Richard Neal	55	Ag lab	Charles Neal	29	Ag lab	Hannah Gaydon	75	Pauper
32	John Reason	69	Coachman	John Reason	80	Former coachman	Barbara Day	70	Pauper
The Cottage	Frederick Silvester	23	Farmer	Frederick Silvester	34	Farmer	(uninhabited)		
33	John Taplin	44	Mason's Lab	(demolished)					
34	(uninhabited)			(demolished)					
35	(uninhabited)			(demolished)					
44 (Beer House)	Robert Fletcher	55	Carpenter, Publican	Robert Fletcher	64	Beerhouse Keeper	Robert Fletcher	75	Carpenter
The Old Vicarage	Jane Smith	68	Landed Proprietor	Jane Smith	79	Annuitant	Charles Quesnel	55	Vicar
36	Elizabeth Webb	70	No Occupation	William Pitt	30	Ag lab	Joseph Salmon	43	Gardener
37	Richard Horseman	65	Ag lab	Giles Samman	30	Ag lab	Kendrick Paxford	28	Ag lab
38	Joseph Phipps	52	Ag lab	John Flowers	63	Ag lab	Sarah Hughes	58	Monthly Nurse
45, The Old Forge	Henry Bryan	69	Smith	James Bryan	38	Blacksmith	Amos Winter	38	Blacksmith
Park Farm	Giles Smith	29	Farmer	Giles Smith	39	Farmer	Giles Smith	50	Farmer
39	George Wheeler	34	Painter	George Wheeler	44	Painter	George Wheeler	54	Painter
Dame School	Elizabeth Salmon	69	No Occupation	(demolished)					
40	John Walton	44	Ag lab	John Walton	56	Ag lab	John Walton	65	Ag lab
41, Top Lodge	William Harwood	52	Gardener's lab	Henry Whitrod	52	Gamekeeper	Henry Whitrod	51	Gamekeeper
UN	Hannah Harwood	78	No Occupation	(demolished)					
42, The Old Thatch	John Norledge	36	Ag lab	John Taplin	55	Ag lab	Thomas Walton	29	Ag lab
43, Priest's Cottage	Mary Marwell	61	Widow	Thomas Gibbins	31	Lab	Thomas Gibbins	41	Ag lab
44	George Day	32	Ag lab	(demolished)					
48, Locke's Farm	William Hewins	52	Roadman	William Hewins	61	Ag lab	William Hewins	71	Road Contractor
49, Locke's Farm	William Riley	45	Ag lab	Thomas Pitt	36	Ag lab	Mary Ann Herbert	58	Charwoman
47, Locke's Farm	Henry Gibbs	27	Ag lab	Sarah Davis	67	No Occupation	Hannah Neal	65	Pauper
46, Locke's Farm	William Wheeler	72	Ag lab	Thomas Garrett	43	Ag lab	Thomas Garrett	53	Ag lab
50, The Bakehouse	Elizabeth Davis	50	Baker	Ann Hone	48	Baker and Grocer	James Hone	32	Baker
51, Church Farm	John Dodd	32	Carpenter	Catherine Smith	65	Former Farmer	Ann Hone	58	Former Shopkeeper
UN	William Paxton	26	Carpenter	William Ingles	53	Waggoner	(gone)		
1 Silvester's Row	David Hancock	55	Ag lab	Frederick George	31	Wheelwright	Elizabeth Gibbins	62	Pauper
2 "	John Bishop	43	Carter	John Bishop	51	Ag lab	Martha Hancox	65	Pauper
3 "	William George	55	Wheelwright	William George	61	Wheelwright	(uninhabited)		
4 "	Giles Horseman	35	Sawyer	Charles Dyer	30	Ag lab	(uninhabited)		
5 "	Mary Bromwich	57	No Occupation	Mary Bromwich	67	No Occupation	Thomas Burrows	66	Ag lab
6 "	David Hughes	48	Shepherd	Thomas Mumford	41	Bricklayer's lab	John Parker	82	Former Ag lab
7 "	John Monk	34	Ag lab	John Monk	43	Ag lab	John Monk	52	Ag lab
8 "	Thomas Mumford	32	Mason's Lab	John Davis Phipps	42	Ag lab	(uninhabited)		
9 "	Thomas Norledge	32	Ag lab	Thomas Norledge	41	Ag lab	(uninhabited)		

Ag Lab: Agricultural Labourer

	1891 census			1901 census			1911 census		
	Name	Age	Occupation	Name	Age	Occupation	Name	Age	Occupation
1	Giles Horseman	65	Ag lab	Giles Horseman	75	no occupation	William Gibbins	41	Woodman
2	Ann Hone	62	own means	Daniel Hopkins	39	Carter	Daniel Hopkins	49	Waggoner
3	Giles Samman	51	Sawyer	Giles Samman	61	Sawyer	Giles Samman	71	Labourer
4	John Gibbins	34	Ag lab	John Gibbins	43	Ag Lab	John Gibbins	53	Farm Lab
5	Henry Job	38	General lab	Mary Job	52	Laundress	Mary Job	64	Laundress
6	Daniel Greenway	50	Sawyer	Daniel Greenway	59	Sawyer	Ann Greenway	69	No occupation
7	Kendrick Paxford	39	Ag lab	Kendrick Paxford	50	Woodman	Kendrick Paxford	58	Farm Lab
8	Jesse Dyde	52	Ag lab	Aubrey Porter	40	House painter	Aubrey Porter	50	House Painter
9	William Dyer	60	Ag lab	William Dyer	70	No Occupation	Fanny Hawkins	61	No occupation
10	Sarah Davis	54	Seamstress	Giles Horseman	38	Sub postmaster	Giles Horseman	48	Sub Postmaster
11	Harry Wright	34	Plumber and painter	Arthur Ainley	26	Estate Agent's clerk	Arthur Ainley	36	Land Agent's Clerk
12	William Fletcher	47	Carpenter	Albert Jackson	39	Electrical Engineer	Percy Dove	37	Electrical Engineer
13	William Riley	69	General lab	William Riley	84	No Occupation	George Burrows	44	Baker's assistant
14	Thomas Pitt	56	Ag lab	Thomas Pitt	66	Ag Lab	Thomas Pitt	76	Farm Lab, ret'd
15	Benjamin Brothwell	35	Bricklayer	George Goodall	49	Gardener	George Goodall	59	Gardener
16	Amos Seal	37	Coachman	Edwin Howes	40	Groom	Richard Parker	30	Groom
17	William Timms	44	Ag lab	William Emms	52	Shepherd	David Rimell	64	Stockman
18	William Paxton	56	Carpenter	William Paxton	66	Carpenter	Ellen Paxton	69	No occupation
19	Joseph Webb	56	Schoolmaster	George Clarke	40	Schoolmaster	George Clarke	50	Head Teacher
20	Hannah Paxford	70	own means	Hannah Paxford	80	No Occupation	Job Paxford	67	Farm Lab (H. Ashby)
21, Old Manor	Charles Dyer	46	Shepherd	Charles Dyer	57	Dom Serv	Frederick Dyer	45	Bricklayer's Lab
22, Old Manor	Elizabeth Davis	84	own means	Jesse Dyde	62	Ag Lab	Frederick Dyde	37	Insurance Agent
23, Old Manor	John Horseman	25	Shepherd	Frederick Dyde	27	Ag Lab	Joseph Hopkins	70	Stockman
The Gables	(uninhabited)			(in occupation)			Sarah Mansell	69	Own Means
The Dell (1)	Frederick George	49	Carpenter, wheelwright	Frederick George	59	Carpenter, wheelwright	Frederick George	69	Carpenter
The Dell (2)	John Dodd	62	Carpenter	(in occupation)			(uninhabited)		
Lower Farm	Thomas Hemming	68	Waggoner	Henry Gould	52	Farmer	Henry Gould	61	Farmer
Silvester's (23)	Sarah Timms	72	No Occupation	George Bennett	60	Carter	George Bennett	70	Waggoner
Silvester's (24)	Thomas Harrison	71	Ag lab	Joseph Coldicott	62	Ag Lab	Joseph Coldicott	72	Farm Lab
Silvester's (25)	Hannah Garrett	65	No Occupation	Hannah Garrett	75	No Occupation	William Garrett	42	Farm Lab
Silvester's (UN)	Hannah Neal	74	No Occupation	(demolished)					
28, The Steps	Henry Gibbs	55	Ag lab	Henry Gibbs	66	No Occupation	Rose Ann Gibbs	73	Pensioner
29, The Steps	George Rouse	79	Former gardener	Arthur Hathaway	25	Drainer (J.R. West)	George Sparrow	41	Farm Lab
30	Hannah Nobes	68	charwoman	Louisa Whitrod	78	Laundress	Frederick Fletcher	39	Shepherd
31	Hannah Gaydon	85	No Occupation	Emma Gaydon	57	No Occupation	Emma Gaydon	67	Former Dressmaker
32	Barbara Day	80	No Occupation	George Burrows	34	Baker's assistant	Mary Ann Emms	66	Duties at home

	1891 census			1901 census			1911 census		
	Name	Age	Occupation	Name	Age	Occupation	Name	Age	Occupation
The Cottage	James Stokes	50	Estate Agent	(in occupation)			Robert Burra	36	Land Agent
44 (Beer House)	George Goodall	39	Gardener	Arthur Ryman	37	Woodman	Arthur Ryman	48	Farm Lab
The Old Vicarage	John Monk	61	Ag lab	William Hall	76	Caretaker	John Seal	63	Farm Lab
36	Joseph Salmon	53	Gardener	Joseph Salmon	63	Gardener	Joseph Salmon	73	Farm Lab
37	Samuel Garrett	33	Gardener	Samuel Garrett	43	Gardener	Samuel Garrett	53	Garden Lab
38	John Dyde	51	labourer	Sarah Hughes	78	No Occupation	Charles Dyer	43	Garden Lab
45, The Old Forge	Amos Winter	49	Blacksmith	Amos Winter	59	Blacksmith	Thomas Winter	41	Smith
Park Farm	Giles Smith	58	Farmer	Thomas Smith	39	Farmer	Thomas Smith	49	Farmer
39	George Wheeler	64	Painter	(in occupation)			(uninhabited)		
40	Elizabeth Walton	80	No Occupation	Thomas Walton	49	No Occupation	Thomas Walton	59	Carrier
41, Top Lodge	Henry Hibberd	33	Gamekeeper	Henry Hibberd	42	Gamekeeper	Frank Noyce	28	Gamekeeper
42, The Old Thatch	Thomas Walton	39	Ag lab	William Edmunds	32	Groom	William Reason	33	Groom (T. Smith)
43, Priest's Cottage	Ann Gibbins	51	No Occupation	Ann Gibbins	60	No Occupation	George Gibbins	36	Farm Lab
48, Locke's Farm	Mary Herbert	68	No Occupation	Albert Horseman	45	Stockman	Albert Horseman	55	Farm Lab
49, Locke's Farm	(uninhabited)			Mary Herbert	77	No Occupation	Edward Herbert	61	Roadman
47, Locke's Farm	Elizabeth Smith	71	No Occupation	William Gibbins	31	Ag Lab	Mary Horseman	85	No occupation
46, Locke's Farm	Thomas Garrett	64	Ag lab	Thomas Garrett	74	Ag lab	Catherine Garrett	76	No occupation
50, The Bakehouse	Richard Beavington	27	Baker and grocer	Richard Beavington	37	Master Baker	Richard Beavington	47	Baker
51, Church Farm	William Higgins	28	Engine driver	John Perkins	71	No Occupation	Mary James	61	No occupation
1 Silvester's Row	Richard Horseman	69	Former Ag lab	Stephen Hall	47	Ag Lab (R. Mansell)	Stephen Hall	54	Groom
2 "	Stephen Hall	37	Ag lab	William Payne	66	Ag Lab	William Payne	76	Waggoner ret'd
3 "	(uninhabited)			Mary Ann Hewitt	67	Own means	Selina Clements	75	No occupation
4 "	(uninhabited)			(uninhabited)			Ellen Dyer	75	No occupation
5 "	Thomas Burrows	76	Former Ag lab	Mary Ann Fletcher	57	Charwoman	(uninhabited)		
6 "	?			Charles Dyer	34	Cattleman	Frederick Moore	31	Farm Lab
7 "	?			Charles Roberts	29	Carter (R. Mansell)	Emily Richardson	44	No occupation
8 "	?			Esther Monk	74	No Occupation	Charles Roberts	42	Odd man at mansion
9 "	?			(demolished)					

	1932 estate survey		1957 local history survey	
	Names	**Occupation**	**Names**	**Occupation**
1	Richard & Yvonne Bannister	Ag Lab (AWM Spencer)	Sidney & Annie Ashfield	Farm worker (RM Spencer)
2	Daniel Hopkins	Former Ag Lab	Bill & Lillian Walton	Metal Polisher
3	Nurse Ballard	Nurse	Nellie Smith	Pensioner
4	John & Jane Gibbins	Former Ag Lab	Fred & Eliza Hartwell	Roadman
5	Jack & Lucy Bloxham	Gardener (Alscot)	Emily & Bertie Maton	
6	Charles & Ellen Dyer	Former Ag Lab	Bill & Gladys Gibbins	Clerical Officer, MOD
7	Jim & Annie Paxford	Garden Lab (Alscot)	Cox	
8	Charles & Rose Horseman	Gardener (Alscot)	Charles & Rose Horseman	Gardener (Alscot)
9	Ernest & Phyllis Ashfield	Painter & Decorator	Ernest & Phyllis Ashfield	Painter & Decorator
10	Sarah Horseman	Postmistress	Lucy Horseman	Postmistress
11	Arthur & Ada Ainley	Clerk (Alscot)	George & Rose Handy	Groom
12	Estate Office		Dennis & Eileen Maton	Farm worker (RM Spencer)
13	Sarah Burrows	Pensioner	Griffiths	Farm worker
14	Charlotte Pitt	Pensioner	Michael & June Matthews	Salesman
15	Frank Goodall	Postman	Eric & Connie Reason	Gardener
16	Richard (Jack) Robinson	Former Roadman	Walter & Lillian Keene	MOD work
17	Albert Sparrow	Ag Lab (AWM Spencer)	Eric & Mary Dale	Farm worker (RM Spencer)
18	William & Gladys Horseman	Housekeeper (Alscot)	Dick & Margaret Beavington	Baker
19	Harry & Emily Lord	Head Teacher	Nellie Bulbick	Head Teacher
20	Mrs Cleaver	Pensioner	George & Elsie Harding	Bus Driver
21, Old Manor	Lillian, Fred, Thos & William Dyer		Stanley & Muriel Carvell	Plumber
22, Old Manor	Fred & Emily Dyde	Insurance Agent	Emily Dyde	Pensioner
23, Old Manor	Mrs S Walton		William & Ethel Hicks	Chauffeur (Alscot)
The Gables	Henry Ashby	Former Farmer	Kinchin	
The Dell	Miss Kate Smith	Own Means	Bob & Doreen Stredder	Accountant
Lower Farm	Harvey & Nellie Smith	farmer	Harry & Peggy Smith	Farmer
Silvester's (23)	Albert & Dora Lowe	Gamekeeper (Alscot)	Sarah Dale	Pensioner
Silvester's (24)	Anna Gibbins	Pensioner	George Gibbins	

	1932 estate survey		1957 local history survey	
	Names	Occupation	Names	Occupation
Silvester's (25)	Eliza Garrett	Pensioner	Sidney Garrett	Bakery worker
28, The Steps	George 'Topper' & Annie Walton	Employed on estate	Reg Kempson	Salesman
29, The Steps	Harry Westbury	Ag Lab	Peter & Jeanne James	Brewery Work
30	Julia Fletcher	Pensioner	Sarah Jobe	Pensioner
31	Martha Brookes	Pensioner	Lucy Bloxham	Pensioner
32	Ann Seal	Pensioner	Ted & Queenie Coomber	MOD work
The Cottage	Mary Knottesford-Fortescue	Private Means	Mary Knottesford-Fortescue	Private Means
44 (45A) (Beer House)	Arthur & Ellen Ryman	Ag Lab (Alscot)	Guy & Frankie Spencer	Farmer
The Old Vicarage	Harry Gould	Former Farmer	Reg & Molly Asbby	Farmer
36	George & Elizabeth Walton	Ag Lab	Elizabeth Walton	Pensioner
37	Frances Garrett	Pensioner	Bill & Connie Paxford	Gardener (Alscot)
38	John & Charlotte Bishop	Former Ag Lab	Charlotte Bishop	Pensioner
45, The Old Forge	Thomas & Emma Winter	Blacksmith	Freda & Margaret Schofield	Secretary (Alscot)
Park Farm	Alwyn & Elsie Spencer	farmer	Robert & Joan Spencer	Farmer
40	Thomas 'Tat' & Hannah Walton	Carrier	George & Molly Nason	Decorator
41, Top Lodge	Myra Noyce	Pensioner	Myra Noyce	Pensioner
42, The Old Thatch	William & Mary Reason	Ag Lab (AWM Spencer)	Bill & Mary Reason	Farm employee (RM Spencer)
43, Priest's Cottage	George Gibbins	Ag Lab	Elsie Spencer	Pensioner
48, Locke's Farm	John & Alice Mutlaw	Employed on estate	(office)	
49, Locke's Farm	Percy Davis	Chauffeur (Kate Smith)	Miss Wells	
47, Locke's Farm	Henry & Ada Garrett	Carpenter (Alscot)	Mrs Plummeridge	
46, Locke's Farm	Phoebe Smith	Own Means	Dorothy Unett	Former Schoolmistress
50, The Bakehouse	Richard & Elizabeth Beavington	Baker	Percy & Millie Beavington	Baker
51, Church Farm	Jack & Louisa Day	Woodsman (Alscot)	Cyril & Mary Wood	Engineer
1 Silvester's Row	Lavinia Roberts	Pensioner	Jim Ashfield	Shopkeeper
3 "	William & Gladys Gibbins	Woodsman (Alscot)	Percy & Minnie Armitt	Chauffeur (Alscot)
4 "	Boys Club & Girls Friendly Society		Peter & Kath Jones	
6 "	Sidney & Annie Ashfield	Gardener (Alscot)	(combined)	
7 "	A Payne	Employed on estate	Harry & Dorothy Westbury	Builder
8 "	Ernest & Emily Maton	Ag Lab	George & Dora Beauchamp	Bin Man

Bibliography and Further Reading

Joseph Arch, *From Plough Tail to Parliament: An Autobiography*, 1986, The Cresset Library.

EAB Barnard, *The Sheldons of Worcestershire and Warwickshire*, 2013, Cambridge University Press.

J. Harvey Bloom, *A History of Preston upon Stour in the County of Gloucester,* 1896, British Library Edition.

J. Harvey Bloom, *Folklore, Old Stories and Superstitions in Shakespeare Land,* 1929, Mitchell, Hughes & Clarke.

Ursula Bloom, *The Changed Village*, 1945, Chapman and Hall Ltd.

British History Online www.british-history.ac.uk/vch/glos/vol8/pp81-89

HM Colvin, *A Biographical Dictionary of English Architects 1660-1840,* 1997, Yale University Press.

Pamela Cunnington, *How Old is Your House?* 1980, Alphabooks.

Ethel Davies, *The Life and Times of Joe Newland*, Self-published.

Ethel Davies, *Under the Thatch*, Self-published.

C.R. Elrington, *A History of the County of Gloucester vol.8,* 1968, Victoria County History London.

John Field, *English Field Names: A Dictionary,* 1972, David and Charles Ltd.

Stephen Friar, *The Local History Companion,* 2001, Sutton Publishing Ltd.

Margaret Gelling, *Signposts to the Past,* 1978, Phillimore & Co. Ltd.

Richard Harris, *Discovering Timber-Framed Buildings,* 1978, Shire Publications Ltd.

Basil Duke Henning, *The House of Commons 1660-1690,* 1983, Secker & Warburg, London.

WG Hoskins, *The Making of the English Landscape,* 1955, Pelican Books Ltd.

Annie Langley, *Joseph Ashby's Victorian Warwickshire,* 2007, Brewin Books.

Susanna Wade Martins, *Farmers, Landlords and Landscapes: Rural Britain 1720-1870,* 2004, Windgather Press.

Oxford Dictionary of National Biography (www.oxforddnb.com)

JEC Peters, *Discovering Traditional Farm Buildings,* 1981, Shire Publications Ltd.

John Stoppard, *A Warwickshire Lad,* 2006, Self-published.

Mike Woods, *Almost All from Memory,* 2004, Kerenza J Ltd.

Index of Surnames

Day; Days 17, 69, 70, 85, 137, 141, 184

Dee 221

Dodd 6, 192

Dove 78

Dudley 34, 35, 152

Dyde 75, 76, 78, 85, 106, 215, 217

Dyer 71

Elson 60

Elvins 6, 193

Emms 18

Farr 58, 59, 68, 194, 195

Felton 102, 104

Fletcher 8, 20, 157, 165, 179, 180, 199, 212, 217, 218, 232

Flower 158

Forster 89

Fortescue 7, 48, 53, 229

Francis 98-100, 101, 180, 200

Gamble 105, 180

Gardiner; Gardner 6, 193, 198, 221, 222

Garfield 58, 59, 65, 189, 191

Garrett 70, 87, 94, 98, 106, 216

Gasey 65

George 6, 9, 91, 92, 98, 184, 198, 199, 226-228

Gibbins 7, 10, 77, 172, 179, 183, 224, 230, 238, 239

Gibbs 59

Gibson 109

Gilks 193

Goodall 97, 218

Gould 6, 53, 163

Greenway 15

Greville 34, 36

Hall 104, 220, 226

Hancox 7

Hand 99

Handy 54, 66, 99, 101, 106, 238

Harding 76, 81, 158, 221, 230, 238, 239

Harris 18, 85

Hartwell 54, 58, 59, 65, 99, 101, 195, 196, 200, 220

Hathaway 101, 104, 105

Hawkins 85, 109

Hayward 85, 205

Herd 218

Hewins 199, 200

Heydon 1, 15, 22, 93

Hiatt; Hyatt 109

Hibberd 209, 210

Hicks 239

Hone 197, 204

Hopkins 73, 80, 168, 199

Horseman 4, 77, 83, 84, 101, 102, 105-108, 163, 164, 173, 181, 192, 201, 202, 207, 216-218, 220, 225, 230, 236, 238

Howes 104

Hoyle 102

Hughes 27

Hulbert 77, 101, 105

Humphries 153

Hunckes 34-36, 66, 127

Hunt 101, 108, 221, 229

Hutchings 201

Jackson 4, 78, 157

James 15, 53, 99-101, 105, 154, 180, 202, 221, 231, 235

Jaques 15, 53, 74, 76, 77, 157, 166, 182

Jeffe 37

Jilks 89

Job; Jobe 14, 73, 99, 101, 216, 217

Jones 21, 101, 139, 180, 182

Kedward 97

Kenwrick 159

Kilby 59

Kingston 13, 190, 215